PAUL I:
A REASSESSMENT OF HIS LIFE AND REIGN

edited by Hugh Ragsdale

University Center for International Studies
University of Pittsburgh

UCIS Series in Russian & East European Studies

Number 2

Library of Congress Cataloging in Publication Data

Main entry under title:

Paul I, a reassessment of his life and reign.

(UCIS series in Russian and East European studies ; 2)

Bibliography: p.

1. Russia—History—Paul I, 1796-1801—Addresses, essays, lectures. 2. Paul I, Emperor of Russia, 1754-1801—Addresses, essays, lectures. 3. Russia—Kings and rulers—Biography—Addresses, essays, lectures. I. Ragsdale, Hugh. II. Series: Pittsburgh. University Center for International Studies. UCIS series in Russian and East European studies ; 2.

DK186.P38 947'.07'0924 [B] 78-14893

ISBN 0-916002-28-4

Additional copies are available from:

University Center for International Studies
Publications Section
University of Pittsburgh
G-6 Mervis Hall
Pittsburgh, PA 15260
USA

TABLE OF CONTENTS

"I do not share the rather common disdain for the significance of this short reign. It is a mistake to consider it some kind of accidental episode of our history, as the sorry trick of a malevolent providence, having nothing to do with the foregoing period and leaving nothing to the succeeding one. No, this reign is organically linked with the previous one as a protest [against it], and with the succeeding one as the frustrated first experiment with a new policy, an edifying lesson for posterity."

Kliuchevskii, *Kurs russkoi istorii,* V, 189.

PREFACE

Paul I occupies a special place in the historiography of Russia. On the one hand, he has been vilified as a despotic madman whose rule threatened the stability of the empire. On the other hand, he has been lauded as something like a clairvoyant who almost alone designed a constructive policy to reconcile the great social disparities and conflicts that eventually did destroy the empire. But these are the views of a generation of historians now long past: in our own time, Paul has been, above all, neglected.

The only biography of Paul of any academic pretensions in English is that of Waliszewski (1913). The last substantial book of research explicitly devoted to Paul in any language was that of Klochkov (1916). Soviet historians have, of course, contributed quite valuable research on the period—especially Stanislavskaia has—but their works have not emphasized the personal outlook and the policy of Paul as autocrat.

Several years ago, I was invited to participate in a panel on Paul at the annual meeting of the Northeastern Slavic Studies Conference in Montreal, and I was surprised at the extent and variety of research being done on him by Western historians. It occurred to me that a book bringing together some of this research would be useful. I organized a further panel on Paul which took place at the 1976 meeting of the American Association for the Advancement of Slavic Studies in St. Louis. Six of the nine contributions in this volume were originally presented on one of those two panels. Three of the papers from the Montreal panel were previously published in a special issue of *Canadian-American Slavic Studies* (Vol. VII, No. 1, Spring 1973). The others were written specifically for the St. Louis meeting and/or this volume. One of the three previously published papers has been revised.

The authors of this book have had several objectives in mind. First, we have sought to exploit a richer and more diverse selection of sources on Paul than his previous historians did. In some measure, we have succeeded. In the old literature, the Russian scholars used very little unpublished foreign material, and the foreign scholars used nearly no unpublished Russian material. Several of the authors of the studies published here have done research on Paul in the Soviet Union. Though none of us has been able to use manuscripts there nearly so extensively as Klochkov, Miliutin, or Stanislavskaia did, there is a vast amount of material rich in Russian history in other European archives, and here we have advanced far beyond what was achieved in the older histories.

In addition, we have sought to apply more modern techniques and viewpoints. Though psychological studies of Paul were in vogue long before they became the rage of recent American historical writing, the modern rage has curiously not yet taken Paul into account. Thus a contemporary approach to the problem of Paul's mental stability is some seventy years more up to date in the issues of mental illness than the only other studies of this kind that we have. Paul's older historians were rather conscientious in taking a variety of approaches to their subject. They devoted appropriate attention to economic, social, and administrative history. But our more recent concept of modernization is an even more illuminating way to study the puzzle of Paul's political intentions.

Finally, we have sought through these approaches to begin to grope our way out of the confused polarization of opinion in the controversy which surrounds Paul. We hope to loosen some of the worn old wrappings in which the subject has been virtually mummified for more than half a century and to stimulate a modest awakening of new discussion and research. We hope that this work will be welcomed by our colleagues as well as by their students in advanced history classes.

INTRODUCTION

Hugh Ragsdale

The Russian variation on the western European theme of enlightened absolutism was played out rather awkwardly some years before the end of the eighteenth century. Peter I had spoken, after the fashion of illustrious Western monarchs, of the "*obshchee blago*" and the "*obshchaia pol'za*" of his people.[1] In pursuit of these foreign conceptions, however, he had followed relatively traditionally some of the practices of his Russian predecessors. Though he had resorted to new devices, his Table of Ranks and law on entail would probably have been recognized by Ivan III, Vasily III, and Ivan IV as something akin to their own harnessing of the Russian nobility in pursuit of the secure establishment of absolutism, or the "hypertrophy" of the Russian state apparatus.[2] After Peter's time, much of his handiwork suffered a fate like that of the work of Louis XIV, and the nobility reasserted itself to throw off some of the controls of the state.

Catherine II, it seems, aspired to halt this progressive liberation of the nobility and to pursue a more nearly egalitarian social policy in keeping with the pretensions of enlightened despotism. It has been pointed out how reluctant she was to confirm Peter III's scrapping of compulsory state service. She did not succeed in persuading the *dvoriane* delegates in the Legislative Assembly to do anything to improve the degraded condition of the serfs, and she evidently did not feel strong enough to proceed on such a course alone.

When Pugachev declared his revolt in 1773, he named both the monarch and the nobility as agents of popular oppression. Pugachev roused Catherine from her political ambivalence and hesitation. She turned to the nobility for a joint defense, and their interests were never separated again. The Law on the Administration of the Provinces of 1775 and the Charter of the Nobility of 1785 symbolize their alliance.

> The alliance between the state and the serf-owning nobility . . . that had lasted from the beginning of the eighteenth century to 1762 had tied the right to exploit land and serf labor to

> service, to a positive contribution to the welfare of the state. The alliance formulated in the 1770s and 1780s on the other hand, was defensive and reactionary in that it tied those same rights of exploitation to the defense of the state against its own subjects. At that point the autocracy ceased to be the progressive force that it had been throughout most of Russia's history ; it . . . devoted its energies and resources to the defense of the status quo.[3]

This withdrawal from enlightened principles was soon encouraged by the French Revoluton. What had begun in France as perhaps the kind of nobles' revolt against monarchy that Catherine had feared in the 1760s soon became a popular revolt against both monarchy and nobility of the kind that she experienced in the 1770s. Thus as European thought turned increasingly liberal and democratic, it lost its former luster and became the ideological enemy at Catherine's court. As she watched the Revolution run its frightful course, she retreated ever further from her previous pretensions into a kind of incoherent hysteria of denunciation and repression.

There matters stood when she died. Enlightenment, Western-style, had been understood in Russia to be the agency of progress. Yet progress at the price of the French fruits of Enlightenment was intolerable. The articulation of a policy to deal with this complex of issues would be perhaps the greatest challenge of Paul's reign. Paul was as alarmed as Catherine by the French Revolution, but he was entirely dissatisfied with her arrangement with the pampered and parasitic Russian nobility.

Catherine's legacy in foreign affairs appeared to be much more satisfactory. She had destroyed Poland. She had established Russian superiority over the Turks. She had reached something like the natural limits of easy expansion on the European frontier. This state of affairs demanded a revision of Russian aspirations. Paul had been convinced for some time—and for reasons other than the hardening of opposition on the frontier—that a more pacific foreign policy was in order. Here, however, the course of developments in the French Revoluton made unexpected demands of him.

Paul, of course, may not have been his father's son. The story of his doubtful paternity is well known. More dubiously, he may not have been his mother's son, either. He may have been expropriated from the nearby Finnish countryside—a *chukhonets*, as the story has it—to replace his mother's stillborn child. Whatever the truth of the matter, he was born in 1754 into almost morbidly inauspicious circumstances.

His parents had been married for nine years and were entirely incompatible. He was taken away from them, for better or worse, on the day of his birth, to be raised under the supervision of Empress Elizabeth. He apparently spent his early childhood in the midst of a variety of transient and anonymous women. In her memoirs his mother expressed considerable regret at being removed from him. So far as we know, his father expressed none. When Elizabeth died, Peter III did not exercise his right to designate Paul as heir. When Catherine turned Peter off the throne, she did so name him. The hopes and fears that these events evoked in him we can only imagine.

In 1760, Elizabeth had appointed Nikita Ivanovich Panin as Paul's tutor and *Oberhofmeister*. Catherine left him in the same charge. Panin had been educated in the French spirit of the age among the Germans of Russia's Baltic provinces. He had spent much of his life in the diplomatic service in Scandinavia and was a distinguished political figure, widely experienced and widely cultured. He was one of the leaders of the coup that brought Catherine to the throne.

Paul seems initially to have regretted the more disciplined regime that Panin required of him. Eventually, however, relations of respect and devotion developed between them. Panin became perhaps the most important and supportive person in Paul's life.

In July 1764, Mirovich tried to liberate Ivan VI, and Ivan did not survive the attempt. Catherine thus disposed of the second of three pretenders to her power, and Paul was the only one who remained.

We know from the diary of one of Paul's teachers, Poroshin, something of the content of his education and something of his behavior at the age of ten to eleven. The child's life and schedule were heavy and grave. He had very few playmates. Dinners were arranged with visiting dignitaries, and the conversation that was carried on at the table was designed to be edifying. Paul was encouraged not to imitate his father's excessive taste for things military, but in vain. He did his lessons fitfully and inconsistently.

His behavior was generally impatient. He hurried from one activity to another, was tense, and sometimes frenzied. He had a very short attention span and his feelings for people were quite volatile. He was easily disappointed. He had a lively imagination, full of fantasies, some of which he dreamed.

At a slightly more advanced age, when, because of the departure of Poroshin, our information about him is much poorer, we still know something about the content of his education, though much less about his behavior. He read extensively in the literature of the French Enlightenment, especially Voltaire, Montesquieu, Rousseau, Diderot, d'Alembert, Helvétius, the *Encyclopédie.* He also read Blackstone and Hume. He was adept at foreign languages, and cared nothing for science or fiction.

Panin had very strong ideas about Russian politics, and he influenced Paul accordingly. Panin admired the service ethic that Peter I had encouraged in the Russian nobility. He had seen it for himself in exemplary form at the court of Denmark. He despised the laziness and uncouthness of the Russian nobility and expected enlightened standards of the Russian monarchy and serious devotion to duty. One such duty was to inspire a conception of civic virtue in the disappointing nobility. He deplored the abuses of favoritism at the Russian court, the petty tyranny of upstart lovers-statesmen, and he thought that the monarchy was obliged to bring such evils under control.

Panin exhorted Catherine to espouse his views and proposed a means to implement them: the State Council project of 1762. Catherine seemed impressed and gave indications of accepting the idea, but she changed her mind at the last minute. This issue was confused with another. Panin had long thought that Catherine should serve not as empress but as regent for Paul. She showed no interest in doing so. Panin's reform project and his protection of the interests of Paul eventually alienated Catherine, and Panin soon centered his hopes for the realization of his program on Paul. This circumstance aggravated relations between mother and son. Paul was not invited on his eighteenth birthday, as he was expected to be, to enter the councils of state and to learn the business of government.

In 1773, he married a princess of Hesse-Darmstadt. When the wedding was over, Panin was given a variety of ceremonial honors and retired as head of Paul's household. His place was taken by Nikolai Ivanovich Saltykov, a distinguished military man. It was soon rumored that Saltykov served as Catherine's spy, and the sour relations between the two courts grew worse.

Paul's marriage ended tragically. Nataliia Alekseevna died in childbirth in 1776, and Paul subsequently discovered that she had become the lover of his own close friend, A. K. Razumovskii. Within months, Paul married again. He and his new wife, Mariia Fedorovna, a princess of Württemberg, were quite happy. The marriage produced the desired heirs, Alexander in 1777 and Constantine in 1780, and it continued harmoniously for a long time. The birth of the children, however, further estranged their parents from Catherine, for Catherine now did to Paul's family what she had so much regretted when it was done to her own: she removed the children to the court to take charge of their education.

Perhaps to ease this conflict, perhaps to reorient Paul away from his Prussophile tendencies in foreign policy at a time when she was preparing to drop the Prussian for an Austrian alliance, Catherine arranged for Paul and Mariia Fedorovna to take an extended trip to western Europe in 1781. They were forbidden to visit Prussia, and spent much time in Paris, Italy, and Vienna. In Paris, Paul's thorough conversancy with French culture made an enviable impression. He was also well received elsewhere, though his rather candid criticism of his mother's policies and favorites raised eyebrows. All of this was reported to Catherine, as were similar references in the correspondence of his entourage.

Paul returned home to find himself in trouble with Catherine for his indiscretions. His mentor Panin died soon afterward. He was now politically isolated in the country where he was born to rule. Paul and Mariia Fedorovna spent the bulk of their time on their two estates, Gatchina and Pavlovsk. Mariia Fedorovna turned Pavlovsk into a bucolic fantasy, while Paul made Gatchina into a drill field and military camp. He complained pathetically in 1784, "I am already thirty years old, and I have nothing to do."

When the Turkish war broke out in 1787, Paul asked for service with the army. Catherine sent him to the Swedish front the following year. He did not see much action there, but he was invited by the Swedes to entertain peace overtures. He properly rejected these, but Catherine was frightened, and Paul saw no more military service.

In the meantime, he contracted a strange liaison with one of Mariia Fedorovna's ladies-in-waiting, Catherine Nelidova. It was rumored that she was his mistress. This was probably not the case, but his hitherto happy marriage soon began to show the strain. The little court divided into two parties, those for and against Mariia Fedorovna. In 1795 Mariia Fedorovna and Nelidova were reconciled, and Mariia Fedorovna actually began to rely on Nelidova to represent her viewpoints to Paul.

In 1796 Catherine evidently decided to dispossess Paul of the succession and to bestow it on Alexander instead. It was rumored that a decree of 1 January 1797 would announce new succession arrangements. Catherine died on 6 November 1796, and Paul quickly gave orders to seal the papers in her cabinet. If there was among them a decree on the succession, it has not survived.

When Paul came to the throne in 1796, he brought a political program that had evolved through a systematic education, and he was very impatient to get on with the business of implementing it. The first year of his reign was exceptionally full of reform legislation. He issued a new law on succession, designed to end the era of palace revolutions, a legacy of the law of Peter I of 1722. It ended all but the one against himself. He found the Senate with a big backlog of business. He reformed its procedures, divided it into several departments, increased its staff, and greatly expedited the efficiency of its operation. He instituted a close scrutiny of the administrative activity of the governors of the provinces.

He regarded the army at the end of Catherine's reign as quite lax and undisciplined and issued a new field manual modeled after that of Frederick II. He put the army through extensive maneuvers in the fall of 1797. Very pleased with the result, he distributed decorations liberally.

Some of his legislation was rather petty. He stipulated, for example, how houses might and might not be decorated. He regulated permissible styles of clothing and banned words reminiscent of revolution. Children were forbidden to play unsupervised in the streets. He instituted strong surveillance over cultural activities and especially over the influx of what he considered malevolent ideas from the West. Eventually, he banned the import of any printed material from western Europe, including even sheet music.

Perhaps the most provocative feature of his reign was social policy. He soon acquired the reputation of being generous to the peasants. He issued a famous law limiting the *barshchina* that might be required of serfs in the Ukraine. He took a special interest in the enlisted ranks in the army, and he made it possible for enlisted men to bring complaints against officers. Of course, he awarded thousands of state peasants to persons enjoying his favor and did not hesitate to use the army to suppress peasant rebellions. Still, he has gone down in Russian mythology as a generous friend of the *narod*.

At the same time, he was severe with the *dvorianstvo*. He required army officers to carry out their duties or resign their commissions. He disregarded the privileges guaranteed by Catherine's Charter of the Nobility and subjected nobles to corporal punishment and exiled them to Siberia. He insisted that they must be of some use to the state, that they must perform some service to justify their privilege of serf-owning.

In foreign affairs, he set out ardently to distinguish himself from his mother. He declared, in rhetoric reminiscent of his education under Panin, that Russia had had war enough to bring the society to the verge of ruin, that it was time to inaugurate a period of peace and to use the respite to restore the order and prosperity of the nation. He recalled the fleet operating with the English in the Channel and the corps under Zubov in the Caucasus. He decided against sending the promised corps to assist in the coalition against France. At the same time, proclaiming and demonstrating his devotion to peace, he remained concerned about the threat of the Revolution in the West, and he offered, in 1797, to mediate peace between Austria and France. Bonaparte forced the Austrians to make peace at Campoformio before mediation materialized.

In 1798, Bonaparte seized Malta and landed in Egypt. By this time, Paul, because of his generous settlement of issues outstanding between Russia and the Maltese Knights since the partitions of Poland, had received the title of protector of the order. Perhaps for this reason, perhaps for reasons of more traditional Russian concern for the balance of power in the eastern Mediterranean, Paul joined the Turks in a campaign against the French in the Ionian Islands. Malta was his next objective. Before long, French aggression in Switzerland, Rome, and the Low Countries brought the Austrians to consider renewing the war. Paul decided that it was time to curtail the ambitions of the French and to protect the defenseless small states of Europe from the Revolution. The Second Coalition was formed. The Anglo-Russian campaign in the Low Countries came to nothing but disaster. Suvorov's campaign in Italy was a brilliant success, but he was then defeated in Switzerland. In the meantime, Austria had refused to undertake what Paul assumed to be one objective of the campaign: i.e., the restoration of the dispossessed princes in Italy. This fact persuaded Paul to withdraw from the coalition without having achieved his aims. He was left, for a time, without any role in European affairs.

In the summer of 1800, he received the well-known overtures of Bonaparte. Simultaneously, Malta fell to the English, who refused what they had previously agreed on, that is, to admit a partially Russian garrison to the island. This action provoked the completion of Paul's reversal of sentiments, and he formed the League of Armed Neutrality. In the winter of 1800-1801, the Austrians were forced to make peace with France, the English were desperately pressured by both the French and the league of northern naval powers, and the appearance of French and Russian cooperation seemed to carry all before it.

By this time, the more politically conscious element of the Russian public, the nobility about the court, apparently became convinced that a continuation of Paul's rule was not in the best interests either of the country or of the class itself. The nobles clearly felt the burden of Paul's somewhat egalitarian social policies. And most of them evidently lived in mortal dread of his capricious punishments. They might be one day at the sovereign's elbow, the next day in Siberia.

The conspiracy was a long time in maturing. Alexander's sentiments had to be taken into consideration. He was finally persuaded to consent to a coup d'état on the understanding that his father would not be harmed. The overthrow was masterminded by Counts Nikita Petrovich Panin and Peter Pahlen. Pahlen, as military governor of the city, had little trouble penetrating the defenses of the Michael Palace, and Paul was strangled to death in his bedroom.

The *dvorianstvo* rejoiced, the *narod* sulked, and the literary reminiscences of the reign were obviously not provided by the *narod*.

The memory of Paul and history's treatment of him are based to a great extent on the memoirs of his assassins,[4] who portrayed him as a passionate person, generous and noble-minded on the one hand, on the other hand vindictive, whimsical, and cruel. He had some aspirations to do good, but these were overborne by an uncontrollable vanity and a suspicion that he was not held in high esteem. Much of this point of view is reflected in the historical literature on Paul, and the biography that best exemplifies it is a work that is in great part a compendium of the memoirs: N. K. Schilder, *Imperator Pavel I: istoriko-biograficheskii ocherk* (St. Petersburg, 1901).

Schilder is often called a court historian, and in fact he did not venture far from the confines of dynastic history and diplomacy into the areas of social and economic history more in vogue since his day. Nevertheless, it is easy to underestimate his contribution to Russian historiography. He worked widely in the published sources and the archives, and he compiled great masses of data on the sovereigns whom he studied. It may be significant that his work on Paul followed a biography of Alexander. In any case, court historian or not, he was not sympathetic to Paul, and he constantly flattered both Catherine and Alexander. Though Schilder maintained a measure of impartiality until he began to describe Paul's reign, he could not thereafter suppress his growing disgust and contempt. Paul's statecraft, Schilder thought, was an exhibition of nonsense. This assessment is implied rather than explicit, and it rests chiefly on the testimony of the memoirists, many of whom figured in the conspiracy. Hence it raises the question whether the historiography has been corrupted by the biases of the memoirists. Has Paul's reputation, like that of his father, rested too largely, and unjustly, on the press agentry of his assassins, who wished to justify themselves by denigrating him?

The thoughtful student of this subject must answer, No, not entirely. Of course, many of the stories of the memoirists are repeated so often from one account to another as to suggest either that they can only have had a common origin in the rumor mill or that they borrowed heavily from one another. Some of these stories are too colorful to be easily resisted by writers whose success depends in part on a good story. It may be doubted whether Paul actually ordered the flogging of a horse that stumbled during military drill. It may be doubted whether chocolates sent through Father Gruber persuaded Paul to seek an alliance with Bonaparte. But a review of the observations of Paul's contemporaries and intimates who had every personal reason to be grateful to him and to flatter him leaves no doubt that something of the image of the man portrayed by the memoirists was real. Poroshin told Paul: "With the best intentions in the world, you will make yourself hated, Monseigneur." Twenty-five years later, Rostopchin described how Paul was "destroying himself and contriving the means of making himself hated":

> It is impossible to observe what the grand prince does without shuddering and pity . . . . He is obsessed with the idea that people

> do not respect him and that they scorn him. Proceeding from that [assumption] he fusses over everything and gives orders indiscriminately. Having four marine battalions of 1600 men and three squadrons of horse, he imagines with these forces to imitate the deceased king of Prussia. On Wednesday, he holds maneuvers, and every day he is present for the changing of the guard, and also for punishments, when they take place. The slightest tardiness, the slightest contradiction put him beside himself, and he is inflamed with rage . . . . He pronounces sentences on everyone: now he sends away a whole detachment because it lost an order sent yesterday; now he orders that Count Zinoviev be told that he must show more respect to persons enjoying Paul's favor; or Gurev, that he must not forget the Marshals of the Household, that he will teach them how to serve . . . . He threatened to beat Bush, the gardener at Tsarskoe Selo, with a stick because he sent fruits to [Mariia Fedorovna] . . . . Countess Shuvalova, arriving somewhat late [for a formal function] was . . . told that she must hurry for Paul because she had always carried out all that Prince Potemkin had told her to do.

Finally, Rostopchin said, Paul lacked the capacity to restrain and control himself.[5] (According to the Danish ambassador, the number of persons returning to the capital from exile in the wake of Paul's death in 1801 was so great that the price of food and lodging rose astronomically.)

The memoir of General N. A. Sablukov—not one of the assassins—is one of our most valuable on Paul's reign.[6] Sablukov served in the Horse Guards and was in a position to observe Paul intimately over a long period. He indicated that Paul was often decent and generous and even had a sense of humor. He saw him one day emerge hurriedly from Nelidova's apartment with a high-heeled slipper flying over his head. The next day, as Sablukov stood guard duty near the same spot, the emperor "came up to me and whispered: 'Mon cher, we had a little quarrel yesterday.'—'Yes, sire,' I answered."

Sablukov was an amateur artist. He had made some sketches of Paul, and they were obviously reported. One day, Paul appeared unexpectedly in Sablukov's room and asked what he was doing. "I am drawing, Sire." "Have you ever drawn my . . . ?" "Many times, Your Majesty." Paul laughed loudly and turned to the mirror, remarking, "What a face for a portrait." Then he slapped Sablukov on the shoulder in a friendly fashion and went out, laughing heartily.

In spite of his friendly attitude toward the emperor, Sablukov never went to the drill field without money in his pocket, lest he be sent straight from there to Siberia. His father, vice-president of the College of Manufacturing, was unable to provide enough dye on short notice for the new Prussian style of army uniforms, and he was therefore peremptorily exiled from the capital though he was ill at the time.

If friendly observers left reports such as these, then we cannot set aside the whole corpus of memoirs as a simple lie. On the other hand, they do not tell the whole story. The image of Paul drawn by the memoirists, and therefore by Schilder, is not wrong, but it is far from balanced.

D. F. Kobeko, *Tsesarevich Pavel Petrovich, 1754-1796* (St. Petersburg, 1882), drew a more sympathetic picture of Paul. He concentrated on the unfortunate conditions of Paul's life: his removal from the care of his mother at birth, the neglect by his father, the rivalry with Catherine later, the uncertainty of his succession. He pointed out how intensely Paul felt his exclusion from affairs of state. Kobeko found faults in Paul's education. Panin, he thought, was neither a thoroughly serious preceptor nor a good moral example. Kobeko did not analyze Paul's personality or his political program, though he gave an account of them. He simply told a straightforward story. Still, his work serves as an appropriate antidote to the more tendentious aspects of Schilder.

Pierre Morane, *Paul I de Russie, avant l'avènement, 1754-1796* (Paris, 1907), covers the same ground as Kobeko. He used a few additional documents that appeared in Russian publications since Kobeko's work as well as French diplomatic reports. His treatment of Paul is similar to that of Kobeko—it is sympathetic—but there are notable differences. Morane added a psychological interpretation based on an idiosyncratic and now outmoded French theory about "degenerates of a high type." It is not a useful concept, and it does not contribute to our understanding of Paul.

But Morane had important insights missing from other accounts of Paul. "It has . . . been observed that Paul enjoys giving advice. It amuses him to think that he possesses the truth, that he has superior views on what moral beauty consists of. He is a philosopher. There is in him a great flowering *(floraison)* of elevated ideas *(hautes pensées)*. He loves wisdom, or rather he adores it; but he banishes it from his life. He is consequently quite unequal to himself. Face to face with the grandeur of his soul and the misery of his life, he is confused and frightened." He had enormous pride in his morality and his conscience (p. 335). In these things he was very much the exemplar of the Enlightenment. He reflected, however, not the disciplined pursuit of reason allegedly characteristic of the age but the raptures of romanticism that would soon undo it. "The century, in its decline, took leave of the masters who had fashioned its youth." It was a time of Masonry and Mesmerism, of Rosicrucians and theosophists. Svedenborg and Cagliostro were popular, and Julie von Krüdener would soon be. "A mania for the supernatural began to become a sort of epidemic in the courts [of Europe]" (pp. 336-338).

Paul was pious and given to prayer. He did not like frivolity and unbelief. "Imaginative, exalted, the Grand Duke Paul was a prey designed for the reveries of ideas; he preferred the perplexing complications of theosophy to the simplicities of Orthodoxy." One of his intimate friends and correspondents was Frederick William of Prussia, whose court was dominated, in Mirabeau's words, by "magicians, visionaries, and gallant women." Paul's own malady, Morane argued, was to

> presume to reach too high, to dream of the inaccessible, the impossible, the sublime. He had to escape from ordinary sentiments! He could not hold to a Christianity that satisfied the needs of the ordinary man: he needed, in his nervous exaltation, a superior Christianity, rich in mystical emotions . . . . There is never

to be found in him a firm purpose, a brave resolution to make modest efforts, to practice common virtues . . . . But he exhausts himself in chimerical quests of unmixed blessings (*bien sans mélange*). It is astonishing . . . that with such exalted ideas he leads such a mediocre life. [pp. 336, 341, 349.]

This is eloquent analysis, and the studies that follow will provide much evidence on these judgments.

The best of the biographies sympathetic to Paul, the one most consistently careful and thoughtful, is E. S. Shumigorskii, *Imperator Pavel Pervyi: zhizn' i tsarstvovanie* (St. Petersburg, 1907). Shumigorskii's work covers the period of Paul's reign as well as the earlier part of his life. Though it is short, it is a more mature historical product than Kobeko and Morane, and not only because it includes the reign. Shumigorskii brought some decided strengths to the study of Paul. He had previously worked extensively in the private correspondence of Paul's family, and he had already published biographies of Mariia Fedorovna (1892) and of Nelidova (1898). In these three works, and in summary form in the biography of Paul, he gives us the most authoritative account that we have of the crisis of the Nelidova affair. The scope of Shumigorskii's authority here sheds much light on family intrigues and court cabals. This is a by no means negligible contribution. On the other hand, as one of his critics observed, this viewpoint severely restricted his appreciation of Paul's administrative system.

Shumigorskii has a relatively limited account of Paul's education. He followed here Petr S. Lebedev, *Grafy Nikita i Petr Paniny* (St. Petersburg, 1863), who maintained that N. I. Panin was a frivolous debauché who scorned Russian culture, admired only the Western world, and poisoned Paul's regard for Catherine. Most of this interpretation does not stand up under careful examination. David L. Ransel has recently provided a thorough critique of it, *The Politics of Catherinian Russia: The Panin Party* (New Haven, 1975).[7] What the Panins taught Paul was a serious political program, and what he learned from them was a good deal, if not enough.

It is only fair to point out that Shumigorskii was aware of some of the shortcomings of his work, in particular those that Klochkov later pointed out: "One may say with certainty that a full and authentic history of the *reign* of Emperor Paul still rests in state and family archives" (p. 5). And he called attention to something worth examining more fully, that Paul spent his life wrestling with the awkward juxtaposition of the advanced political and cultural ideas of western Europe and the backwardness of his native Russia (p. 6). Shumigorskii's work gives us a much more judicious appreciation of Paul than Schilder and the memoirists.

Kliuchevskii[8] selected several themes of Paul's reign for special emphasis. "The instinct for order, discipline and equality was the leading incentive of the activity of this emperor; the struggle with class privileges, his chief problem. Because the exclusive position attained by one class had its source in the absence of fundamental laws, Emperor Paul began the formulation of such laws." The law on succession, the law on three-day *barshchina*, and the abrogation of the privileges guaranteed the nobility in 1785 represented the beginning of this process. But Paul turned the pursuit of equality of rights into a general void of rights. His "convictions degenerated into aimless caprices and fruitless impulses and only introduced new contradictions (the law on succession and the thought of dispossessing Alexander, the three-day *barshchina* and the distribution of serfs, the idea of order and the breaking of the laws by personal order)."

Kliuchevskii thought that Paul was not mentally abnormal but "morally abnormal." His deficiencies stemmed from the fact that he not only did not know "the rules of human society" but that he did not want to know them: he did not want to be constrained by them. "It is difficult for imperial (*tsarstvennyi*) personages, by virtue of their very position, to learn their way in human society. Their position places them above simple people but does not raise their understanding of human relations; it rather alienates them from society . . . . In Paul, this moral solitude became a kind of timorous asylum . . . . In his nature, generally rather meagerly endowed, one quality not from the higher order of talents stood out: excitability."

Nevertheless, Kliuchevskii characterized Paul's political program as the "frustrated first experiment with a new policy, an edifying lesson for posterity" (pp. 189-190, 439-440).

Some of Kliuchevskii's pithy suggestions were picked up and amplified in the imposing study of M. V. Klochkov, *Ocherki pravitel'stvennoi deiatel'nosti vremeni Pavla I* (St. Petersburg, 1916). Klochkov opened up a previously neglected perspective on Paul's reign. He undertook a serious exploitation of the records of imperial administration, and what he found there significantly revised the previous understanding of Paul. Klochkov was very critical of the memoirists and of the histories of Paul that relied heavily on them.

The most important feature of the reign, in Klochkov's opinion, was the emphasis on legality and order. The second most important feature was its military character. Other important themes were the centralization of power, the growth of the bureaucracy, a conspicuous concern about balancing the equation of the privileges and services of different classes in relation to the state, and efforts to improve the administrative efficiency of the government and to encourage the prosperity and well-being of the whole population. Klochkov showed that the Senate reorganization made it more efficient and that officers and officials everywhere became more responsive to the concerns of the populace and the capital. He pointed out that Paul was the first Russian sovereign to do more than merely think about improving the lot of the serfs. Many of these archival findings, Klochkov said, reflected the teaching of the Panins as embodied in Paul's youthful policy papers. Here, poor Paul I becomes something like a pigmy Peter the Great.

There is much in the work of Klochkov that the modern researcher can agree with. Klochkov gives us the most authoritative study of Paul's internal policy, but he was as misled by his particular selection of sources as Schilder was by his. It is not that Klochkov did not read the other sources; rather, he allowed the new findings to dominate the old. We can sympathize with his enthusiasm for the new materials without succumbing entirely to his point of view. As was suggested above, some of the considerable consensus about Paul's unfortunate behavior will simply not argue away, and yet that behavior is not reflected in Klochkov's work. Klochkov was looking at Paul's principles and intentions and the very formal and abstract manifestation of them in cold and studied, black and white bureaucratese. It is impossible to imagine a selection of sources that would reflect Paul's peculiar personality more flatteringly. He is shown to be conscientious, which he was, and concerned about his people, which he was. What is missing is the unvarnished human impulse unmediated by bureaucratic formalities and rhetoric. We are much in Klochkov's debt, but to capture the whole of the elusive spirit of Paul we must take a broader view of things.

Probably the most widely read study of Paul in the English-speaking world is Kazimierz Waliszewski, *Paul the First of Russia* (London, 1913), a translation of the French edition of the year before. It is an attractively written book, full of human interest. But it is deeply flawed in a number of respects. First, the author contradicted himself. On the one hand, Paul "was neither insane, in the pathological sense, nor even weak-minded." He was rather, Waliszewski asserted, the product of the political and moral hysteria of the age (p. 3). On the other hand, "he was capable of the most astounding madness and folly . . . . He was the victim of morbid tendencies which inevitably resulted from such an abnormal constitution of mind, and were aggravated by the influence which the political and moral exaltation of the age necessarily exercised on so impressionable a temper" (p. 478). In Waliszewski's introduction, Paul is almost sane; in his conclusion, he is not. This is hardly a consequential view, and yet it is the natural result of a book that is itself a product of methodological inconsequence. It is an uninterrupted chronicle of madness, petulance, and trivia. While no responsible student of Paul would deny that there was such a dimension to him, there is clearly more to the problem than that. Chapters entitled "The Reformer" or "Paul's Methods and Ideas" do not tell us about these things. They are, like the other chapters, undigested collections of gossip. Waliszewski did not take a serious look at Paul's education, and his references to Paul and the Panins are mere glosses. The author had no grasp of the historical virtue of collation. He too often did not ask himself the meaning of the paradoxical manifestations of Paul's policies and behavior.

Still, if the plethora of confusion can be overlooked, there is one glimmer of insight in Waliszewski's outlook that is worth consideration. He pointed out, as Shumigorskii also had briefly, the clash between the French and German education of Paul and the Russian environment in which he was called on to govern, the "romantic and humanitarian ideas of the Latin West" and the backward recalcitrance of Russia: "civilisation and barbarism jostled in him" (p. 478). Perhaps Waliszewski thought that Paul aspired to use an old autocratic political principle to bring to his people a conception of social and political happiness that was decidedly eighteenth century and modern—and foreign as well. If this was his thought, it is a point worth pondering.

A related view of Paul was expounded by Valentin Graf Zubow, *Zar Paul I: Mensch und Schicksal* (Stuttgart, 1963). The title is a bit misleading: it is really an account of the conspiracy and the assassination, preceded by a brief biographical introduction. The part of the work dealing with Paul's personality and policy is suggestive rather than persuasive: Zubow found Paul to be a modernizer. There is enough truth in the observation to warrant some consideration. Paul desired to make his government machinery more efficient, to centralize power, and to design regular bureaucratic processes. He did not, as Zubow asserted "liquidate the old regime" (p. 40); he did not do for Russia what the Revolution did for France. Paul was perhaps a modernizer in material matters, but he exemplified anything but a modern European spirit in his conception of politics and the role of government in society. He would share his power with nobody. He could conceive of a career open to duty rather than talent. Even so, Paul's peasant conscripts did not carry a marshal's baton in their knapsacks: only the *dvoriane* could become officers.

Few historians have failed to mention Paul's mental condition, and several have devoted considerable attention to it. The best of their studies is V. F. Chizh's "Imperator Pavel I: psikhologicheskii analiz," *Voprosy filosofii i psikhologii* (1907). As biography, this is a good piece of work. Chizh reconstructed the record of Paul's behavior in detail and collated the various paradoxical aspects of its scrupulously. His verdict on Paul's mental condition is, however, vague and ambiguous, and his psychology is now outdated and useless. Morane's dubious observations on Paul's psyche have been mentioned. P. I. Kovalevskii, *Imperator Petr III, Imperator Pavel I: psikhiatricheskie eskizy iz istorii*, I (St. Petersburg, 1909) is not a professional piece of work.

According to Florinsky, "The foreign policy of Paul displayed none of the unity of purpose and inner consistency that some of the students of Russian government have observed in his administrative reforms."[9] This is a very general opinion. It is supported by the rather casual historiography of Paul's foreign policy in the older western European diplomatic histories of the period.[10] These histories emphasize what was evident to western European observers at the time, the contradictions and the apparent volatility and inconsequence of Paul's policy. They point to his early professions of peaceful intent, his mysterious obsession with Maltese affairs, his crusading zeal in the Second Coalition, the abrupt break with Austria and then with England, the expulsion of Louis XVIII from Russia, the formation of the League of Armed Neutrality, and finally the rapprochement with Bonaparte. Admittedly, if there was method in this apparent madness, it is by no means obvious.

Yet this view of the matter was expressly challenged by one of the early and still important studies of the subject, D. A. Miliutin, *Istoriia voiny Rossii s Frantsieiu v tsarstvovanie Imperatora Pavla I v 1799 g.*, 5 vols. (St. Petersburg, 1852-1853). It is a fervently patriotic account. Though his subject was military history, Miliutin placed it appropriately in its diplomatic context, and his account of Paul's foreign policy is relatively extensive. Paul, he said, tried to mediate the peace of Europe in 1797 and early 1798 because "his constant aim was to secure a general peace" (I, 58-59). But his good intentions were frustrated by French expansionist ambitions. Bonaparte's conquest of the Ionian Islands and of Malta offended him, and he became the moving force in the Second Coalition. At this point, Miliutin's view of what Paul consistently sought shifted slightly. Though he still "constantly had in view one single thing—the pacification of Europe," it was now to be done "by the restoration of the royal throne in France" (III, 150). His policy remained as disinterested as ever. "Paul I did not seek any compensation for the success of the common cause; with all his forces he sought to strengthen and broaden the alliance. Unalterably true to his goal, the Russian monarch always acted frankly, openly, and did not admit any ambiguity into his diplomatic relations" (III, 217-218).

Miliutin was not at all disturbed by Paul's desertion of the coalition. It was the perfidy of his former allies that caused it, and Paul's reaction was perfectly natural. He was committed to "save Europe, whether from the French or from the Austrians" (III, 254). "It is vain for foreign writers to attribute the rupture of the alliance to the passionate character and the wilfulness of Emperor Paul" (III, 265). He always stood staunchly by what he believed. The hopes of all the small states of Europe centered on him. He never hesitated between honor and interest.

When Paul received the French offer to return the Russian prisoners, he "accepted the proposal of Bonaparte with great joy" (V, 265). "The reconciliation of Russia with France apparently did not encounter any difficulties and did not even require very extended negotiations." But this abrupt reversal of alliances still did not signify for Miliutin any change in Paul's policy: "Paul did not wage war for his own benefit; he wished a general pacification of Europe, and he did not cease to concern himself with the fate of those weak states which had sought his powerful protection" (V, 266-267). Miliutin's account of the French rapprochement is full of the spirit of enthusiasm and triumph. Paul had used his forces "exclusively for the restoration of a stable peace and legal order; he constantly protected the weak states against the power-loving pretensions of the strong, and through all the changes in political relations, he unequivocally followed his goals with disinterest and sincerely chivalric stubbornness" (V, 287-288). By this time, Miliutin had apparently forgotten the "constant aim" of the restoration of the French monarchy.

> Those who judge actions by their results observe, of course, that the good intentions of Emperor Paul were not attained; that he, becoming the head of the imposing alliance against the French Republic, was himself the first to disrupt this alliance ... and [make] peace with the former general enemy. But the whole history of the war serves as an obvious justification of the foreign policy of Emperor Paul; all the documents ... prove without a doubt the justice of all his deeds and show clearly who was to blame for the break-up of the coalition and for the fact that it did not attain its goal. [V, 311.]

This account is deficient in several obvious ways. Miliutin relied almost exclusively on Russian documents and not on all of those. He represented Paul's policy exactly as Paul did, citing nothing more than Paul's own pronouncements to explain the sudden shifts of policy that were so incomprehensible to his contemporaries. Moreover, Miliutin evidently did not notice the contradictions and inconsistencies in his own acccount. For example, he maintained first that Paul's sole and constant aim was general pacification, subsequently that it was to achieve the restoration of the French monarchy as well, and last, and most ironically, that it was to attain good legal order in Europe by dealing with Bonaparte, a usurper who blocked the road to restoration. Finally, Miliutin did not explain how the Maltese affair, the Armed Neutrality, and the expulsion of Louis XVIII, to cite only the most obvious examples, contributed to Paul's allegedly constant aim of restoration of peace and good order.

Subsequent documentary discoveries have also damaged Miliutin's views. First there was the notorious Rostopchin memorandum that proposed an alliance with the French based on a partition of the Ottoman Empire.[11] Later, research in the French and Russian archives turned up clear evidence that the alliance between Paul and Bonaparte, which, in Miliutin's phrase, "did not encounter any difficulties," in fact faced the most serious obstacles.[12]

Still, Miliutin's work retains considerable value. It contains much valuable documentation, it is the only emphatic defense of Paul's foreign policy, and it provides one essential dimension—the moral one—of any serious effort to understand Paul's policy. In its emphasis on pious rhetoric and ideological animus, it is consonant with the outlooks of Morane, Shumigorskii, and Kliuchevskii.

The Soviet view of these things, best represented by Avgusta Mikhailovna Stanislavskaia's *Russko-angliiskie otnosheniia i problemy Sredizemnomor'ia, 1798-1807* (Moscow, 1962),[13] is quite different. Though Stanislavskaia used Miliutin's work, she obviously was not much impressed with his interpretation. She was fully conversant with the documentary publications that superseded parts of his work, and she used at least selected parts of the Russian archival materials more thoroughly than Miliutin had. The focus of her work is different, and yet much of the subject matter overlaps with Miliutin's. The Mediterranean element of Paul's policy was too prominent to allow her to neglect any significant part of his European policy. Hence her work, like Miliutin's, is much more broadly cast than the title suggests. She was not so much concerned with the personal element in Paul's policy; yet, by Soviet standards, she devoted a great amount of attention to the personal dimension.

Not surprisingly, she maintained that the "aggressive wars of tsarism served the interests of the governing class." In particular such a policy in the age of Catherine had served the grain-exporting interests of the Russian nobility, who sought an entrance into the markets of southern Europe (pp. 23-26). In Paul's reign a more pressing concern was the threat represented by the French Revolution to Russian serf law and to Russian Poland. Two different groups of nobility gathered about these issues to influence foreign policy at Paul's court. One of them, consisting of the Vorontsovs, N. P. Panin, A. K. Razumovskii, and I. A. Osterman, stood for war with France as the best means of containing the threats of territorial expansion and political radicalism. The other, consisting of A. A. Bezborodko, V. P. Kochubei, and A. B. Kurakin, thought that French principles posed no threat to the peculiar kind of country that Russia was—cold, conservative, and far away—and that it would be more dangerous to Russian interests to fight France than to remain aloof from the struggle (pp. 89-96). Paul was influenced by both groups at different times.

Paul's Maltese interest, Stanislavskaia explained, derived from two factors. First, "In Russian policy, Malta was closely connected with the Ionian Islands. The establishment of a protectorate over the Ionian Islands attracted the attention of Paul to Malta [which] in anyone else's hands became a threat to Russian interests on the islands" (p. 140). She cited no evidence to support this view, and, in fact, there is abundant evidence that Paul's interest in Malta antedated the French conquest of the Ionian Islands. The second factor, Stanislavskaia maintained was Paul's wish to use the chivalric character of the knights for a more effective and comprehensively European struggle against the Revolution and revolutionary ideas. "His Maltese plan was a link in the general system of legitimacy" (p. 141). This idea is not unusual and not without some foundation.

Stanislavskaia's account of Paul's break with Austria and England is familiar. She insisted, however, that Paul did not, as soon as he withdrew from the coalition, throw himself blindly into the arms of Bonaparte. The Russo-French negotiations of 1800-1801 were protracted and difficult, and the disagreements between the parties were never overcome (pp. 160-163). She maintained that the famous Rostopchin project for a Franco-Russian alliance and a partition of Turkey had an "incidental, episodic character" (p. 112), and she cited much evidence from the Russian foreign affairs archives to show that relations with Turkey continued to be good throughout this period and that Paul's solicitude for the protection of the Turks continued undiminished.

Stanislavskaia's research is quite valuable. Her view of Paul's policy, however, attributes to him two motivations that are not compatible: a policy of expansion and one of conservative legitimacy. Perhaps she did not do well to ignore Miliutin's explanations of Paul's motivation.

Norman E. Saul, *Russia and the Mediterranean, 1797-1807* (Chicago, 1970), covers much the same territory as Stanislavskaia. Saul's views of Paul's policy are both similar to and different from Stanislavskaia's. Professor Saul speaks of these matters for himself in the second part of this volume.

Where does this leave us with respect to Paul's foreign policy? It seems clear that it has not received as much attention as his internal policy. How might it be studied more advantageously?

Miliutin and Stanislavskaia used unpublished sources from Russian archives alone. There are many other pertinent archives to consult. Of course, Western scholars have made extensive use of English, Austrian, and French papers, and we already observed that these sources have yielded little more than well-worn clichés about Paul's foreign policy. Even so, there is much rich material in the repositories of Sweden, Denmark, Prussia (archives in the DDR), Sardinia-Piedmont, Naples, Malta, the papacy, and Turkey. The authors published here have used materials from all of these except the last.

From this analysis of the best-known literature on Paul, we may safely conclude that his life—both childhood and adulthood—was quite unfortunate. His behavior was often bizarre. His education was impressive. He had strong principles and great moral drive of some kind, but it is by no means always clear what his principles and objectives were. They were often obscured by his impulsive and apparently contradictory behavior. And they have been much disputed.

The research that follows provides much new information, and even new light, on the life and reign of Paul.

NOTES

1 N. I. Pavlenko, "Petr I: k izucheniiu sotsialno-politicheskikh vzgliadov," in *Rossiia v period reform Petra I: sbornik statei* (Moscow, 1973), pp. 40-102. See also Reinhard Wittram, *Peter I: Czar und Kaiser,* II (Göttingen, 1964), 120-123.

2 Richard Hellie, *Enserfment and Military Change in Muscovy* (Chicago, 1971).

3 Robert E. Jones, *Emancipation of the Russian Nobility, 1762-1785* (Princeton, 1973), pp. 293, 295.

4 A convenient collection is *Tsareubiistvo 11 marta 1801 g.: zapiski uchastnikov i sovremennikov*, 2nd ed. (St. Petersburg, 1908).

5 *Arkhiv kniazia Vorontsova,* VIII (Moscow, 1880), 76; and *ibid.*, XXIV, 257-258.

6 *Zapiski* (Leipzig, n.d.).

7 Ransel's article here is in great part a revision of a section of his book based on archival discoveries made after the book appeared.

8 V. O. Kliuchevskii, *Sochineniia,* V (Moscow, 1958).

9 M. T. Florinsky, *Russia: A History and an Interpretation,* I (New York, 1955), 617.

10 E.g., Albert Sorel, *L'Europe et la Révolution française,* 8 vols. (Paris, 1885-1904); Edouard Driault, *Napoléon et l'Europe,* 5 vols. (Paris, 1910-1927); Adolphus W. Ward and G. P. Gooch, eds., *The Cambridge History of British Foreign Policy,* I: *1783-1815* (New York, 1922). The documentary collections are entirely consonant with this point of view. E.g., *Correspondance de Napoléon I,* 32 vols. (Paris, 1858-1870); *Lettres inédites de Talleyrand à Napoléon, 1800-1809,* 2nd ed. (Paris, 1889); Walter Fitzpatrick, ed., *The Dropmore Papers: The Manuscripts of J. B. Fortescue Preserved at Dropmore,* 7 vols. (London, 1892-1910); Hermann Hüffer, ed., *Quellen zur Geschichte der Kriege von 1799 und 1800,* 2 vols. (Leipzig, 1901); F. T. Piggott and G. W. T. Omond, eds., *Documentary History of the Armed Neutralities* (London, 1919); James Brown Scott, ed., *The Armed Neutralities of 1780 and 1800; A Collection of Official Documents . . .* (New York, 1918); Alfred von Vivenot, ed., *Vertrauliche Briefe des Freihernn von Thugut,* 2 vols. (Vienna, 1872); Paul Bailleu, ed., *Preussen und Frankreich von 1795 bis 1807,* 2 vols. (Leipzig, 1881-1887); Hansard's *Parliamentary History of England* . . . .

11 *Russkii arkhiv,* 1878, I, 102-110.

12 A. S. Trachevskii, ed., *Diplomaticheskiia snosheniia Rossii s Frantsiei v epokhu Napoleona I,* I (St. Petersburg, 1890). (Vol. 70 of *Sbornik IRIO.)*

13 S. B. Okun', *Ocherk istorii SSSR: konets XVIII-pervaia chetvert' XIX veka* (Leningrad, 1956), is very general and not very probing or persuasive on Paul. Two major collections of private papers of persons prominent in the politics of the era do not throw much light on the problem. See Petr Bartenev, ed., *Arkhiv kniazia Vorontsova,* 40 vols. (Moscow, 1870-1895), and Alexander Brückner, ed., *Materialy dlia zhizneopisaniia grafa N. P. Panina,* 7 vols. (St. Petersburg, 1888-1892). Trachevskii's *Diplomaticheskiia snosheniia* is informative but does not enable us to make much sense of Paul's foreign policy.

I
EDUCATION AND PERSONALITY

1

AN AMBIVALENT LEGACY: THE EDUCATION OF GRAND DUKE PAUL*

David L. Ransel

Historians invariably remark on the contradictory influences in Tsar Alexander I's upbringing: his education at Catherine's court under the Swiss liberal La Harpe and the severe, authoritarian life at his father Paul's Gatchina estate. Seldom has it been noted that Tsar Paul also received an ambivalent legacy. In Paul's case the contradictions were not spatially defined, as in Alexander's divided loyalties, but reposed in the tension between two sets of ideas and models he was encouraged to emulate. His mentors prepared him first and foremost to be an enlightened constitutional monarch. They even went so far as to draft a constitutional project for his later implementation. At the same time, for reasons connected with their own political battles at court, they encouraged him to adopt Peter the Great as his chief role model, perhaps not fully realizing how ill the despotic power of that monarch accorded with their own aspirations for constitutional government. Certainly they gave too little thought to the difficulty that an impressionable young man like Paul would have in reconciling these two contradictory influences. Although Paul ultimately resolved this tension in favor of the autocratic alternative, his thinking first took a remarkable turn in the direction of constitutional government, as the following survey of his education and early political writings demonstrates.

There is no need to dwell on Paul's early childhood. This period was spent among female caretakers, with the addition in time of a male preceptor to instruct him in the rudiments of reading, writing, and the psalter. Formal education began at the age of six or seven, the customary time for boys of high station to be removed from their previous surroundings and thrust into an almost exclusively male milieu where they were expected to go about the serious business of training for their future role in life. For an heir to the throne this naturally involved special arrangements, including a separate court with its complement of servants, cooks, and orderlies, a full tutorial staff, and

---

*** Editor's note: Old Russian orthography has in this article been modernized.**

an *Oberhofmeister* or governor who administered the "young court" and served as the boy's principal guardian and mentor. In 1760, when Paul reached the age of six, Empress Elizabeth conferred this coveted post on Nikita Panin, a diplomat just returned from an extended tour as Russian minister in Sweden.

Panin was the senior member of an important Petrine clan, which is to say, a family that had risen in state service by virtue of the system of merit promotion introduced by Peter the Great. Panin was a great admirer of Peter I and identified closely with the service ethic and westernizing values of the Petrine reform period, attitudes which, as noted earlier, he would strive to inculcate in his charge Paul.

Panin's appointment as governor owed something to his personal and kinship ties with powerful Petrine servitors at Elizabeth's court. The choice was nevertheless a wise one. Few men were better prepared to undertake the guidance and training of the young heir. Among the best-educated men of his time, Panin commanded a thorough knowledge of science, politics, literature, and the arts. Moreover, he was a man of considerable experience in government. Following an initial stint in the imperial guards, he moved rapidly up the court and civil service hierarchies, attaining the post of special diplomatic envoy at the age of twenty-nine. After twelve years abroad, he returned home to the *Oberhofmeister* job through which he was able to aid Empress Catherine II in her coup d'état of 1762. He then capped his career by becoming senior minister and director of Russian foreign affairs during the first twenty years of her reign.[1]

Panin's first assignment as governor of the grand duke was to produce a prospectus of his educational plans and philosophy. Past Russian examples being inadequate, he looked to the West for his models. Here Panin's mission abroad had prepared him admirably. During his stay in Sweden the parliament (Riksdag) and royal family had bitterly fought out the issue of Crown Prince Gustav's education, and in reporting on this dispute Panin was able to acquire much information on princely upbringing. Not only did he examine the various projects employed in Gustav's training, but he also took note of their practical application and knew many details of the subjects taught, exams taken, and books read. Another source at his disposal was Leibniz's well-known tract *De educatione Principis commentario.* Though first published in 1787, the plan circulated widely in manuscript copies at several northern European courts, and in Russia Jacob von Stählin had used its precepts in a belated and vain effort to improve the education of Peter Fedorovich (later Peter III).[2]

The Leibniz commentary and Swedish plans were progressive documents incorporating the new educational ideas of the late seventeenth and early eighteenth centuries. These new views, which began with Rabelais and Montaigne, received fuller definition in the writings of Locke, Comenius, and Fénelon. These men sought to replace the former scholastic methods of rote learning and dry-as-dust drill in classical languages with living knowledge. Two means were proposed. The first called for basing instruction on visual experience: observation of nature, copper engravings, mechanical devices, globes, and the like. Comenius especially stressed this point. A concomitant approach was to encourage the child to develop his own thoughts and apply himself to independent study. For example, the teaching of language was to rely heavily on the pupil's immediate participation in conversation and the composition of brief epistles. Latin would give way to a greater emphasis on the native tongue and living foreign languages. In teaching history the instructor was to dispense with the memorization of dates and facts, using instead the child's own reflections as a point of departure for discussions and essays. Another innovation was for the governor and teachers to shed the role of stern fathers and become "friends" of their charge, an attitude better suited to an education whose purpose was to cultivate judgment rather than stuff the child's head with learned pedantry. These modern methods, which prepared the ground for Rousseau's revolutionary restatement of educational philosophy, exerted an unmistakable influence on Nikita Panin's thinking and formed the basis of his plan for Paul's education.

In line with contemporary educational models, Panin's prospectus stressed moral and religious training first.[3] Since a good ruler, in Panin's view, had to be "God-loving, just, and kind," the governor's primary duty was to protect his charge from spiritual corruption and to provide a setting that would develop his desire to imitate honor and goodness. Religious training in Orthodox Christianity and the Scriptures naturally was basic. More interesting was Panin's insistence on a religious instructor free of prejudice and superstition. Clerics of this caliber were not readily available at the court of Empress Elizabeth, whose own religious attitudes were unsophisticated. Not until the accession of Catherine II did Panin find an instructor of the desired quality. This was the monk and later metropolitan Platon Levshin, one of the rare Russian churchmen familiar with the literature of the Western Enlightenment. Under his direction Paul developed an unusually tolerant and yet deeply pious religious outlook.

The remaining subject matter outlined in Panin's prospectus had a modern ring. Mathematics was to occupy a central place, as its concepts "purified reason and trained in the bases of truth." History received the next highest priority. The means proposed for its instruction were brief essays with particular attention to the history of Russia. The stress on Russian history, though natural enough, also reflected the growing sense of national pride particularly evident among Petrine dignitaries like Panin and the adherents of his court party. It revealed itself as well in his remarks about the teaching of the native tongue, where he praised the writings of Lomonosov and Sumarokov as models to be employed in Paul's instruction. As for foreign languages, French and German took precedence, and Panin typically advised a modern conversational approach to their instruction. Beyond these basics, he proposed cavalry exercises, dance, and artistic drawing to provide relief from the pressure of academic studies. Likewise, funds were needed for the "acquisition of books, mathematical and physical instruments, guns, copper engravings, collections of paintings and other works of art, which if collected little by little before [His Highness'] eyes can imperceptibly give him a general inclination, love, and curiosity for all the sciences and arts."

Only after Paul had mastered the basic educational program was he to be introduced to the special study of statecraft. This subject, Panin advised, should include a "knowledge of commerce, fiscal affairs, domestic and foreign policy, naval and land warfare, institutions of manufacture and factories, and other sectors constituting the government of his state and the power and glory of the monarch." While military science was common to much earlier instructions on monarchical education, the remaining categories were somewhat novel and testified to a new appreciation of the ruler's important role in fostering the economic and industrial development of the country. No longer was it sufficient merely to have a military leader and tax collector at the head of government; the monarch had to be versed in all facets of modern administration.

Finally, with regard to the grand duke's daily regimen and living conditions, Panin's educational plan held to the Spartan ideal recommended by such writers as Locke and Leibniz. The best results could be achieved "if every overindulgence, splendor and luxury which tempt youth were kept from him and considered by him in no other wise than as the hope of future reward for zealous compliance" with the wishes of his superiors. His court should correspond to his rank, but with decency and good behavior as its principal decoration.

In brief outline, this was Panin's plan for rearing Paul. He did not present a systematic philosophy of education or even go into much detail on the specific points proposed. He merely set forth the precepts he intended to follow without elaborate design or exhaustive justification. Still, his plan expressed a clearly defined approach to childrearing, a set of learning priorities, and a considered method, all of which demonstrated his sympathy with the advanced educational ideas of the time. It should also be noted that Panin was something of a pioneer in this respect, as he was one of the first Russians to put these ideas into written form.

It is much easier to sketch the contents of an educational plan than to evaluate its implementation and influence. The scattered sources available, nevertheless, suggest that Panin and his staff honestly strove to realize in Paul their exemplar of an enlightened monarch. They gave him a firm grounding in the essential skills of language, mathematics, and military science, as well as a broad understanding of modern statecraft in both its theoretical and practical aspects. Paul likewise became well versed in the principal literary and philosophical writings of the age. The diary of one of his teachers provides an intimate glimpse of his education at age ten and eleven and shows him following regular courses in physics, astronomy, mathematics, and history while at the same time cutting his teeth on the writings of David Hume, Buffon's *Histoire naturelle,* Voltaire's *Dictionnaire philosophique* and other Voltairian writings, plus a heavy diet of neo-Stoic moral works, especially those of Racine and Fénelon.[4] Another memoir on the grand duke's education during his middle teens shows him engrossed in studies of European history, the important sources at this stage being the works of the Scottish historian Robertson and biographies of famous monarchs and ministers.[5] At about the same time Paul began his practical training in statecraft. Here the main work was done by Grigorii Teplov, a state secretary and specialist on commercial affairs, who introduced Paul to the details of office procedure and the form of government papers and official documents. Guidance on the broad principles of government came primarily from Nikita Panin and the diplomats and ministers working under him.[6] The governor's brother, Peter Panin, a senator and highly decorated general, counseled Paul on military affairs and gentry service, and for a short time in 1772-1773, Empress Catherine herself took the grand duke in hand and instructed him in the day-to-day operation of imperial decision-making.

In addition to his formal studies, discussions and conversations at the grand ducal dinner table unquestionably played an important role in Paul's education. Nikita Panin presided there and daily brought visitors from among government officials and court dignitaries as well as writers, scientists, and foreign representatives. This exposure gave Paul an exceptionally broad acquaintance with world affairs, current politics, and new cultural and scientific developments. Political and administrative topics regularly touched on included law, commerce, factories and manufactures, village economy, land surveying, and bureaucratic organization and personnel. Panin often illuminated these issues with remarks about conditions in other countries or by drawing on his own experience and giving examples from Russian and European history. As for cultural life, Paul had at his disposal the offerings of the court ballet and drama theater, and he often finished his day with attendance at the theater. With all these advantages it was scarcely surprising that during his tour of Europe as a young man Paul made a very favorable impression on his hosts with his refinement, linguistic skills, and highly cultivated and knowledgeable conversation.[7]

As Paul advanced into manhood he began to develop and articulate views on government policy and political reform, views that were unquestionably shaped by his training with Nikita Panin and his circle. This influence was all the more profound by virtue of the fact that Paul, having lost his own father and been neglected by his mother, formed a strong personal attachment to his guardian and even commented that Panin had served in the role of a father.[8] Certainly Panin, for his part, strove to instill in Paul an appreciation of his basic principles in the conduct of domestic and foreign policy. It would therefore be helpful at this point to review briefly Panin's political stance and policy orientation.

Panin was first of all a political reformer whose ideas earned him a place among early Russian constitutional thinkers. At the beginning of Catherine's reign he had tried to win acceptance of a reform plan involving the establishment of a state council for reviewing legislation and coordinating executive action. His object was apparently to make this a permanent body whose membership, while selected by the ruler, would be subject to censure and removal only with consent of the Governing Senate. A second part of his plan called for dividing the Senate into functionally differentiated departments with considerable discretion in resolving appeals from lower courts and administrative agencies. Though more in the nature of an administrative reform than a constitutional check on autocratic power, the reform, had it been instituted as Panin wished, would have confined government action within clearly defined channels and thereby made law something more than the arbitrary pronouncement of the ruler or her court favorites. Legislation would have become the product of a strictly regulated process requiring the review and sanction of established government bodies. The proposal was defeated, or, more accurately, it was implemented in a way that rendered its central provisions ineffective. Since Panin had in the meantime risen to senior minister for foreign affairs, he understandably ceased to advocate a reform that would only have served as a check on his own power.[9] Not until several years later, when his enemies gained ascendance, did he return to these ideas and expand them into a full-fledged constitutional reform program that he hoped his pupil Paul would someday institute.

In the area of foreign affairs Panin was more successful. He went some distance in establishing his "Northern Accord" policy, a conservative alliance of northern states aimed at offsetting the power of the Habsburg-Bourbon alliance in central Europe. With this shield he hoped to give Russia a long period of peace in which to build an effective domestic administration and reestablish an economy reeling from the effects of the Seven Years' War. Within a few years, however, troubles in Poland and the meddling of young courtiers ambitious for imperial glory undermined this policy and led in rapid succession to a draining conflict with Ottoman Turkey (1768-1774) and the widespread popular rebellion of Emelian Pugachev (1773-1774) at home. Ironically, the government's success in meeting these challenges, exhausting though they were, simply whetted appetites for further aggrandizement and resulted in a gradual abandonment of Panin's conservative program of peaceful development. In consequence, his leadership was steadily phased out during the 1770s.[10] Despite this setback, Panin held steadfastly to his original foreign policy principles, and these too he bequeathed to Paul in hopes that he would eventually return Russia to the proper course.

The Panin circle also had strong views on the role of the nobility. They wanted the Russian nobility, or at least its upper echelons, to occupy a position similar to that of its Western counterpart: to be a recognized estate (*Stand*) with all that implied by way of rights and obligations. In the Petrine spirit, they regarded state service as the very first principle of noble life. They not only disdained those who avoided service, but, as Peter Panin resolutely stated in his letters to Paul, they preferred to see well-born malingerers read right out of the ranks of nobility.[11] In their view, a noble also had the duty to be educated and enterprising, a bearer of Western culture as Peter the Great insisted, and a citizen who contributed by his personal initiative to the well-being of the entire nation. Nobles should uplift their fellow countrymen morally, culturally, and materially. In return, they received certain distinctive rights and privileges, among them the right to own serfs. It should, however, be noted that in regard to the serf right the Panins were somewhat in advance of their fellow noblemen in wishing to see serfdom regulated so as to end the abuses of unscrupulous landlords. Finally, they aspired to a special role for the elite of serving nobles. Men like themselves who were distinguished by education, culture, and long years of loyal service were, to their minds, entitled to special consideration in the governing councils of the empire and should have the leading positions reserved for them and their progeny. In this connection, the Panins were particularly hostile to the young favorites granted office and influence by Catherine, and Nikita Panin's constitutional proposals were designed in large measure to exclude these "unworthy upstarts" from power.

While these attitudes and policy differences would in themselves have provided Paul with an independent position from which to judge his mother's regime, the Panin circle added a still broader critical perspective by suffusing his education with the neo-Stoic ideal of an enlightened monarch ruling through an administration articulated on the basis of natural law and Christian morality. The tutors and young writers gathered under Panin's leadership at the grand ducal court were much devoted to this brand of political morality and frequently discoursed on one of its basic themes, the contrast between the good ruler and the despot. The virtuous ruler devoted his energy to maintaining peace and promoting wise legislation that would secure his subjects their lives and possessions. His rule was characterized by personal moral rectitude and a concern for popular welfare. A despot, on the other hand, abandoned himself to his passions, set himself above the law, and sacrificed the people's welfare to the whims of his favorites. Instead of securing justice and prosperity, he preferred the role of military conqueror and in the interests of an adventurous foreign policy brought ruin to the country. There can be no doubt that Paul took these lessons to heart. Nor could he have missed their practical significance when Catherine in the late 1760s abandoned her program of legislative reform to concentrate on war with Turkey and the partition of Poland. This change was accompanied by a downgrading of the Panin party's influence at court, and the resulting critical tone toward Catherine that began to characterize the grand ducal court at this time was also evident in Paul's early political writings, which date from this period.

The first example, written in 1772, is a school exercise on the "Principles of Government." Paul began by sketching a Hobbesian explanation of the origin of government, to the effect that in a state of nature the weak select rulers to protect them and voluntarily submit to the rulers' directives. In time, however, it becomes necessary to develop the concept of law and establish limitations on the supreme power, Paul continued, because "the rulers, growing powerful and seeing nothing that could set limits to their passions, allow themselves to give vent to them and commit excesses. The society then takes care to moderate this power and prescribe limits for it, and that is the beginning of law . . . . It is the foundation of accumulated laws . . . that serves as a guide to the ruling power and [is] what one calls the principle of government." Then Paul concluded on a critical note. "I am not at all speaking here of the abuses of the laws and of power, for to speak of the abuses would be like counting the drops of water in the sea."[12]

While none too sophisticated, the essay accurately reflects the *Rechtstaat* notions of enlightened government that Panin had advanced early in Catherine's reign, especially the need to set recognized bounds to keep the ruling power within the framework of established law. Paul's final remark shows that he understood the difference between the enunciation of these principles and their actual implementation, a possible reference to the gap between Catherine's enlightened public pronouncements and the actual governing practices of the time.

More interesting is Paul's second memoir, entitled "A Consideration of the State in General." He composed it in the summer of 1774 and evidently intended it as a serious proposal for governmental reform. The timing was important. It was not only the first political project of Paul's majority but it came in a moment of acute crisis. The first Turkish war was just drawing to a close in the south, while Pugachev and his rebel legions threatened the center of the empire. The memoir spoke directly to these issues, appealing for support of Panin's goal of reestablishing a long period of peace. "Although the war had been to our advantage, how much we have at the same time lost through poor harvests, the plague—which was, of course, a result of the war—internal disorder, and, even more, through military recruitment! Now all that remains is to wish for a long peace whereby we could attain a respite to restore calm, bring affairs into order and finally enjoy full public tranquillity."[13] Although the desire for peace was scarcely controversial in 1774, Paul's initiative implied a criticism of the war policy and especially of the mismanagement that accompanied it.

Pursuing this thought, he inveighed against the imbalance in priorities and misallocation of resources. "Everything is done with the last [available] means," he wrote, "and nothing is held in reserve. So if a breakdown occurs in some area, we have next to nothing with which to recover there; it is necessary to withdraw our resources from another place, thereby weakening it." This was a clear reference to the war, which by fully engaging the army and heavily taxing the people had led to the massive rebellion under Pugachev. Paul stated this directly. The primary treasure of the state is its people, he wrote, and their preservation is the state's salvation. Yet the people were overburdened, they abandoned their settlements, left the land uncultivated, and finally went into revolt. Paul then suggested a formula to remedy the situation. "The state should be regarded as a body. The ruler is its head, the laws are its soul, morals its heart, wealth and abundance its health, military power its arms and all other parts serving its defense, and religion is the law under which everything is constituted." These sections must be in proper balance. If too many resources are committed to military power, the health of all the other members suffers and undermines the overall strength of the state. The government should therefore allocate only sufficient resources for the external defense and maintenance of internal order without unnecessarily burdening the population. Paul then followed these remarks with a number of specific proposals for bringing about a balanced arrangement of military and police forces.

While evidently meant to be helpful and instructive, the memoir had unmistakable political overtones. In repeating many of Panin's arguments for a properly regulated government and the need for peace and internal development, it demonstrated Paul's endorsement of his mentor's principles and gave notice that he intended to speak out when he saw them violated by the ambitious imperial policies of Panin's enemies. But if Paul expected his mother to respond favorably to his advice, he was gravely in error. The memoir must have convinced her more firmly than ever of the need to remove him from the influence of the Panin circle and prevent his meddling in government affairs. Indeed this period marked the beginning of Paul's long exile on his Gatchina estate, whence he was invited to the capital only for infrequent ceremonial appearances.

Despite his separation from government affairs, Paul persisted in his desire to be useful. Within the limited scope allowed him he faithfully implemented many of the principles of enlightened governance acquired through his education. His Gatchina administration was characterized by religious tolerance, comprehensive welfare facilities, establishment of manufacturing enterprises, and a progressive educational system, including schools for peasants. In fact, he managed his small domain so well that his administrators had difficulty stemming the tide of peasants from nearby areas who wanted to settle there.[14] At the same time, Paul's contact with members of the Panin group continued through a correspondence in which he tested his ideas on larger questions of military and state policy. His most frequent exchanges during this period were with Peter Panin and another adherent of the party, General N. V. Repnin.[15] But by far the most striking instance of the Panins' continued influence came by way of a face-to-face meeting between Paul and Nikita Panin in the early 1780s. His former guardian, having finally worked out his ideas for political reform in detail, used this opportunity to persuade Paul to adopt a fully articulated plan of constitutional government for Russia.

This episode only recently came to light. Historians have long known that after his ouster in 1781 Panin returned to his earlier reform proposals and sought to extend their constitutional implications. Yet the surviving documentary record from this period was so scant as to leave doubts about the precise nature and extent of his reform program. Apart from an electrifying preamble, which catalogues the abuses of despotic rule, affirms the right of rebellion against tyrants, and closes with the promise of concrete reform proposals to follow, about all that survived was a bare constitutional outline containing little more than article headings. These documents were found in the nineteenth century among Paul's papers together with some notes and letters from Peter Panin stating that his brother Nikita had not been able to complete the project before his death in 1783.[16] It now appears that Peter Panin's statement was merely a blind to cover his own decision to suppress the project rather than forward it to Paul, as originally intended. Another set of the grand duke's papers recently uncovered in the Soviet archives makes clear that the constitutional program was fully worked out by 1783. Although the document containing Panin's project has been lost,[17] the basic intent of his program and Paul's response to it can be reconstructed on the basis of two papers in this newly discovered archival collection.

The first document is a memorandum entitled "Discussions held on the evening of March 28, 1783."[18] It contains notes hastily jotted down by Paul immediately after a visit with Nikita Panin just two days before the latter's death. Paul wrote that they had gone into some detail on the abuses of the present form of government in Russia and, comparing it with conditions in other countries, "We found it best to bring the monarchical executive power indispensable to such a large state into conformity with the advantages of that freedom necessary to each estate for its preservation from the despotism either of the ruler himself or of some private [power]." The first step, the essential foundation for any reform, the two men agreed, was the establishment of an immutable succession law that would forever end the chaotic succession practices of recent history. They then went on to discuss the structure of the new constitutional order, especially the need for a separation of legislative, judicial, and executive power. As before, executive power was to remain the prerogative of "the ruler predestined to govern the state." Legislative authority too was to continue to repose in the hands of the ruler but could only be exercised, as the memorandum rather oddly phrased it, "with the agreement of the state." Judging from subsequent fragmentary remarks, the two men were here referring to a state council of the kind Panin had tried to introduce twenty years earlier. Finally, the judicial authority was to reside solely with the "entire nation" and would be exercised by representatives elected from among the nobility of each province and confirmed by the ruler. A little further on in the memorandum it becomes clear that the franchise would be rather narrow. Paul noted that this body, to be known as the Senate, would derive its membership from an election among the first three ranks of the service hierarchy. In other words, "the entire nation" was understood to include only the topmost elite of serving nobles. Although the memorandum also includes places in the Senate for one public prosecutor from each province elected on a somewhat broader franchise (the choice in this case being left to an assembly in each province consisting of nobles of the first six ranks), these officers were evidently not to enjoy the same authority as senators, as their principal duty was to communicate and report on provincial affairs to be litigated in the Senate. This arrangement, the two men concluded, would conduce to the best cooperation among the various branches of government and serve as a pledge of the firmness of statutes, for there would always be an assembly of men to protect the general welfare by preserving the laws.

While the memorandum leaves little doubt about the basic drift of the conversation between Paul and Panin, it nevertheless omits some important information. One difficulty is that the first part, which contains general principles, employs the first person plural ("we," "our," "we shall strive," etc.), whereas the second part, outlining specific changes, uses the first person singular ("I shall institute," "I propose," "I understand," etc.).[19] It is therefore unclear whether the reform under discussion was one designed by Nikita Panin and written down by Paul partially in the first person singular or whether Paul was sketching his own reform plan and receiving comments on it from Panin, not all of which were noted down in the memorandum. In any event, the reform lacked significant operational definitions. It said nothing about the functions of the Senate elected from among the nobility and failed to explain what was meant by the ruler's need to exercise the legislative power "with the agreement of the state." These matters only received clarification in a second document written by Paul. Though composed soon after the memorandum and bearing the unmistakable imprint of the ideas discussed there, this second proposal was carefully thought out and reworked several times. It may therefore be taken as Paul's considered view of government reform at this period.[20]

The reform plan speaks first of the state council, and in doing so it clearly marks the turn toward a ministerial administration. This system, not officially introduced until Alexander I's reign, was advanced in Paul's later legislation, and this 1783 project shows that he was thinking along these lines much earlier. He called for the establishment of departments of justice, revenue, finance, budget, commerce, navy, army, and foreign affairs. Each would be headed by a minister or chief, who would meet to discuss affairs in an institution to be known as the state council (*gosudarev sovet*). Although Paul did not define the competence of this body, its similarity to the one Panin had earlier proposed leaves little doubt that it was intended as an institution for developing and coordinating legislative policy. This then is what Paul's memorandum of 28 March meant by "the agreement of the state," a council of ministers to consult on legislation.

Turning to the Senate, Paul first described its current role as both a judicial institution and the leading administrative agency of the state. He now proposed instead to transform it into a supreme court with a chancellor of justice as its chief executive. But, like the present-day United States Supreme Court, it was not only to serve as the highest court of appeal. It would also possess important review functions. As Paul explained, such an institution was necessary in cases where the ruler might pass a law or issue an order that would "of itself or in its execution present difficulties or be able to cause by itself or its consequences some kind of harm or evil." Prior to such a law's promulgation the Senate would have time to make representations to the sovereign through the chancellor of justice and thereby avoid unfortunate consequences for both the state and the ruler.

With regard to the structure and composition of the Senate Paul proposed to establish it with four branches, one each in St. Petersburg, Moscow, Kazan', and Glukhov.[21] Each branch would be divided into two departments (criminal and appeals), composed of seven members elected in the following manner: as soon as a Senate seat fell vacant, the nobility of the provinces in that Senate district would assemble and elect three candidates from among its members occupying the first three ranks on the state service hierarchy. The results would be forwarded to the St. Petersburg Senate for presentation to the sovereign, who would then choose one of the three candidates to fill the vacancy. The St. Petersburg Senate was to be the senior branch and had the duty of deciding cases that the other branches could not satisfactorily resolve on their own. If the St. Petersburg Senate also proved deadlocked, the case went to the sovereign for final decision.

While these procedural changes would have greatly expanded access to justice at the highest level and improved the Senate's ability to cope with its heavy caseload, the most striking and innovative features of the proposal were unquestionably the elective nature of the Senate and its judicial review function. It should be added that Paul was remarkably generous in his definition of this latter competence, which was to cover all areas of state administration save for foreign affairs. As he noted a second time, "It is necessary that the Senate possess the right to make representations to the sovereign ... concerning the establishment, amendment and nullification [of edicts] ... relating directly to the administration and the people, such as those in the departments of revenue, finance, treasury, budget, commerce, and [army and navy] (as regards taxation and recruitment)."

It was in this fashion that Paul faithfully embodied the ideas developed in his conversation with Panin. Despite the alteration of a number of details, he remained true to the basic premise expressed in the earlier memorandum, that the legislative power was "to repose in the hands of the ruler but with the agreement of the state, for otherwise it will turn into despotism. The depository of laws must be in the hands of the entire nation and the executive power in the hands of the ruler predestined to govern the state."

The memorandum and reform plan written by Paul in 1783 went as far as he was ever to go in considering a constitutional order for Russia. Yet even if the two documents represent a temporary aberration influenced by immediate contact with his ailing mentor and his own frustrating isolation from government affairs, Paul's papers stand alone in the annals of Russian autocracy as a personal written commitment to grant his subjects a constitution based on separation of powers and elected representation at the national level.

From this point, one observes a return of Paul's thinking to the more familiar structures of autocratic politics. While still clinging to Panin's general policy orientation, Paul soon abandoned his mentor's constitutional ideas. This change occurred even before his accession, as is clear from an "Instruction" he wrote in 1788. This document was composed on the eve of Paul's departure for the Swedish war front and was intended as a policy guide for his heirs should he die in battle. It was the last political project written by Paul before his elevation to the throne, and it reveals a significant modification of the reform aspirations of his mentors.

As just noted, Paul remained faithful to the Panin group's basic policy recommendations. Among other things, the 1788 Instruction follows closely earlier Panin proposals for defining peasant obligations in law and protecting serfs from the unbridled caprice of their overseers; in this respect it foreshadows Paul's later efforts to ease peasant burdens.[22] Similarly, the sections on financial policy, taxation, and encouragement of commerce and manufactures faithfully reflect the notions advanced by his mentors. In the area of foreign affairs Paul repeated more or less word for word Nikita Panin's *dicta* on morality in international relations and Russia's reliance on its own great strength within the framework of an alliance among the northern powers. By the time Paul came to the throne, the French Revolution and the worldwide struggle between France and Britain added new dimensions to this picture, but, as Klochkov argues, Paul worked to incorporate this broader foreign policy configuration into the Northern Accord system, which he saw as Russia's best hope of remaining powerful and at peace.[23]

It is when Paul's Instruction turns to the question of government structure that the fundamental change in his views becomes evident. In contrast to the concern he had expressed under Panin's guidance just five years earlier for constitutional rights and guarantees against arbitrary state power, Paul now made no reference to rights as such. Instead he spoke of the contributions each estate must make to the general good of society. While his definitions of the functions of the estates may have implied rights, the stress fell heavily on the obligations of each to serve for the good of all. The best indication of the change in Paul's views may be seen in his general definition of government. He dropped altogether the Panin formulation that Russia should be "a monarchical government with fundamental, immutable laws" and announced, in full conformity with his mother's views, that "there is no better form [of government] than autocracy, for it combines the strength of the law with the executive dispatch of a single authority." In line with this formulation, the council he proposed was to possess none of the review functions that Panin desired but would simply be another executive agency submissive to tsarist orders. At the same time, Paul abandoned the idea of *pouvoirs intermédiaires*, the assembly of men elected to supervise the laws. He now located the depository of laws in the bureaucracy and thus showed no inclination to advance beyond the "legal despotism" practiced by his mother. Panin had wanted a supervisory organ to be the eye of the law. Paul kept it as it had been, the "eye of the sovereign" whose personal will alone determined the validity of statutes.

Although Paul's retreat from the reform aspirations of his teachers seems sudden, it would be more accurate to view it as the product of a long period of preparation to which those very same teachers had contributed. The principal factor was their exploitation of the Petrine myth in their battles with opposing court parties. The Panin family and many of its political adherents had been beneficiaries of the system of merit promotion introduced by Peter the Great, and they naturally identified closely with the style and values of the Petrine reform period. They frequently boasted of their Petrine pedigree and liked to contrast their long years of loyal service with the quick rise of the young officers in Catherine's favor, the men who challenged and eventually overturned the Panin dominance in government. Nor did the Panin party allow Paul to forget his direct descent from Peter the Great and the expectations his Petrine birthright imposed. This was both an accepted form of legitimizing Paul's claims as future ruler and a veiled criticism of Catherine's abandonment of the Panin party's leadership in favor of "unworthy upstarts." For the Panins, given their family and service background, this was a natural stance, and they were never in danger of confusing the despotic Petrine legacy with their own constitutional modification of it. Yet they were not sufficiently alert to the impact of this powerful myth on Paul or aware of how desperately and uncritically he clung to his identification with Peter I.

The most compelling motive in Paul's adulation of Peter the Great was probably his personal insecurity and corresponding need for legitimation. The frequently whispered doubts about the legitimacy of his birth could not have escaped his attention and must have been reinforced by his parents' hostility and neglect. He was no doubt frequently plagued with the question of whether he had the right to rule. More frightening still, after the overthrow and assassination of his father and the killing of the imprisoned emperor Ivan VI, it was clear that "rights" in themselves provided an insufficient protection even for already consecrated rulers. If the problem of his right to rule were not enough to arouse Paul's fears and insecurities, he also had to contend with doubts about his ability to govern. Catherine had spurned his proposals and made clear how unwelcome was his advice and participation in government; her court adopted a similar sneering attitude toward Paul's qualifications; even the Panins, it seems, harbored doubts about his earnestness and stability.[24] In this swamp Paul's one solid foothold was his Petrine heritage. It is not surprising that he cultivated an identification with Peter that went beyond what might normally be expected. He frequently referred to Peter in his writings and conversation and announced that his "greatest ambition was to resemble [Peter] one day and to continue the work he had begun."[25] According to Baroness Oberkirch, Paul even reported having a vision in which Peter appeared and offered advice about his future actions as tsar. After coming to the throne he symbolically proclaimed his association with Peter's work by having Rastrelli's equestrian statue of Peter moved to the entrance of his Michael Palace and engraved with the words: "To Great-Grandfather from Great-Grandson."[26]

Paul was confronted with a sharply conflicting legacy. He was encouraged to rule as an enlightened constitutional monarch, and he in fact moved very far in that direction, even committing to paper a plan for representative government and checks on autocratic authority. At the same time, he was taught to rule in the Petrine spirit. In nurturing this identification with Peter the Great, Paul's mentors sought above all to bolster the grand duke's legitimacy and to establish a critical contrast with Catherine's policies. With regard to Paul's personal attitude, they intended the Petrine myth to serve merely as a model of service and selfless devotion to duty. Indeed they were largely successful in this effort. Like his great-grandfather, Paul saw himself as first servant of the state, a ruler above class, and a reformer with the task of creating a stable, modern government order for Russia. But the use of the Petrine myth also courted the very disaster the Panins feared most. They too quickly forgot that Peter was also a ruthless despot, and one day Paul would succeed to that same despotic power much distressed with what he had been taught to perceive as an intolerable deterioration of the Petrine system. What motivation would he then have to restrict the powers necessary to return the state to its proper course? To rule in Peter's spirit he needed Peter's authority.

Indeed this is exactly what happened. After coming to the throne, Paul forgot entirely his commitment to political reform. Apart from instituting a stable succession law—admittedly an important and much needed contribution—he shunned all reform of a constitutional nature. He failed even to seek the cooperation of the leading estate or major interest groups and attempted to rule with only the crude force of personal autocracy. The result was a despotism unknown in Russia since the time of Peter the Great. Paul was so averse to any division of his authority that he confined the discretion of his ministers within even narrower limits than had Peter I. Finally, where his mentors had sought to create respect for law by the institution of permanent fundamental statutes, Paul turned the idea inside out. He flooded his chancelleries with a stream of contradictory decrees, abolishing today what he had yesterday erected; he demanded strict conformity to a seemingly endless series of idiotic norms in dress, speech, and behavior; and eventually he created the very nightmare of despotic rule and personal insecurity the Panins had hoped so much to prevent.

Why Paul took this despotic turn remains something of a mystery. Some argue that the French Revolution caused him to recoil from the notion of constitutional order and impressed him with the need for urgent counteraction and executive force. Others hold that Paul suffered a mental breakdown once the full burden of supreme authority fell on his shoulders. At any rate, the grand duke's training and its result supply a useful corrective for one of his century's most cherished myths, the power of education to mold an individual in the image designed by his mentor.

NOTES

1 For a fuller treatment of Panin's career as well as several other points in this essay, see my study *The Politics of Catherinian Russia: The Panin Party* (New Haven, 1975).

2 Gustav's education is discussed in chapter 1 of Beth Henning, *Gustav III som kronprins* (Uppsala, 1935); the projects for his education are in Johañ Göransson, *Svea Rikes Konungars Historia ok Ättårtal ifran 2200 år före Skriftum intil 1749* (Stockholm, 1749), pp. 271-277, and in Panin's translation in the archive of the Leningrad Sector of the Institute of History, Soviet Academy of Sciences (*LOII*), fond 36, opis' 1, delo 1132, pp. 93-99. Leibniz's plan is published in *Magazin für das Kirchenrecht, die Kirchen- und Gelehrten-Geschichte,* I (1787), 177-196. On Peter II and Stälin, see Peter Petschauer, "The Education and Development of an Enlightened Absolutist" (Ph.D. diss. New York University, 1969), pp. 278-279.

3 Panin's plan, entitled "Vsepoddanneishee pred"iavlenie slabogo poniatia i mneniia o vospitanii ego imperatorskogo vysochestva, gosudaria velikogo kniazia Pavla Petrovicha," edited by T. A. Sosnovskii, is published in *Russkaia starina,* 36 (Nov. 1882), 315-330; the unattributed quotes that follow concerning the prospectus are from this plan.

4 S. A. Poroshin, *Zapiski* (St. Petersburg, 1881); references on the content of Paul's instruction are too numerous to list, but see especially the entries for 24 Sept., 20 Oct. 1764; 8 Jan., 24 Mar., and 24 June 1765.

5 Edmund Heier, *L. H. Nicolay (1737-1820) and His Contemporaries* (The Hague, 1965), pp. 32-33.

6 D. F. Kobeko, *Tsesarevich Pavel Petrovich (1754-1796),* 2nd ed. (St. Petersburg, 1883), pp. 53-56.

7 David M. Griffiths, "Russian Court Politics and the Question of an Expansionist Foreign Policy under Catherine II, 1762-1783" (Ph.D. diss. Cornell University, 1967); p. 61n.; L. Maikov, ed., "Graf i grafinia Severnye," *Russkii arkhiv,* 1876, V, 46; H. L. Oberkirch, *Mémoires de la Baronne d'Oberkirch* (Paris, 1853), I, 237, 303; II, 2-3.

8 The remark is in a letter from Paul to Peter Panin, cited in Ia. Barskov, "Proekty voennykh reform tsesarevicha Pavla," *Russkii istoricheskii zhurnal,* 1917, III-IV, 117. See further comments on their close personal relationship in Cathcart to Rochford, St. Petersburg, 17 Mar. (N.S.) 1769, *Sbornik IRIO,* XII, 431-432, and in Poroshin, *Zapiski, passim.*

9 This point is developed in detail in my *Politics of Catherinian Russia,* chapters 4 and 5.

10 For an excellent treatment of the Northern Accord system, see Griffiths, "Russian Court Politics"; the standard pre-Revolutionary studies are: N. D. Chechulin, *Vneshniaia politika Rossii v nachale tsarstvovaniia Ekateriny II 1762-74* (St. Petersburg, 1895), and P. A. Aleksandrov, *Severnaia sistema* (Moscow, 1914).

11 See especially Peter Panin's letter to Paul, "Pis'mo k Nasledniku Prestola dlia podneseniia pri zakonnom vstuplenii Ego na Prestol," and the accompanying "Formy manifestu," reproduced in E. S. Shumigorskii, *Imperator Pavel I, zhizn' i tsarstvovanie* (St. Petersburg, 1907), appendix pp. 20-32. The Panins' ideas on nobility are treated in great detail in my *Politics of Catherinian Russia*, especially pp. 153-161, 186-190, 268, 274-276.

12 All the quotations above are from Paul's "Réflections, qui me sont venus au sujet d'une expression qu'on m'a fait si souvent sonner aux oreilles, qui est: Principes du Gouvernement," *Russkaia starina*, 1874, IX, 670.

13 "Rassuzhdenie o gosudarstve voobshche, otnositel'no chisla voisk, potrebnogo dlia zashchity onogo, i kasatel'no oborony vsekh predelov," the complete text of which I have found only in manuscript in the archival division of the Gosudarstvennaia Biblioteka SSSR imeni V. I. Lenina (GBL), fond Barsk XVII, delo 10, unnumbered. Lengthy excerpts may, however, be found in P. S. Lebedev, *Grafy Nikita i Petr Paniny* (St. Petersburg, 1863), pp. 184-198. This and quotes in the following paragraph are from the manuscript copy.

14 S. V. Rozhdestvenskii, "Gatchinskaia votchina Pavla I," *Uchenye zapiski RANIION, institut istorii*, 1928, VI, 127-145.

15 Copies of the full correspondence are in GBL, fond Barsk XVII, delo 10, and fond Pan, XIV, delo 13; portions were published in the February and March 1882 numbers of *Russkaia starina*. An excellent survey and analysis of the influence of P. Panin and Repnin on Paul may be found in the article based on this correspondence by Ia. Barskov, "Proekty voennykh reform tsesarevicha Pavla," *Russkii istoricheskii zhurnal*, 1917, III-IV, 104-145.

16 All these letters and projects were published in a 35-page appendix to Shumigorskii, *Imperator Pavel I.*

17 So far as the story can be reconstructed, it seems that a copy of Nikita Panin's constitutional proposals was kept by his secretary and collaborator Denis Fonvizin, who in turn entrusted it to the safekeeping of his brother, P. I. Fonvizin, a former rector of Moscow University. Then in 1792, at the time of the persecution of Freemasonic groups connected with the university, fearing that it would be discovered by police search parties, P. I. Fonvizin destroyed the project. This whole question is treated in detail by the scholar responsible for the recent find, M. M. Safonov, "Konstitutsionnyi proekt N. I. Panina—D. I. Fonvizina," *Vspomogatel'nye istoricheskie distsipliny*, VI (Leningrad, 1974), 261-280. I want to thank my colleague Benjamin Uroff for bringing this article to my attention.

18 "Rassuzhdeniia vechera 28 marta 1783," found by Safonov in Tsentral'nyi gosudarstvennyi arkhiv drevnikh aktov (TsGADA), fond 1, ed. khr. 57, listy 1-4 ob. The following excerpts are from Safonov's article, pp. 266-267.

19 Safonov, "Konstitutsionnyi proekt," p. 267.

20 The document, located in TsGADA, fond 1, ed. khr. 73, listy 12-18, is untitled and undated. The following excerpts are from Safonov, "Konstitutsionnyi proekt," pp. 268-270.

21 The inclusion of Glukhov may seem odd in view of its nineteenth-century status as a small district center in Chernigov province. In the eighteenth century, however, it had served as the residence of the Ukrainian *hetmans* and for a brief period, near the time of Paul's writing, as the capital of the governor general of Malorossiia.

22 This Instruction or *Nakaz* is published along with Paul's will and letters to his wife and children written at the same time in M. I. Semevskii, ed., "Materialy k russkoi istorii XVIII veka (1788 g.)," *Vestnik Evropy*, 1867, II, 297-330; the following excerpts are taken from this source. See also a detailed interpretation of the document by Claus Scharf, "Staatsauffassung und Regierungsprogramm eines aufgeklärten Selbstherrschers, Die Instruktion des Grossfürsten Paul von 1788," in Ernst Schulin, ed., *Gedenkschrift Martin Göhring,* Studien zur europäischen Geschichte (Wiesbaden, 1968), pp. 91-106. I want to thank Professor Marc Raeff for bringing this article to my attention.

23 M. V. Klochkov, *Ocherki pravitel'stvennoi deiatel'nosti vremeni Pavla I* (Petrograd, 1916), p. 133.

24 This at least was Peter Panin's evaluation of Paul's contribution to their written exchanges on military reform. In a letter to N. I. Panin, 31 Dec. 1778 , GBL, fond 222, papka xv, list 6; also cited in Safonov, "Konstitutsionnyi proekt," p. 279n.

25 Oberkirch, *Mémoires,* I, 272, and for other references to his attachment to Peter I, I, 300; II, 122.

26 On Paul's vision, Oberkirch, *Mémoires*, II, 96-100. Psychological studies have differed on the issue of Paul's hallucinations. P. I. Kovalevskii, "Imperator Petr II, Imperator Pavel I," *Psikhiatricheskie eskizy iz istorii,* I (St. Petersburg, 1909), 61-172, accepts them as authentic material for analysis; V. F. Chizh, "Imperator Pavel I, psikhologicheskii analiz," *Voprosy filosofii i psikhologii,* 1907, Nos. 88, 89, 90, however, questions the validity of this particular vision (see especially No. 90, pp. 672-674). For Paul's discussion of Peter in one of his early political writings, see Lebedev, *Grafy Paniny,* pp. 232-235. The equestrian statue is discussed in B. N. Kalinin and P. P. Iurevich, *Pamiatniki Leningrada i ego okrestnostei* (Leningrad, 1965), pp. 159-161.

2

THE MENTAL CONDITION OF PAUL

Hugh Ragsdale

Paul I was notoriously a madcap. Historians have treated him, with varying degrees of explicitness, as insane.[1] There is at the same time an undercurrent of suspicion that his reputation has been too much influenced by the memoirs of his assassins. In fact, there were many other contemporaries who largely shared his assassins' opinion of Paul.[2] It is impossible to read far in the sources, other than in official Russian state papers, without finding examples of Paul's bizarre and eccentric behavior.[3] Nevertheless, in order to review responsibly the issue of Paul's mental condition, it is probably better to avoid the often partial accounts of the memoirists. V. M. Klochkov has pointed out their shortcomings,[4] and there are several other kinds of sources that are less suspect in the question of Paul's sanity. These include the observations of his tutors, records of his appearances at public ceremonies, acts of state, Paul's own writings, and the reports of foreign diplomats.

In a study of the scope of this paper, the selection of evidence from such a variety of sources is an awkward problem. There is no room for a biography, yet biographical data are essential. I have chosen to rely primarily on the evidence provided by Paul himself in his own writings. This approach, like all approaches that ignore alternatives, entails obvious disadvantages. To take what is probably the most obvious one, it emphasizes the period when the writings were done, i.e., 1772-1788. Perhaps most of us would prefer to examine instead the period of his reign, a much more complex undertaking. It might be argued that Paul's condition deteriorated, even to the point of breakdown, under the burdens of office. I believe that Paul's foibles, or abnormalities, were played upon very unfortunately and likely aggravated, certainly made more conspicuous, by the factionalism that developed at court during his reign. But I am tentatively of the opinion that his condition was stable throughout his life. There is the distinct possibility that the conspirators who took his life were careful to justify the deed beforehand by misrepresenting his behavior, that Pahlen in particular was in a sufficiently advantageous position to create disastrous impressions of him and to make him appear more bizarre than he actually was. But these problems cannot be treated adequately here.

My method here is to select a part of the biography and a part of the diagnostic spectrum to show how the question ought to be approached and what the proper diagnosis of Paul is. I hope only to achieve a result that the reader will find plausible and persuasive. Subsequently, I plan to do more.

Four of Paul's writings are drawn on here. The first example is his student notebooks from about the age of eighteen.[5] These exhibit a certain reserve and inhibition. He observed that there were two kinds of pleasure, spiritual and physical. Spiritual pleasure was the kind experienced when "doing good or listening to the story of some beautiful deed . . . . The physical pleasures . . . are livelier and more impetuous (*poryvistee*) . . . . And thus there is no doubt that every right-thinking (*blagomysliashchii*) person prefers the former, which . . . are higher than the latter."

He was evidently afraid of his own notorious impetuosity. "Happy are the people who can reason in that decisive moment when the passions—the inevitable consequences of strong sensual impressions—struggle with reason and too often dominate it."

He felt very strongly about duty. "Satisfaction (*dovolstvie*) is nothing more than the sweet feeling of joy that we experience upon fulfilling our obligations, both in respect to others, and in respect to ourselves." He evidently feared that he might not be adequate to fulfilling his duties. "Sometimes, wishing, even with all our heart, to do something, we meet with an obstacle in inadequacy of means [that] deprives us of the possibility of doing what we want . . . . we prevent ourselves, not doing everything in our power, out of weakness or some other reason."

In a similar way, he was on his guard against idleness. Nothing, he believed, was more harmful. "It is the product of a weak and lazy mind to which every serious occupation is aversive."

He reflected on the power of monarchs. Laws, he said, must be laid down to prevent monarchical excesses. He very much admired the conduct of Henry IV and especially his application to the business of state. Henry had concerned himself, Paul remarked, not with his own glory, but with the well-being of his people.

In 1774, Paul made his first venture into politics. He submitted for his mother's consideration what amounts to a policy paper. It was entitled "Reflections on the State in General,"[6] but it had to do especially with military affairs. Paul wrote: "Our kingdom is now in a situation that requires peace (*pokoi*)." The Turkish war of five years, the Polish disturbances of the past eleven years, and the Cossack rebellion on the Yaik were sufficient reason to think of peace,

> for all these things drain the kingdom of people (*iznuriaet gosudarstvo liudmi*) and thereby diminish the tilling of the soil and devastate the land. Although this war [turned out] in our favor, we

> have at the same time suffered harvest failures [and] an ulcer which was of course a consequence of the war, internal disturbances, especially [difficulties] in recruiting. Now it remains only to hope for a long peace, which would give us complete rest, in order to . . . put things in order. . . . To achieve this, it is necessary to begin with the restoration of internal calm.

Paul appealed for lower taxes and the end of recruiting levies, for thus the chief causes of dissatisfaction would be removed. "Our people is such that the smallest satisfaction makes it forget years of discontent and even calamity. But we have this time, relying on the obedience and naturally happy disposition of the people, taken everything and saved nothing." The patience of the people, he said, had been stretched to the breaking point, and the state would therefore be unprepared in the eventuality of any genuinely unexpected emergency.

> The preservation of the kingdom is the preservation of the people; the preservation of the people is the preservation of the kingdom. The kingdom should be considered like a body; the sovereign is the head; the laws are the soul; morals are the heart; wealth and abundance are health; the military forces are the arms and all the members that serve for protection; and religion is the law under which all is comprised. The wise man will consider the preservation of his health and the strength of his body as the first thing on the physical side. We apply the same thing to the kingdom and it turns out that in it, it is necessary to try above all to preserve wealth and abundance (that is, agriculture and industry [or handicraft; literally in modern Russian, needlecraft—*rukodelie*] and the armed forces). . . .
>
> Supposing the military forces [to be like] the arms and the other limbs serving for defense, they should be, following this analogy, maintained exactly in that condition in which the members of a healthy body are [maintained]; that is, strong and powerful without excess, for if there is an excess [evidently an excess of power in one of the members of the body], then, of course, it will damage the remaining members, taking from them, for its superfluous strength, the nourishment (*soki*) necessary for the equal satisfaction of all the members. . . . Thus there is balance in all parts of the body.

It must be obvious by now that Paul had a penchant for loose argument that relied heavily on analogy and clumsy figures of speech. His thought was not thoroughly logical and clear. He implied that the limbs of the body were exclusively for its defense. Whatever he was trying to say about balancing the nourishment of the different limbs of the body was barely comprehensible and scarcely articulate. His writing was extremely awkward.

Equally obvious—and this is a theme that will recur again and again in Paul's thought—is a sensitive concern for the well-being of the Russian people and the Russian state. Paul had written a condemnation of the foreign policy of aggression and aggrandizement and an invidious comparison of Catherine's reign with an imagined reign of peace and prosperity.

To remedy the deplorable state of affairs that he described, he set down rather explicit recommendations:

1. To repudiate all offensive war and to deploy the entire armed force of the nation for defense. A series of fortresses should be built along the borders. They should be supported by formations of the army drawn from the local population, which would naturally know the enemy on its part of the border well and which would fight more bravely for its own homes than for strange territory.

2. To arrange the defense of the nation so that it would not be a burden on those who did not require it by deploying the army primarily on the borders and in force like that deployed against it on the other side of the border: one army against Sweden, one against Austria and Prussia, one against Turkey, and one in Siberia. The reserve forces should be scattered through the kingdom and supported by the province in which they were quartered.

3. Once the regiments were settled into permanent quarters, to replace deceased and disabled soldiers by drawing new recruits from the children of the soldiers themselves. The families of the soldiers were to be settled in military colonies with them. Thus the regiments would sustain themselves.[7]

4. To provide detailed manuals and instructions and especially "to prescribe to all, beginning with the field marshal, ending with the common soldier, all that they must do"; thus each one may be held precisely responsible for his duties, and the quality of the regiments ought to be maintained uniformly high.

5. By strictly subordinating everyone in the regiments to the manual of instructions, to avoid the discontent caused by personal preferment and commanders' caprices; and thus to make everyone more eager to serve and to serve well.

These proposals embody Paul's penchant for schemes exalting precise system and fastidious good order. He evidently imagined that important and complicated affairs could be rendered reasonable and orderly by a sufficiently reasonable and orderly approach to them. Personal pull and arbitrary command could be controlled by a proper field manual.

The third document embodying Paul's outlook was occasioned by his second marriage.[8] He was evidently concerned to avoid this time the difficulties that his first wife had had in adjusting both to her Russian surroundings and to her new mother-in-law. So he composed an "Instruction" for the benefit of Mariia Fedorovna, a treatise that was intended to acquaint her with the customs and peculiarities of her new land, with the character of Catherine, with his own, and with what was expected of her in her new duties.[9]

Paul urged Mariia Fedorovna to take Russian Orthodoxy very seriously and to practice it very piously. He urged her to "draw near" Catherine and "gain her trust." "In relation to the empress, the princess must be attentive and gentle. . . . Thus [the princess] will spare herself many intrigues that would not be long in involving her." Concerning her conduct in relation to Paul himself, he thought it "appropriate for her above all to arm herself with patience and meekness (*krotost'*), in order to tolerate (*snosit'*) my ardor (*goriachnost'*) and volatile disposition (*izmenchivoe raspolozhenie dukha*), and, equally, my impatience . . . . I wish her to be on a completely friendly basis with me, not however transgressing decency and decorum in society. Moreover, I want her to express to me directly and candidly all that she does not like in me."

He was exceptionally fastidious about the couple's finances. They would receive money, he said, every four months. It would be necessary to manage their budget very carefully in order not to run out of money. Part of it must be divided up to devote to various expenses. Then, "the remaining sum must be deposited in savings (*vnesena v khranenie*): this will be money for a rainy day (*eto budet dengi na chernyi den'*)." The accounts for a given four-month period were to be presented and paid on the first or second day of the succeeding period, and they must be verified with care.

Next he took up the subject of their schedule. "Our manner of life must be strictly regulated (*strogo opredelen*) . . . . Subjecting ourselves (*podchiniaias v zhizni*) to well-known rules, we protect ourselves from our own fantasies, which frequently become caprices, and together with this, we give an example to other people, who are obliged to subject themselves to the same rules." Particular days must be designated for receptions, lunches, and dinners, and all this should take place in a strongly ordered fashion, "without changes, because any change in these things appears in the eyes of the public as a caprice." Thus it was necessary to establish two orders of etiquette: one for reception days and holidays, the other for ordinary days. "We will in no way depart from etiquette." If receptions proved sometimes monotonous, he and Mariia Fedorovna must comfort themselves with the thought that they were doing their duty and that it would be doubly sweet to retire to the freedom of their own apartments when their duties were finished.

> I said above that the exact fulfillment of the rules is one of the chief conditions that it is necessary to observe in life; I repeat this again, especially relative to the domestic regime (*obikhod*). While we hold to established rules, we spare ourselves much, including tedium, one of the chief enemies of man—it does not have, so to speak, power over us. Therefore I consider it my duty to ask the princess to subject herself . . . to the established rules both in her manner of life and in regard to her duties in particular. I advise the princess to get up rather early, in order to have time to do her hair, to use an hour or two for her duties and then to complete her toilette, all the more in that my own passage of time is distributed such that, beginning at 10:00, when I am completely dressed, and until noon, I do not have a minute of free time . . . . I strongly request her to be ready at noon, and on Sundays and holidays at 10:30. After lunch I ask her to occupy herself with reading, music, and other things that she will find helpful and pleasant; in the course of her morning duties, I beg the princess to appoint an established time for [the study of] the Russian language and other subjects in order to acquire some understanding of the history, politics, and geography of our country, and also our religion and church services.

In view of the fact that the princess would be extremely busy with her duties and her social life, Paul suggested that she should spend a few minutes a day entirely alone, without even her service staff present. Any circle of intimates that she established about herself except that which was appointed for her would cause suspicion in the eyes of the public and give rise to gossip. "Concerning bedtime, *I beg the princess to submit to my custom of a regular life* (which in the beginning will be awkward for her), the more so since in consideration of my health and my morning duties, I do not have the possibility, in spite of my young years, of staying up all night." Finally, she should not do anything, even in her own room, that might seem secretive or give rise to the suspicion of secretiveness.

In summary, Paul's instruction for his new wife tells us that he designed their life, like the life of his regiments at drill, and, if possible, the life of Russia from Vilnius to Vladivostok, to be a model of order, routine, and regularity.

In 1788, Paul wrote the last of the documents that serve as our sources here. He was about to depart for the Swedish front and wished to leave, in the event that he was killed, an order of succession and a political testament that he recommended to his son Alexander. The object of the document on succession was to bring order out of the chaos of eighteenth-century succession crises, perhaps to condemn Catherine by invidious example, and to spare his successors the agonizing uncertainty that had been inflicted on him. It is what we would expect of him. The political testament is more interesting.[10]

> The object of every society is the happiness (*blazhenstvo*) of each and of all. Society cannot exist unless the will of everyone is directed to a common goal. This is what a governent is for, any kind of government. The best is that which most directly and most advantageously reaches its goal [i.e., the happiness, or blessedness, of all]. [In pursuit of this end] various kinds of government arise. The larger the land, the more difficult the means of fulfilling [the goal of happiness]; consequently the first care (*pervoe popechenie*) must be to facilitate them (*oblegchat' ikh* [evidently to facilitate the means of achieving social happiness]). The simplest means [of doing so] is to entrust power to a single person, but there are human inconveniences (*neudobstvami chelovechestva*) connected with it.

Paul thought that the best form of government was autocracy because "it unites in itself the force of the laws and the efficiency (*skorost'*) of the power of one person." The major duty of the autocrat was to see that the laws were observed and that the different classes of society did the duty that their station prescribed for them.

The first estate of the land, Paul wrote, was the nobility. It was the mainstay of the state and the sovereign. It must be concerned with the quality of the estate and not admit superfluous or unworthy persons to its ranks. The second estate was the clergy, whose holy duties were quite demanding. It must teach a proper understanding of God and not superstition. The next estate was the commercial and industrial class. Its duties were to encourage economic development and the prosperity of the land. The remainder of society consisted of the peasantry, worse condition was worthy of special respect. To deserve this respect, it must work better and provide a steady supply of provisions.

But the mere definition of the duties of these estates was not sufficient. It was necessary for them to fulfill their proper functions, which was not possible unless every member of every estate learned through education the scope of his duties. The first duty was serving the well-being of society. This could not be achieved without education, from which an understanding of the law came. Without education, people were corrupt. Thus it was necessary to found schools, "based on the rules of government," so that everyone, according to his social station, could learn his appointed duties and how to fulfill them for the betterment of society.

Ordering the business of the state as described could not fail to produce moral and physical balance leading to "general good faith" everywhere. Someone must oversee all this, for the attainment of peace and bliss (*blazhenstvo*) of each and all and of the purpose of God's law was the first object of statecraft.

Paul was sure, in conclusion, that when "all parts of the state have been led in an orderly fashion to the good balance in which they should be, such that the balance can not be broken or damaged, then one may say that the society has been directed onto its proper path of the well-being of each and of all, which is in accord with the law of God and consequently can not fail to be blessed in everything by his Heavenly Hand."

While he waited to govern Paul had, as he said, nothing to do, that is, nothing to do except to fantasize, to dream of the day when, if fortune spared him, he would have a sovereign's business of state to do. In the meantime, he drilled his troops, and he fretted over a fussy schedule. He did not spend his enormous leisure in a conspicuously constructive way. In many respects, the observation that Martin Malia made of Herzen and the gentry socialists of that generation applies as well in a slightly different sense to Paul:[11]

> Where the entire order of the world, in every detail of its organization, is an affront to the dignity of the [legitimate sovereign], the formulation of a specific set of grievances is impossible, and the cry of protest can only find expression in generalities . . . . under such circumstances . . . to approach politics pragmatically was in effect an abdication of hope, if not downright collaboration with the existing order. Therefore the only thing left to do was to think in terms of general principles; and principles, the longer one lives with them, without any possibility of application, become increasingly pure, ideal, sweeping, and, most crucial of all, uncompromising. The reformer turns intransigent and will settle for nothing less than the complete destruction of the "old" corrupt world and the creation of a totally "new" one.

The two chief malefactors in the old corrupt world were the immoral empress and the pampered nobility. The two chief sufferers were the masses and the heir. Paul's aim would be to undo the work of Catherine, to harness the nobility to state service, and to provide justice and *blazhenstvo* for the people. Such a program was at the very least painfully naive. Was it insane?

Among psychologists and psychiatrists, *insane* is strictly a legal term, a term for the criminal court. The standard terminology of mental illness in the United States is that of the American Psychiatric Association's *Diagnostic and Statistical Manual of Mental Disorders* (2nd ed. Washington, 1968).[12]

What we have seen of Paul's attitudes and ideas suggests that he falls in the category of personality disorders. This particular terminology was first adopted by the APA relatively recently, in 1968. Naturally, several years passed before it began to be reflected significantly in the literature, and it is still slighted in the conventional textbooks.

This state of affairs is recognized by the editor of an important new book on the subject: "This book is designed to fill a void in the literature regarding personality disorders and their clinical care. As a teacher and therapist I have become more aware of deficits in both psychiatric training and treatment of this very large group of patients about whom much less has been studied than neurotic and psychotic disorders [*sic*]."[13]

Personality disorders are "characterized by deeply ingrained maladaptive patterns of behavior that are perceptibly different in quality from psychotic and neurotic symptoms. Generally, these are life-long patterns, often recognizable by the time of adolescence or earlier."[14] They are perceptibly different from neuroses and psychoses in that they are less severe, in the opinion of most specialists. They are different, too, in that they are not distinguished for the perceptual skew of the psychoses or for the strident anxiety of the neuroses. In many cases, however, they display the same kind, if not the same degree, of abnormal behavior as is sometmes found in psychoses or neuroses.

There are quite a variety of personality disorders. The kind that best describes Paul's behavior is obsessive-compulsive personality.[15] "This behavior pattern is characterized by excessive concern with conformity and adherence to standards of conscience. Consequently, individuals in this group may be rigid, over-inhibited, over-conscientious, over-dutiful, and unable to relax easily."[16] Personalities with obsessive-compulsive tendencies are easily recognized: "they are excessively cleanly, orderly, and conscientious, sticklers for precision; they have inconclusive ways of thinking and acting; they are given to needless repetition. Those who have shown such traits since childhood are often morose, obstinate, irritable people; others are vacillating, uncertain of themselves and submissive."[17]

These characteristics are, however, fairly common in the population at large, and to some extent, they are even fortunate. "Most of us have obsessional traits and lead an obsessional way of life; we are preoccupied with clock time and with problems of order and orderliness in our paper subculture. In a sublimated way, obsessional values are part of our middle-class social character. At their best, the operation of these values gets things done, particularly the routine ones, makes the world move more smoothly—so to speak, the trains run on time."[18]

The distinction between a normal and abnormal level of such traits is determined by the degree of disability and by character rigidity. "If fear of closeness and a need to control others keeps the compulsive at a distance from family and prevents him from forming close friendships, it is reasonable to consider his behavior as deviant."[19]

The obsessive-compulsive's behavior is driven and full of effort: it lacks spontaneity. There is in his behavior a "trend toward the replacement of 'I want to' or 'I enjoy' with 'I ought to' or 'I should' . . . . Tragically, he often does things for or with others mainly because he feels *required* to do so."[20] He is burdened with a great weight of duty and obligation.

The obsessive-compulsive person is concerned to control his own personality and its impulses on the one hand and his environment on the other hand. He wants to render his experience as little spontaneous and accidental and as much predictable as possible.

> The [obsessives] tend to increase the predictability of life events by ensuring that their room is always the same from day to day, that clothes are taken off in the same order and that the daily constitutional is taken at the same time and along the circumscribed routes. By doing this they are reducing the chances of being caught unawares by an event which may present difficulties of interpretation. . . . If the world ceases to be orderly, if prized possessions are moved, then chaos throughout their whole environment is a possibility.[21]

If the things in their environment depart slightly or greatly from their preconceived notion of proper and secure order, then such persons experience considerable consternation and frustration.[22] They tend to concern themselves in an increasingly self-centered and eccentric fashion with premeditated order. In the words of Fransella, "obsessional thinking is concerned more and more with less and less."[23]

> When forced to work under circumstances over which he has no control and which may vary unpredictably, the compulsive personality may become anxious and disorganized . . . . As a supervisor, he is one who breathes down the necks of his subordinates and drives them to distraction by his attention to petty detail and his insistence on following the letter of the law. His need for perfection and order always carries with it the potential for conflict with others who may view him as obstructionistic, petty, inordinately scrupulous, and irascible.[24]

He maintains a hyperalert vigilance, for he is consumed by doubt as to whether other persons and the world in general are friendly or hostile. To structure a confident relationship between himself and others, he is constantly in search of the "right rules."[25]

A wide variety of research during the past two decades has showed that obsessive-compulsives have stronger feelings of ambiguity about many things than other persons do. They also have a stronger need for certainty and therefore a stronger need to avoid ambiguity. For example, in tests involving faint auditory signals, administered simultaneously to groups of obsessive-compulsives and to controls, the obsessive-compulsives asked for the repetition of the signals much more frequently than the controls and left many fewer answers marked "not sure." The researchers concluded that obsessive-compulsive ruminations are "the result of an overpowering need for certainty in decisions to terminate quite ordinary activities."[26] Other studies show that obsessive-compulsives repeat this same pattern of avoiding ambiguity in tests discriminating for differences in weight, length, block shapes, etc.[27] Similar tests show that they err in the direction of symmetry in visual problems more than other people do.[28]

Hojer-Pedersen found that his obsessive-compulsive patients tended to regard themselves as altruistic and yet to behave in a quite narcissistic manner. They reflected the same ironic paradox with respect to generosity-stinginess. Even more interestingly, all of them were ambiguously dependent and independent,[29] that is, they protested their independence to a suspicious extent.

The evidence that Paul was an obsessive-compulsive personality is abundant and unambiguous. It is hardly necessary to dwell on his rigid adherence to standards of conscience and his imposition of his own conscience on others. He was dutiful in the extreme, and he admired monarchs who were known for devotion to duty.

Just as conspicuous was his quest for order and perfection. Contemporaries spoke of the "Gatchina spirit" that pervaded both his military concerns and other affairs of state. The French Revolution he dreaded in part for its threat to the good order of Europe. When Bonaparte appeared, Paul entertained some thought that he would make himself an absolutist and thus tame the Revolution and restore good order. His note to Mariia Fedorovna to acquaint her with the strange land to which she had come and the imposing duties that she had assumed dwelled emphatically on order in their schedule as in their monetary accounts.

The "right rules" were the burden of that document. Russians could be received on certain days, and foreigners on other days. If it all seemed too much to bear, she should consider that the rules themselves would, if adhered to, provide them the refuge that they could not otherwise have. The new army field manual, the new field maneuvers, the new law on succession—all these things represent salvation by rules. This is not to say that these things were not useful or appropriate. Rather, they represent the extreme degree of service that Paul expected of right rules. The Maltese Order had good rules, rules of service and religion. That was not its only virtue, but it was important for that reason.

No one would deny that Paul was vigilant and hyperalert, that he was a mobilized personality. He scanned the environment intently for signs of disrespect for himself, as well as for signs of disorder. Because he read the environment for those signals in particlar, he often misinterpreted it. Further he was, according to even the most friendly observer (e.g., Sablukov), an irascible supervisor.

He was more concerned to structure his life to preempt personal spontaneity than he was to experience the feelings of persons ostensibly close to him. He was demonstrably afraid of his inner impulses and kept them under tight rein. "Our manner of life must be strictly regulated . . . . Subjecting ourselves to well-known rules, we protect ourselves from our own fantasies, which frequently become caprices, and together with this, we give an example to other people, who are obliged to subject themselves to the same rules." This is a classic confession of the obsessive-compulsive outlook, one that the clinician might well regard as the rarest articulation of the unconscious. All must be arranged just so, "without changes, because any change in these things appears in the eyes of the public as a caprice." Paul did not want to be capricious, or, worse, appear capricious.

The findings of Hojer-Pedersen are especially interesting for Paul's case. Paul's own expression is full of intentions of generosity and self-sacrifice and of the ideal of service on his part to the suffering nation. He was, he thought, an altruist. This pose was accepted by the common people who rarely came into contact with him. It was repudiated in morbid fashion by those who dealt with him daily. For them, his touchy narcissism was only too apparent. The ceremonies that he loved, the care that he lavished on them, the fanfare of the Maltese Order, all of these things manifested a wounded vanity seeking compensation.

Even more telling is Hojer-Pedersen's observation on ambiguous dependency. Paul was so childishly dependent, and so much in need of being demonstratively independent, that he was putty in the hands of clever intriguers about him. He required Panin's support against Catherine, the support of religion and principle against his evil enemies, and finally the support of his barber-lackey Kutaisov against those persons, Mariia Fedorovna, Nelidova, and the Kurakins, whose support had been essential until he was required to recognize it.[30]

By way of fathoming the murky mysteries of Paul's disconcerting behavior patterns, I offer the following suggestion. He was born into a situation in which he was exceptionally important and exceptionally insecure. He early developed traumas over what might happen to him. He soon evolved a characteristic paradigm of dealing with his actual problems and his no less real traumas at once. He exalted pious principles, principles so high and mighty that they were invulnerable to attack. He proclaimed his own unflinching attachment to these, he required it of others, and he rewarded and punished accordingly. To the extent that he could structure his environment according to his favorite moral standards, he achieved good order and submission to himself. Most important, he achieved his own safety. Paul's environment, however, was peculiarly vast. From 1796, he had to manage the whole of the Russian Empire. From about 1798, in his opinion, events beyond his borders threatened his imperial environment. Hence he aspired to impose his paradigm on the entire continent. Only thus could he secure himself, i.e., only by threatening everyone else. His psychological processes were a catalyst of conflict, and the reign was a short one.

NOTES

1 S. F. Platonov, *A History of Russia* (Bloomington, 1964), p. 304: "When he ascended the throne at the age of forty-two, Paul was a broken man, physically, mentally and spiritually." Kazimierz Waliszewski, *Paul the First of Russia* (Philadelphia, 1913), p. 478: "He was the victim of morbid tendencies which inevitably resulted from . . . an abnormal constitution of mind . . . . When the teaching of the jacobins of the West and the revolutionary tradition of Peter the Great converged in one mind the end could not fail to be insanity." Geoffrey Bruun, *Europe and the French Imperium, 1799-1815* (New York, 1938), refers to Paul, p. 40, as the "pathologically unbalanced son" of Catherine II. The examples could be multiplied endlessly.

2 For a convenient introduction to a part of that opinion, see the study of Roderick E. McGrew, "A Political Portrait of Paul I from the Austrian and English Diplomatic Archives," *Jahrbücher für Geschichte Osteuropas*, XVIII, No. 4, n. s. (Dec. 1970), 503-529.

3 "The madness of this unfortunate sovereign (there is no doubt that he was not in his [right] mind) reached such lengths (*predielov*) that it could no longer be borne." Aleksandr Fedorovich Lanzheron, "Iz zapisok," in *Tsareubiistvo 11 marta 1801 g.; zapiski uchastnikov i sovremennikov*, 2nd ed. (St. Petersburg, 1908), p. 176. See also the story of N. A. Sablukov in his *Zapiski* (Leipzig, 1902), pp. 46-52.

4 *Ocherki pravitel'stvennoi deiatel'nosti vremeni imperatora Pavla I* (St. Petersburg, 1916), pp. 1-92.

5 *Russkaia starina*, 1874, IX, 667-683.

6 The full name of the memorandum was "Razsuzhdenie o gosudarstve voobshche, otnositel'no chisla voisk, potrebnago dlia zashchity onago, i kasatel'no oborony vsiekh predielov." Petr S. Lebedev, *Grafy Nikita i Petr Paniny* (St. Petersburg, 1863), pp. 185-199. P. A. Geisman and A. N. Dubovskii, *Graf Petr Ivanovich Panin, 1721-1789; istoricheskii ocherk voennoi i gosudarstvennoi deiatel'nosti* (St. Petersburg, 1897), pp. 88-98. "Velikii kniaz' Pavel Petrovich; perepiska v. k. Pavla Petrovicha s gr. Petrom Paninym," *Russkaia starina*, 1882, XXXIII, 403-418, 739-764.

7 The analogy with Alexander's idea is obvious.

8 His first wife died in 1776.

9 E. Shumigorskii, ed., "Instruktsiia Velikago Kniazia Pavla Petrovicha Kniagine Marii Fedorovne (1776)," *Russkaia starina*, 1898, II, 247-261.

10 M. I. Semevskii, ed., "Materialy k russkoi istorii XVIII veka (1788)," *Viestnik Evropy*, 1867, I, 297-330. I am indebted to Sergei Ignashev for checking my translation of this material.

11 Martin Malia, *Alexander Herzen and the Birth of Russian Socialism* (Cambridge, 1961), pp. 55, 118-119.

12 Hereafter *DSM*-II. It is coordinated with, but not identical to, the World Health Organization's *International Classification of Diseases*, 8th ed. There are ten broad categories: (1) mental retardation; (2) organic brain syndromes; (3) psychoses not attributable to physical conditions; (4) neuroses; (5) personality disorders; (6) psychophysiologic disorders; (7) special symptoms (enuresis, tics, disorders of sleep and feeding); (8) transient situational disorders; (9) behavior disorders of childhood; (10) conditions without manifest psychiatric disorder. The reader will easily see why at least some of these do not apply to Paul. I hope that I will be excused for not examining each of the categories individually.

13 J. R. Lion, ed., *Personality Disorders: Diagnosis and Management* (Baltimore, 1974), p. v.

14 *DSM*-II, p. 41.

15 There are two other kinds of personality disorders that are of considerable interest where Paul is concerned. The first of these is hysterical personality. "This behavior pattern is characterized by excitability, emotional instability, over-reactivity, and self-dramatization. This self-dramatization is always attention-seeking and often seductive.... These personalities are also immature, self-centered, often vain, and usually dependent on others" (*DSM*-II, p. 43). I have not pursued this diagnosis here because it is almost invariably applied to women. I am aware of the controversial nature of such a statement these days, but I would like to plead that it is not my fault. See David Shapiro, *Neurotic Styles* (New York, 1965), p. 180; M. G. Blinder, "The Hysterical Personality," *Psychiatry*, 29 (1966), 229; J. M. Perley and S. B. Guze, "Hysteria—the Stability and Usefulness of Clinical Criteria," *New England Journal of Medicine*, 266 (1966), 423; O. Arkonac and S. Guze, "A Family of Hysteria," *ibid.*, 268 (1963), 239; S. B. Guze, R. A. Woodruff, and P. J. Clayton, "Sex, Age and the Diagnosis of Hysteria," *American Journal of Psychiatry*, 129 (1972), 745; J. J. Purtell, E. Robins, and M. E. Cohen, "Observation on Clinical Aspects of Hysteria," *Journal of the American Medical Association*, 146 (1961), 903.

The other possibility is paranoid personality: "hypersensitivity, rigidity, unwarranted suspicion, jealousy, envy, excessive self-importance, and a tendency to blame others and ascribe evil motives to them." Many observers of Paul would likely agree that this definition might have been invented to describe him. But what needs emphasis here is the phrase "unwarranted suspicion," for, to continue with the definition, "the presence of suspicion of itself does not justify this diagnosis, since the suspicion may be warranted in some instances" (*ibid.*, p. 42). To take only the most obvious of many examples, we cannot afford to ignore the facts that Catherine's rival pretenders to the throne, Peter III and Ivan VI, were murdered, that she considered dispossessing Paul of the succession, and that he was himself assassinated. Of these four things (and of lesser ones like them), there is a very complex question whether in the case of the last two, unlike the first two (which argue the case against paranoid behavior), suspicion preceded threat—and provoked it—or vice versa. The problem is a subtle one.

16 *DSM*-II, p. 43.

17 A. J. Lewis and E. Mapother, "Obsessional Disorder," in Sir Ronald Bodley Scott, ed., *Price's Textbook of the Practice of Medicine*, 11th ed. (London, 1973), p. 1379.

18 Rose Spiegel, "Psychotherapy with Obsessive-Compulsive Patients," in Max Hammer, ed., *The Theory and Practice of Psychotherapy with Specific Disorders* (Springfield, Ill., 1972), p. 99.

19 Walter Weintraub, "Obsessive-Compulsive and Paranoid Personalities," in Lion, *Personality Disorders*, p. 87.

20 Henry P. Laughlin, *The Neuroses* (Washington, 1967), pp. 326-329.

21 Fay Fransella, "Thinking of the Obsessional," in H. R. Beech, ed., *Obsessional States* (London, 1974), p. 179.

22 H. R. Beech and J. Perigault, "Toward a Theory of Obsessional Disorder," *ibid.*, p. 114.

23 Fransella, "Thinking of the Obsessional," *ibid.*, p. 194.

24 E. Brody and S. Lindbergh, "Personality Disorders, I: Traits and Pattern Disturbances," in A. M. Freedman and H. I. Kaplan, eds., *Comprehensive Textbook of Psychiatry* (Baltimore, 1967), p. 944.

25 Weintraub, "Obsessive Compulsive and Paranoid Personalities," in Lion, *Personality Disorders*, p. 87; E. G. Schachtel, "On Attention, Selective Inattention and Experience; an Inquiry into Attention as an Attitude," *Bulletin of the Menninger Clinic*, 33 (1969), 65-91; H. R. Beech and Andrée Liddell, "Decision-Making, Mood States and Ritualistic Behaviour among Obsessional Patients," in Beech, *Obsessional States*, p. 143.

26 A. D. Milner, H. R. Beech, and V. J. Walker, "Decision Processes and Obsessional Behavior," *British Journal of Social and Clinical Psychology*, 10 (1971), 88-89.

27 V. Hamilton, "Perceptual and Personality Dynamisms in Reactions to Ambiguity," *British Journal of Psychology*. 48 (1957), 200-215.

28 B. G. Rosenberg, "Compulsiveness as a Determinant in Selected Cognitive-Perceptual Performances," *Journal of Personality*, 21 (1953), 506-516.

29 Willy Hojer-Pedersen, "The Compulsive Personality Type," *Acta Psychiatrica Scandinavica*, 44 (1968), 166-167.

30 It is appropriate to make one brief comment on the possibility of obsessive-compulsive neurosis. It is roughly a more advanced degree of the same kind of behavior as that just described. To warrant such a diagnosis, it is necessary to establish, in addition to the symptoms of obsessive-compulsive personality, two others. One is obsessive thinking, the persistent, repeated intrusion of unwelcome or embarrassing thoughts, such as forebodings of danger to oneself or family or the impulse to shout obscenities in solemn assemblies. The other is compulsive rituals, such as repeated hand-washing. In Paul's case, while there is no reason to find these two symptoms implausible, we lack sufficiently intimate evidence of his private habits to decide the question. Neurotics are aware that their behavior is abnormal, they are embarrassed about it, and they try to hide it.

II
FOREIGN AFFAIRS

3

THE OBJECTIVES OF PAUL'S ITALIAN POLICY

Norman E. Saul

The reign of the Emperor Paul witnessed an unprecedented Russian involvement in the affairs of the Italian states. The purpose of this paper is to explore the background of the Russian presence in Italy, the course of its development, the objectives of Russian policy in the area, and the results. Viewing Russia through an Italian prism may also provide another perspective on the character of the Emperor Paul and on Russia's place in European affairs at the end of the eighteenth century. At the same time, it will be possible to examine some of the international implications of the Italian question in the context of Russian policy.

Russia's Italian connections did not begin with Paul but extended back over several hundred years of religious and cultural missions. The Italianate influences on the architectural styles of Old Russia are well known, and the new St. Petersburg was practically built by Italians—Rastrelli, Quarenghi, Rossi. In fact, though the literature on the Western impact on Russia in the eighteenth century is sizable, relatively little attention has been devoted to physical and psychological influences on Russia in architecture, art, and theater, which were largely Italian. Direct political and economic relations between Italy and Russia, however, for all practical purposes did not begin until the last half of the eighteenth century.

The investigation of this subject is as complex as the character of the Emperor Paul, of the political situation within Italy, and of the French Revolution and the Napoleonic Wars in general. Twenty pages could be devoted at this point to an attempt to define Italy—with the probable conclusion that it did not exist. One authority commented, somewhat facetiously, that only the Papal States pursued a modern concept of Italy.[1] Perhaps that is because the Pope lacked the military forces that would either be in confrontation or alliance with the four foreign presences—French, Austrian, Russian, and British. For practical purposes our concern will focus on the three main political entities—the Kingdom of the Two Sicilies, Sardinia-Piedmont, and the Papal States—although it will be necessary to examine in some degree the greater Italian circle that included the Ionian Islands and Malta. This area will not be a major consideration here, since the Ionian Islands were in the process of becoming part of a Greek sphere, and Malta, as far as it relates to Russian policy in this period, is a subject by itself. The focus geographically will then be on the Italy that was later made into a European power.

Another difficulty has to do with the variety of personalities who circulated in and around Italy during these years. On the international level Italy became the battleground of a dynamic and unpredictable French military genius of Corsican background, an inconstant Russian tsar, a stubborn Austrian chancellor, a brilliant but emotional English admiral, and a Neapolitan king whose greatest concern in his perambulations between Naples and Palermo was the state of the local hunting grounds. Appearing from scene to scene in a plot that might just as well have been from one of the many second-rate Italian operas performed in St. Petersburg are the Duc di Serra Capriola, who began a long diplomatic career in Russia as a Neapolitan dandy at Empress Catherine's court in 1783, and an assortment of Italian missionaries who came to Russia with a variety of projects and proposals both secular and religious. On the Russian side in Italy were a motley group of Russian commanders and diplomats, including the famous but aging Suvorov and the young, bewhiskered Mikhail Borozdin. Romantic interests were nourished by the wife of the British envoy who kissed the blood-stained sword of a Turkish courier bringing a jeweled snuff box from Paul to Nelson; a wealthy Russian widow and niece of Potemkin, in whose quest an influential Milanese nobleman and knight of the Order of Malta came to St. Petersburg in 1795; and a Russian grand duchess, for whose attachment Adam Czartoryski was forced to begin what became an illustrious political career as Russian minister to Sardinia.

The real beginning of Russia's interest in Italy was ushered in by two developments. The first was Catherine II's modern concept of fighting the Turks on two sides, by land from south Russia and by sea from the Mediterranean. The plan involved the sending of emissaries to Italy to arrange for supplies and other support. The second was the partitioning of Poland, which brought Russia much more intimate involvement in the affairs of the Catholic Church. Russian expansion southward and westward obviously brought Italy closer and enhanced the possibilities of direct and indirect trade.

And indeed the annexation of the Crimea and the settlement of the steppe, especially by foreign colonists, led to a spectacular increase in Russian grain exports across the Black Sea and into the Mediterranean. Between the 1780s and 1800 exports of grain from Russian Black Sea ports increased by twenty times while total grain exports from European Russia multiplied fourfold. If wheat alone is considered, the increase is even more impressive. For the period 1796-1801 the Black Sea ports accounted for over half of the Russian grain exports.[2] Details on the proportion going to Italy are not available, since most of the grain was transshipped in Turkish ports, but it was generally known that Italy was one of the major consumers of Russian leather, hemp, and iron, in addition to grain, some of the Italian imports even arriving indirectly from the Baltic ports. By 1800, consuls and merchants in Kherson represented Naples, Genoa, Trieste, and Livorno.[3] And the development of this trade would have led naturally to an increased awareness of Russia in the major ports and cities of Italy. A corresponding increase in the number of Russian consuls in the Mediterranean suggests at least some realization of market potential in St. Petersburg, but there is little evidence to support the contention that economic factors were of major importance in determining Russian policy toward Italy. The most significant effect of expanding trade was the rise in the number of Italians visiting south Russia, facilitated by the friendlier relations between the Italian states and the Ottoman Empire that corresponded with the Russian rapprochement with Turkey toward the end of the 1790s.

Another background factor that is difficult to measure in the forming of Russian attitudes toward Italy was the increase in personal contacts. Many of the Russians who had the means and desire to travel outside of the country in the last half of the eighteenth century visited Italy. An environment that so greatly contrasted with life in Moscow and St. Petersburg seemed to draw Russians like magnets to this region. The Emperor Paul, who included Italy on his Grand Tour of 1781-1782, was certainly no exception in favoring the Italian experience over that of other countries visited. What these exposures did to condition an Italian consciousness in Russia, however, is difficult to determine.

In 1796 the primary Russian interest in Italy was political and strategic. There were, however, additional secondary factors. The inclusion of many Roman Catholics in the empire as a result of the final partitions of Poland was drawing Russia into more regular relations with the Papacy. And the importance of direct and indirect trade with Italy probably registered upon those concerned about Russia's financial condition. Paul came to the throne without any particular Italian objectives in mind, certainly with no influences from that quarter that could challenge his general partiality for things Prussian. In the round of diplomatic courtesies that followed immediately upon his succession, the Neapolitan envoy was unintentionally slighted, for which Paul made the appropriate apology. But the Sardinian representative, Carlo Bossi, was cordially disliked by Paul, a factor that resulted in his recall and clouded Russian-Sardinian relations for over a year.[4]

The first significant event in Russo-Italian relations during Paul's reign occurred indirectly through the efforts of Count Giulio Litta to gain Russian support for the Order of St. John of Jerusalem. Litta arrived in St. Petersburg in October 1795 to negotiate on behalf of the order claims to estates in the territory newly acquired from Poland, but he was unsuccessful until after the accession Paul. The emperor's favorable response to Litta's overtures in December 1796 was due to his predilection for the order and to his previous contacts with its Italian representative. Having enjoyed the hospitality of the Litta family at their villa near Milan in 1782, Paul reciprocated by giving a reception for the young Giulio upon his arrival in Russia in 1789 to receive a commission in the Russian navy and serve in the Russo-Swedish war under Prince Nassau-Siegen. These initial meetings served as a bond between the two men and facilitated the negotiation of the treaty between Russia and the Maltese Order that was signed in January 1797. By the terms of the treaty the emperor was designated a "protector," a separate Russian, Greek Orthodox *langue* was created, and an annual subsidy was granted. As representative of the state that held technical suzerainty over Malta, Serra Capriola assisted in the negotiations, retaining the prominent position in the diplomatic circle of St. Petersburg that he would keep throughout Paul's reign.[5]

Giulio Litta also got from Paul encouragement for his brother, Lorenzo, who was then in Warsaw, to come to Russia to negotiate a rearrangement of the affairs of the Roman Catholic Church in Russia on behalf of Pius VI. The Papal emissary arrived in Moscow in April 1797 in time to assume a high-ranking position among the foreign diplomats at the coronation. Though his initial reception in Russia was quite warm, deliberations on improvements in the administration of the Catholic Church progressed very slowly through 1797 and into the next year, partly because of a rivalry that developed between the Littas and Stanislaw Siestrzencewicz (1731-1826), who as Archbishop of Mogilev held the highest office of the Church in the Russian Empire. Finally, in May 1798, Lorenzo Litta and Alexander Kurakin signed the new regulations that increased the number of Catholic bishoprics from one to five and provided for more autonomous administration under the College of Justice.[6] After awkward communications with a mobile Papacy brought the expected approval, the new "Acts" went into effect in August 1798. For his acquiescence to Litta's project, Siestrzencewicz was elected a Cardinal.

Paul's accommodations with the Roman Church went hand in hand with a shift in mood from peace to war in the Russian capital. For the most part, this change had nothing to do with deliberations in St. Petersburg but was caused by outside events, in particular the victories of the French army under Napoleon Bonaparte in Italy. Though Paul was well aware of French military supremacy in northern Italy and of Austrian peace overtures, he was still quite surprised at the terms of the Treaty of Campoformio and the extent of the concessions granted by Austria. One feature of the treaty that the emperor especially disliked was the partitioning of the Republic of Venice, which resulted in its elimination.[7] Another legitimate state, like Poland, had been sacrificed to feed the appetites of larger neighbors. Paul not only opposed the partition on principle, but he also especially deplored giving the French possession of the Ionian Islands with mainland enclaves in the Balkans. He feared French revolutionary influences upon restless Balkan peoples and a possible strengthening of the French position at Constantinople. In a conversation with the Austrian envoy, Dietrichstein, on 20 November 1797, Chancellor Bezborodko complained, "We did not believe you would forget our interests so quickly in your negotiations." But he added, "The democratization of the Turkish provinces by the establishment of the French in the islands and in Albania was less worrisome for Russia than for the House of Austria."[8]

The obviously increased Russian concern about the Italian situation, indicated by a series of conferences in St. Petersburg, surprised and alarmed the Austrian leaders. Thugut, the Austrian chancellor, could not understand Paul's disinterest in Germany, and asked Francis II to write a personal letter on the subject in February 1798. Cobenzl, the permanent ambassador to Russia, temporarily leading the Austrian peace negotiations at Rastadt, emphasized in a letter to Dietrichstein that "the more that can be done in Germany, the more can be done in Italy."[9] But mention of German affairs only irritated another sore spot with Paul, his exclusion from the Congress of Rastadt.

As he prepared to become more actively involved in Europe in early 1798 by offering asylum to Louis XVIII and Condé's royalist corps and mending fences with Suvorov and other generals, two basic objectives of Paul's policies in relation to Italy emerge: to shield the Ottoman Empire on the Adriatic side from French influences that might damage or destroy the existing friendly relations with that country, and to play a role as arbiter or mediator in the conflicts of other European powers.

Throughout 1798, Russia, with prodding by the French, who were becoming more aggressive in the field in Italy (with the occupation of Rome in February) and at the conference table at Rastadt, moved slowly but surely into measures to secure those objectives. The first important military step was the sending of a squadron of the Baltic fleet in May to the North Sea in order to free English ships for the Mediterranean. And at practically the same time that rumors reached northern and central Europe that a large French force was embarking at Toulon for Malta, the emperor hosted a grand reception for twenty-eight Knights of the Order at his palace in St. Petersburg. This was quickly followed in July by a reinforcement of the Russian squadron in the North Sea and by an offer of naval assistance to the Ottoman Empire and the alerting of an army of 16,000 under Rosenberg on the Austrian frontier.[10] In a letter at this time to his ambassador in London, Paul voiced particular concern about the fate of Italy.[11] And despite the objections of his chief advisers on foreign affairs, Bezborodko and Victor Kochubei, Paul proposed sending armies of 60,000 and 75,000 to Austria and to the Ottoman Empire (to the latter under the impression that the French expeditionary force was headed for the Balkans), providing those powers would supply all of their needs.[12]

The commitment of substantial Russian arms to the defense of neighboring powers was frustrated for the time being by the Turkish reluctance to host a large Russian force and by difficulties over subsidies and rations to support the one intended for Austria. While Paul became exasperated over Austrian delays, a Black Sea fleet under Admiral Ushakov sailed into the straits and, after negotiating an agreement for common action with the Turks, proceeded to liberate the Ionian Islands from French control.

From the first indication of the availability of Russian assistance against France, the Neapolitan envoy was naturally interested in obtaining direct Russian support, but any effort to comply with allied requests was hampered by want of means to get an army into Italy. With the main French campaign launched in Egypt, however, the immediacy of the need to safeguard the Balkans and central Europe diminished, and Paul, whose frustration with Austria continued, listened more carefully to the Neapolitan arguments.[13] A combination of the emperor's growing involvement with the Order of Malta, and consequent desire to free the island from the French, and the diplomatic skill of Serra Capriola resulted in a treaty of alliance between Russia and the Kingdom of the Two Sicilies, the first of several bilateral agreements negotiated in late December and early January that made Russia a keystone of the Second Coalition against France.

In order to cement this new Italian connection Paul ordered a corps of 8,000 to be prepared at Black Sea ports for shipment to Italy.[14] Paul, however, had entered an Italian war that was already reaching a climax. A

Neapolitan army had marched north in November to overthrow the Roman Republic only to be routed in battle by the French and their Italian and Polish allies. As this latter army pushed toward Naples the king and court escaped on a British ship to Palermo, almost on the same day as the signing of the Russian treaty, leaving practically all of mainland Italy in French hands, the king of Sardinia having also fled to an island refuge.

The radically changed situation in Italy alarmed all of the new coalition partners with the result that the outstanding difficulties in the way of the dispatch of a Russian army directly to northern Italy were quickly resolved. Suvorov left St. Petersburg in March 1799 to take command of an army that now included the corps originally intended for Naples. Admiral Ushakov, who had just conquered the last of the Ionian Islands, Corfu (though this was not yet known in Russia), was ordered to extend his activities to patrolling the Adriatic coast of Italy. And at the same time, a new squadron was sent from the Baltic to augment the Russian fleet in the Mediterranean.[15]

With all of these forces bearing down on Italy, questions remained concerning Russian goals and aims. The absence of any precisely stated objectives on the part of the Emperor Paul is one factor that led to difficulties between him and his allies. It was clear that Paul wanted to remove the Frence influence and presence from Italy and to reestablish the old political configuration of the area, but restoration of frontiers could mean many things, depending upon the date selected. Paul was no doubt mindful of this problem and perhaps purposefully and necessarily vague. He did commit Russia, however, to the basic aim of bringing the three chief independent rulers in Italy—Ferdinand IV, Charles Emmanuel IV, and Pius VI—back to their capitals, Naples, Turin, and Rome. But the new Italy could not be simply the pre-Campoformio Italy. Paul had no intention of reviving the Venetian Republic, but exactly what was to happen to the French share of Venice, to the reformed Republic of Genoa, or to Tuscany and the Papal States was unclear, except that Paul himself on several occasions denied any territorial ambitions.[16]

Austria, with long-standing interests in Italy and a large army on Italian territory, was in a position to take advantage of these ambiguities. The fact that the main center of military strategy for the allied campaign had shifted to Vienna also gave Austria an advantage in Italy. The state most immediately concerned about the situation was Naples, which sought to secure the direct assistance that had been promised in December. For this purpose the Marquis di Gallo, a leading Neapolitan diplomat, came to Vienna in March, having been provided safe passage to Trieste on board a Russian frigate. Since Austria found the presence of a Neapolitan envoy unwelcome and was unwilling to divert forces to the south, Gallo decided to travel on to St. Petersburg in his quest for support and because of his belief that only Russia could counteract Austrian power in Italy.[17]

In the meantime another Neapolitan emissary, Antonio Micheroux, negotiated directly with the Russian commander at Corfu for aid to the Calabrian Christian peasant army of Cardinal Fabrizio Ruffo that was making its way slowly from the southern tip of the peninsula toward Naples. The most that Ushakov could spare was a few hundred Russians and Turks under command of Captain Henry Baillie, who landed at Manfredonia in May, joined

Ruffo, and helped liberate Naples in mid-June.[18] On another front Suvorov won Paul's approval of his invitation to the Sardinian king to return to his liberated capital, and Adam Czartoryski left St. Petersburg at the end of June to improve diplomatic contacts with Sardinia.[19]

By the time Gallo arrived in St. Petersburg on 21 June, the main purpose of his mission, the dispatch of substantial Russian forces to Naples, was no longer of pressing concern. In any event Paul, reacting to Suvorov's complaints regarding Austrian behavior and to Serra Capriola's requests, ordered Rhebinder's corps of Suvorov's army to move in that direction.[20] Annoyed by his treatment in Vienna and taking advantage of the anti-Austrian mood in the Russian capital, Gallo pressed the Neapolitan course with renewed vigor and perhaps inspired Paul's call for a general conference at which the representatives of Naples, Austria, Russia, and Great Britain would decide the future of Italy.

During a three-hour interview with Gallo in mid-July, Paul stressed the importance of maintaining a balance of power in Italy and of assuring the commercial vitality of the whole region, for which good relations with the Ottoman Empire was essential.[21] His emphasis on preserving freedom of trade in the Levant indicated the emperor's cognizance of the importance of Russo-Italian trade through the Black Sea. The discussion then concentrated on the future territorial alignment of Italy, with Gallo arguing for a strengthening of the position of Naples by considerable annexation of territory. Paul was at first alarmed—"You would take Rome!" Gallo assured him this was not so, but he insisted that the military security of central Italy necessitated a realignment of frontiers. When Paul continued to uphold the idea of a complete restoration, Gallo pointed out that this was impossible for Lombardy, Venice, Genoa, and the three legations. Paul admitted that his sympathies were with Naples but that Austria had the position of power. "What can one do for the King?"[22] Nevertheless, Paul seemed persuaded of new possibilities for Italy and asked Gallo to submit a detailed memorandum on the subject.

Paul continued to press for a conference that would be aimed at curbing Austrian influence in Italy. During a conversation with the British ambassador, Whitworth, he noted that Austria "betrayed such views of acquisition, as were not only incompatible with the safety of Italy, but even with the general welfare of Europe." He wanted to know each power's objectives in Italy as a preliminary basis for a peace conference,

> for the purpose of defining what may be the views of each in the prosecution of the War, and the extent of indemnification that may be mutually acceded to without losing sight of that balance that it is so much the interest, and ought to be the object of every one to maintain. And this rather with a view to moderate the insatiable spirit of aggrandisement that marks the conduct of the Court of Vienna, than to limit those whose sacrifices have been great, and by whose exertions the contest has been so long and so gloriously supported.[23]

By the end of July, then, Paul was prepared to entertain changes in Italy that would accommodate his goals of eliminating French and curbing Austrian influence in the area.

The memoir that Gallo quickly placed before the tsar proposed that the Kingdom of the Two Sicilies should annex either the three legations or Modena joined to Parma and that Austria should keep only its Venetian territory.[24] This plan won the immediate support of Whitworth, who in a dispatch accompanying a copy of the memoir wrote,

> In order to maintain any sort of balance in Italy, it is necessary that some one of the Italian Powers should be allowed in some degree to keep pace in point of acquisition with the House of Austria; and . . . His Sicilian Majesty may now be considered as a more useful and powerful ally than the King of Sardinia, from the circumstance of his dominions being less under the immediate control of France.[25]

Rostopchin, who was rapidly losing the favor of Paul, wrote separately to Vorontsov in London in a sarcastic vein: "The Marquis di Gallo has presented a memoir on indemnifications at the peace, and, judging from the stupidity of this man, he believes himself to be in the time of caesars."[26]

Paul, however, wished to wait for a general conference of the powers and in the meantime softened his anti-Austrian mood in response to the combined diplomatic efforts of Cobenzl and Dietrichstein, the latter employing his influence with the empress. He agreed to countermand his order to Rhebinder in August, noting that the Russian and British fleets could now take care of the defense of Naples. He also relented to the Austrian desire that the king of Sardinia not be immediately reinstated but warned Cobenzl, "that at a proper season His Sardinian Majesty shall be restored to all his Dominions."[27]

In September, Gallo and Serra Capriola protested the cancellation of the dispatch of Rhebinder's corps so effectively that Paul issued orders for a new Russian auxiliary force of 3,000 to be sent through the Black Sea to Naples. In conversations with Whitworth at Gatchina, Paul indicated more concretely his plans for Italy: Austria could have Venice and Lombardy except that part already claimed by Sardinia, providing it gave up control of the Low Countries; Naples would annex the three legations; and Sardinia would absorb Genoa. The Pope, he added, "would stay in Rome." Russia would take only Malta, "as the property of the Order, of which the Emperor is Grand Master."[28] Paul also turned down a Turkish request for the annexation of the Ionian Islands and prescribed instead an independent aristocratic republic under the protection of Russia and the Ottoman Empire. This appears to be the solution that Paul would have put forth at a general peace conference.

But at the end of September and early in October Paul's dissatisfaction with Austria again increased over the matter of supply for Suvorov's and Korsakov's forces in Switzerland and especially over the Austrian rejection of his call for a conference.[29] On 6 October Whitworth reported, "It is impossible to give an adequate idea of the disgust which the Emperor feels at the general conduct of the Austrian Cabinet . . . . His friendship and confidence in the Court of Vienna are irrevocably lost."[30] Paul, however, was in a delicate position, having previously approved the Austrian offer of a dynastic marriage of his daughter and an Austrian grand duke, scheduled for October. A few days before the ceremony Paul received word of the defeat of the Russian army in Switzerland, fomenting additional consternation, and the emperor again threatened to recall Suvorov's army.[31]

Though Paul was certainly short-tempered, proud, and conceited, he should not be so readily accused of inconstancy and unpredictability. Even Whitworth was probably consciously playing along with the emperor's diplomatic anger. From a glance at the documentary evidence, it would appear that Paul's policies shifted drastically back and forth for the remainder of 1799 and into 1800. Upon closer examination much of the verbal barrage boils down to a matter of which side of the border the Russian armies would encamp on for the winter. New instructions to Admiral Ushakov, issued in early November, ordered him to return to the Black Sea for the repair of vessels of his squadron if the expedition to Malta was unsuccessful and if there was nothing more to be done on the coasts of Italy.[32] The lateness of the date and the length of time needed for communications with Italy meant, however, that the Russian fleet could not be withdrawn to the Black Sea before the beginning of the winter storms and hence not before the opening of spring navigation in the Russian ports.

Communications problems also contributed to the inconsistency of the policies of the other powers in regard to Italy. On 22 October the Austrian ambassador, Cobenzl, assured Panin, the Russian vice-chancellor, that Austria intended to restore all lands occupied during the war. A few days later, apparently after receiving new instructions from Thugut, and, significantly, after the grand ducal marriage had taken place, Cobenzl presented a strongly worded case, again to Panin, for the Austrian annexation of Piedmont, now arguing that Austria must have compensation in Italy for war costs equivalent to what Russia gained in the second partition of Poland and in the annexation of the Crimea.[33] At practically the same time as these conversations were occurring in St. Petersburg, Lord Grenville wrote Whitworth that Britain favored the Austrian annexation of Piedmont in order to form a strong barrier against France. But less than three weeks later, he informed Whitworth that George III now agreed to Sardinian sovereignty over Piedmont with the rest of Italy to revert to status quo ante bellum "with the exception only of such arrangements in favor of Naples, as should, on fair Examination, appear to be just and reasonable, on which point His Majesty would willingly acquiesce in the Judgment of the Emperor of Russia."[34] And the Marquis di Gallo, who had become a key figure in St. Petersburg, received in early November a letter from Acton designating him as Neapolitan envoy for the peace conference with full powers on the same day that Paul received one from Ferdinand IV disavowing his envoy, ordering his recall, and denying any claims to additional territory in Italy.[35]

While Gallo was packing his bags another special emissary from Italy appeared in St. Petersburg. Charles Emmanuel IV of Sardinia, prompted by Suvorov and fearing Austrian designs on Piedmont, decided rather belatedly to treat directly with the Russian emperor. Unfortunately, Gaetano Balbo arrived just as the emperor was withdrawing his forces from Italy. Moreover, the Sardinian envoy was handicapped in his effort to negotiate a defensive alliance with Russia by the Sardinian chancellor's priority on an understanding with Austria.[36] Balbo's project, calling for a mutual guarantee of territory (which would have committed Russia to a complete restoration of Sardinia) and the assistance of 12,000 soldiers, was put forward in January 1800, but his court's authorization for this plan was delayed until April and then included the additional demand that Savoy and Nice also be returned.[37] Though the Sardinian government eventually sanctioned the original terms in June, by that time the Emperor Paul was looking toward the French for a solution of Italian questions.

In the closing months of participation in the Second Coalition against France, Russia's military forces in Italy continued to play a major role even without the presence of Suvorov and the main army. Admiral Ushakov arrived at Messina with the main Russo-Turkish fleet in August 1799, while separate Russian squadrons patrolled both sides of the Italian peninsula. Rear Admiral Pustoshkin assisted the siege of Genoa on one side, and Captain Voinovich attacked Ancona in concert with an Austrian land force on the other. At the same time a detachment of Russian marines assisted the Neapolitan army in the liberation of Rome from the French. Three battalions detached from Suvorov's army arrived at Naples in December under General Dmitri Volkonskii for the eventual garrisoning of Malta. From another direction General Mikhail Borozdin reached Corfu with two more battalions that were destined to form a stabilizing security force for the Neapolitan court. All of these movements, however, brought more problems with allies, and it was at Ancona that the incident occurred that would lead to a final rupture in relations between Russia and Austria: the Austrians overzealously tore down a Russian flag during the capture of the port.

Ushakov continued the mopping-up operations in the Mediterranean in December 1799 by embarking Volkonskii's battalions and setting off for Malta. The arrival of these forces might very well have led to the quick surrender of the long-besieged French garrison, but Ushakov was intercepted by new orders to withdraw to the Black Sea. He interpreted these orders to include the battalions of both Volkonskii and Borozdin. Before a complete evacuation could be effected, new instructions, prompted by Serra Capriola's diplomacy, renewed the assignment of Borozdin to Naples, which he reached with the guard units by the end of March 1800. In fact, Ushakov himself spent the spring and summer months of that year at Corfu tending to complex Ionian affairs and the difficult repair of his vessels for return to the Black Sea.[38]

During 1800 the French took advantage of the withdrawal of most of the Russian forces and the demoralization of the Austrian army to reassert control over most of Italy. The presence of the Russian battalions in Naples, however, was a major factor in the French reluctance to attack that city. The center of Russian diplomatic activity now shifted to Berlin and then Paris, where negotiations for peace and an alliance between Russia and France were being conducted. Having easily attained the concession of Malta from Bonaparte, Paul ordered General Sprengporten to command a detachment of Russian prisoners in France to garrison the island, which, however, was by that time in British hands. The conditions for a French alliance then centered on the Russian insistence upon a French withdrawal from Italy and the restoration of the Neapolitan and Sardinian territories. Russia seemed to be on the path to a "Tilsit-style" arrangement whereby Italy would be divided into Russian and French spheres—an enlarged Sardinia under French protection and greater Naples under Russian. This objective conflicted with Bonaparte's aspiration to dominate the whole of Italy. While a resolution was being attempted, Paul was murdered.

Alexander I, like his father, was at first intent on peace and reform at home and ordered the withdrawal of the last Russian troops from Naples.[39] But his position in the general peace negotiations of 1801 and 1802 was to support the restoration of the Italian kingdoms. It was no accident that when Russia again entered Napoleonic combat, in the Third Coalition, the focus was in the first instance on Italy, and a Russian army was again on the peninsula.

Paul's Italian policies were based on eighteenth-century principles of balance of power—to prevent any preponderant influence from accruing to either Austria or France. This could be achieved only through buttressing the legitimate rulers of Italy by military and diplomatic support. Despite significant initial success, Paul was thwarted in his objectives by the behavior of his allies, in particular by the territorial ambitions of Austria and by the difficulties inherent in making satisfactory arrangements for Italy at a general peace conference in distant St. Petersburg while the fighting continued. Paul also erred in widely publicizing his own policy of refusing annexations for Russia while entertaining schemes of aggrandizement for Naples and Sardinia and even Austria. Above all, Paul had to contend with weak and unstable leadership in all of the Italian states. Though the tsar's interest in Malta intensified his concern for Italy, his objectives and achievements in this quarter had very little to do with his Maltese fantasies or his alleged project for the unification of the Orthodox and Catholic Churches. Paul's Italian policy demonstrates that a rational foreign policy that complemented a reactionary ideological outlook was pursued. Paul's values and general objectives in foreign policy were not strictly limited nor unduly distorted by his peculiar and more "infamous" projects.

What, then, were Paul's achievements in Italy? Russian arms actually did help to secure and to maintain for brief periods the restoration of the weak and disrupted Italian governments on the mainland. Russian policy kept "Two Sicilies" a reality and may have saved the link between Sardinia and Piedmont. It may also have influenced the "Italianizing" of French policy, as for example in the Concordat and in the emergence of the Marquis di Gallo as foreign minister of Joseph Bonaparte's and Joachim Murat's Kingdom of Naples. More importantly, Paul's objectives set a precedent that would be followed by his successor and would influence the leaders of Russia's allies in the coalition wars that followed. Paul would probably have been satisified with the results of 1815.

NOTES

1 Giuseppe Berti, *Russia e stati italiani nel Risorgimento* (Turin, 1957), p. 166. Berti is practically the only modern Italian historian who has examined Russo-Italian relations. Franco Venturi contributed a general, and rather disappointing, survey of this period to a Soviet-sponsored symposium. See "Italo-russkie otnosheniia s 1750 do 1825 g." in *Rossiia i Italiia: iz istorii russko-ital'ianskikh kul'turnykh i obshchestvennykh otnoshenii* (Moscow, 1968), pp. 25-50. More important are the Russian/Soviet analyses of Evgenii V. Tarle, *Admiral Ushakov na Sredizemnom more* (Moscow, 1948) and Avgusta M.Stanislavskaia, *Russko-angliiskie otnosheniia i problemy Sredizemnomor'ia (1798-1807)* (Moscow, 1962). For a background discussion of the issues of the period, see the author's *Russia and the Mediterranean, 1797-1807* (Chicago, 1970).

2 B. N. Mironov, "Eksport russkogo khleba vo vtoroi polovine XVIII-nachale XIX v.," *Istoricheskie zapiski*, 93, 1974, 157-171.

3 Stanislavskaia, *Russko-angliiskie otnosheniia*, pp. 29-30.

4 Cobenzl to Thugut, 26 Dec. 1796, Haus-, Hof-, und Staatsarchiv, Vienna (hereafter HHSA), Russland II Berichte, carton 84.

5 Giuseppe Greppi, *Un Gentiluomo Milanese guerriero-diplomatico, 1763-1839: appunti biografici sul Bali Conte Giulio Litta—Visconti Arese* (Milan, 1896), pp. 42-49, 87-91, 100-103; Pierre Pierling, S.J., *La Russie et le Saint-Siège* V: *Catherine II—Paul Ier—Alexander Ier* (Paris, 1912), pp. 184-194; Litta to Rohan, 7/18 Jan. 1797, in A. F. Bychkov, comp., "Depeshi Grafa Litty poslannika Mal'tiiskago ordena v Peterburge pisannyia v kontse 1796 i nachale 1797 g.," *Sbornik IRIO*, II (St. Petersburg, 1868), 209-237.

6 Pierling, *La Russie et le Saint-Siège*, V, 205-236; Marie Joseph Rouët de Journel, S.J., *Nonciatures de Russie d'après des documents authentiques*, I, *Nonciature de Litta, 1797-1799; Studi e Testi*, 167 (Vatican City, 1943), xi-xlii.

7 Nikolai I. Grigorovich, "Kantsler kniaz' Aleksandr Andreevich Bezborodko v sviazi s sobytiiami ego vremeni," part 2, *Sbornik IRIO*, XXIX, 389-390; Dietrichstein to Thugut, 29 Jan. 1798, HHSA, Russ. II Ber. 87.

8 Dietrichstein to Thugut, 16 Dec. 1797, HHSA, Russ. II Ber. 86.

9 Thugut to Dietrichstein, 17 Feb. 1798, and Cobenzl to Dietrichstein, 27 Apr. 1798, HHSA, Russ. II Weisinger 181. The congress in Rastadt in 1798 was devoted to a resolution of problems of the nearly defunct Holy Roman Empire, but it accomplished little and dissolved in April 1799.

10 Dietrichstein to Thugut, 10 and 27 July 1798, HHSA, Russ. II Ber. 88.

11 Paul to S. R. Vorontsov, 28 July, 8 Aug. 1798, *Arkhiv kniazia Vorontsova*, X (Moscow, 1876), 240.

12 Kochubei to S. R. Vorontsov, 29 July/9 Aug. and 16/27 Aug. 1798, *ibid.*, XVIII, 150-158. The offer of an army to the Ottoman Empire was made under the mistaken belief that Bonaparte's expedition was headed to Salonika, and even several days after receipt of the news of the landing in Egypt, Greece was believed to be the main target. Whitworth to Grenville, 17, 21, and 27 Aug. 1798, Public Record Office, Foreign Office Papers (hereafter PRO, FO), 65/40.

13 Dietrichstein recorded the first Neapolitan request for aid on 30 Mar. and voiced his displeasure on subsequent occasions. Dietrichstein to Thugut, 30 Mar. and 27 July 1798, HHSA, Russ. II Ber. 88.

14 The "Italian" corps under General Herman was to number 9-10,000, according to some accounts, with an additional force of 3,000 for the siege and garrisoning of Malta. Cobenzl to Thugut, 4 Jan. 1799, HHSA, Russ. II Ber. 90; Whitworth to Grenville, 2 Jan. 1799, PRO, FO 65/42.

15 Cobenzl to Thugut, 21 Mar. 1799, HHSA, Russ. II Ber. 90; Paul to Vorontsov, 6/17 Mar. 1799, PRO, FO 65/42.

16 The British ambassador was even convinced that Paul would not accept Malta if it were offered to him: "It is possible that in the opinion of many who are not conversant with the character of the Emperor of Russia, the assumption of the dignity of Grand Master may be construed into a desire of obtaining a preponderance on the Mediterranean. I think I can venture to assure Your Lordship that this is by no means the case. I believe most sincerely that if we were to offer Him the Sovereignty of the Island, He would refuse it without the least hesitation, indeed I am fully persuaded of it. It is simply to His high flown notions of Chivalry, a subject on which His ideas go sometimes beyond enthusiasm that His conduct is to be imputed." Whitworth to Grenville, 25 Jan. 1799, PRO, FO 65/42.

17 Carlo di Somma, *Une mission diplomatique du Marquis de Gallo à Saint-Pétersbourg en 1799* (Naples, 1910), pp. 19-27, 44-49.

18 Benedetto Maresca, *Il Cavaliere Antonio Micheroux nella reazione Napoletana del 1799* (Naples, 1895), pp. 8-11, 59-65; Ushakov to Paul, 24 June/ 5 July 1799, in *Admiral Ushakov*, III (Moscow, 1956), 38-43.

19 Paul to Suvorov, 7/18 June 1799, copy in PRO, FO 65/43; Rostopchin to S. R. Vorontsov, 18/29 June 1799, *Arkhiv kniazia Vorontsova*, VIII, 223.

20 The Austrian diplomatic correspondence places this new disposition of forces on 18 June and Gallo's arrival on 21 June, but this is contradicted by other evidence: an actual order to Suvorov, dated 16/27 June and Gallo's request for such aid, dated 21 June. Dietrichstein to Thugut, 18 and 25 June 1799, HHSA, Russ. II Ber. 91; Paul to Suvorov, 16/27 June 1799, in Tarle, *Admiral Ushakov*, III, 28; and Somma, *Une mission diplomatique*, pp. 330-338.

21 Somma, *Une mission diplomatique*, pp. 72-73, quoting Gallo to Acton, 5/16 July 1799.

22 *Ibid.*, pp. 73-79.

23 Whitworth to Grenville, 17/28 July 1799, PRO, FO 65/43.

24 The text is in Somma, *Une mission diplomatique*, pp. 310-316. A subsequent, more detailed project placed highest priority on the acquisition of Tuscany (Somma, pp. 316-330).

25 Whitworth to Grenville, 27 Aug. 1799, PRO, FO 65/44.

26 Rostopchin to S. R. Vorontsov, 10/21 July 1799, *Arkhiv kniazia Vorontsova*, VIII, 229-230.

27 As reported by Whitworth to Grenville, 22 Aug. 1799, PRO, FO 65/44.

28 Whitworth to Grenville, 14 and 23 Sept. 1799, PRO, FO 65/44.

29 The Austrian rejection appears to have been known in St. Petersburg in early September, but Thugut wrote a detailed explanation that could not have reached the Russian capital before October. Rostopchin to Vorontsov, 25 Aug./5 Sept. 1799, *Arkhiv kniazia Vorontsova*, VIII, 239; Thugut to Cobenzl, 12 Sept. 1799, HHSA, Russ. II Weisinger 184. And the Austrian chancellor followed with a barrage of missiles attacking the intrigues of the "little courts" and depicting Suvorov as senile and affected by the Italian climate. To Cobenzl, 16 and 25 Sept. and 6 Oct. 1799, HHSA, Russ. II Weisinger 184.

30 Whitworth to Grenville, 6 Oct. 1799, PRO, FO 65/44.

31 Whitworth to Grenville, 22 Oct. 1799, PRO, FO 65/44; Dietrichstein to Thugut, 18 Oct. 1799, HHSA, Russ. II Ber. 93.

32 Paul to Ushakov, 23 Oct./3 Nov. 1799, in Tarle, *Admiral Ushakov*, III, 174; Rostopchin to S. R. Vorontsov, 26 Oct./6 Nov. 1799, *Arkhiv kniazia Vorontsova*, VIII, 259.

33 Cobenzl to Thugut, 22 Oct. 1799, HHSA, Russ. II Ber. 92.

34 Grenville to Whitworth, 1 and 19 Nov. 1799, PRO, FO 65/45.

35 Ferdinand IV to Paul, 24 Sept. 1799, in Somma, *Une mission diplomatique*, pp. 219-224; Rostopchin to S. R.Vorontsov, 1/12 Nov. 1799, *Arkhiv kniazia Vorontsova*, VIII, 262. The abrupt turn-about in Naples was caused by Vorontsov's relay of Rostopchin's initial sarcastic reference to Gallo concerning the former Neapolitan ambassador to Britain, Castelcicala. See Panin to Vorontsov, 3/14 Nov. 1799, *Arkhiv kniazia Vorontsova*, XI, 94-98.

36 M. A. Polievktov, *Proekt soiuza Rossii s Sardinskim korolevstvom v tsarstvovanie imperatora Pavla I* (St. Petersburg, 1902), pp. 6-12; Giuseppe Greppi, *Sardaigne, Autriche, Russie: pendant la première et la deuxième coalition (1796-1802)* (Rome, 1910), pp. 93-99.

37 Polievktov, *Proekt soiuza*, pp. 12-17; Greppi, *Sardaigne,Autriche, Russie*, pp. 107-116.

38 Tarle, *Admiral Ushakov*, III, *passim*; M. Polivanov, *M. M. Borozdin, nachalnik okhrany Neapolitanskago korolia, 1800-1802 gg.* (St. Petersburg, 1912), pp. 21-32.

39 Polivanov, *M. M. Borozdin*, pp. 40-42, 61-65.

4

PAUL I AND THE KNIGHTS OF MALTA*

Roderick E. McGrew

Paul I was a profoundly ideological man who judged the world by moral absolutes. His values were conventional, a distillation of two centuries of monarchical doctrines, while the policies he pursued seemed to fall within the boundaries of accepted usage. But Paul's mercurial temperament led him to such exaggerated stands that the familiar became transformed, while his tendency to think in moral imperatives always made what he believed more important than what he might have known. As a result, if we study Paul simply as an administrative centralizer, a fiscal reformer, or a social modernizer, we will miss the special character of his reign. Similarly, if we insist on treating him essentially as a despot, no matter how enlightened, he will also escape us. Paul used conventional political vocabularies in highly unconventional ways. He built up what may have been the first systematic conservative response to the Revolutionary era, but his lack of personal control and his willful identification with anachronistic as well as alien traditions thrust him into isolation and contributed to the motives for his murder. Paul lived in an environment of anomalies and paradoxes. The elements of each, when considered coolly and in isolation, usually show rational patterns, and if what Paul did was not always a model of wisdom, it was generally comprehensible and often defensible. In the aggregate, however, the effect was simply stunning. It is the anomalies that hold the key to Paul's reign, and among them the events that made an orthodox tsar of all the Russias grand master of the Knights of St. John of Jerusalem were one of the most important.[1]

---

*Portions of this paper were read at the 1976 national meeting of the American Association for the Advancement of Slavic Studies in St. Louis, Missouri. Thanks are owing to the American Philosophical Society, whose grant-in-aid helped finance research on the project during 1972 in London, Rome, and Stockholm. A report on that work appeared in the American Philosophical Society *Yearbook* for 1972.

Paul's relationship with the Knights of Malta provides an unusual opportunity to study his political style and ideological commitments. From the beginning of his reign to the very hour of his assassination, the Knights of Malta held a central place in his thinking. This preoccupation had its most obvious effects on diplomacy, including relations with the Vatican, but its most provocative implications concerned the kind of society Paul hoped to see in Russia.[2] The tsar's interest in the knights was of long standing. At the age of ten he was studying Vertot's monumental history of the order, and what he learned there became part of a continuing fascination with chivalry and its ideals that lasted into his maturity.[3] Joseph de Maisonneuve, the émigré chronicler for the knights in Russia, declares that Paul was "perfectly instructed in the science of history" and that he knew "in detail that of the Knights Hospitallers of St. John of Jerusalem." Even allowing for Maisonneuve's sycophancy, it seems certain that Paul was entirely familiar with the knights' tradition, that he approved and supported it, and as soon as he was tsar, he moved to establish a formal association between the Knights of Malta and the Russian Empire.[4]

Russia's interest in the order antedated Paul's by something over six decades.[5] In 1698 Count Sheremetev, in the course of an extended mission to European courts, visited Valletta where he was well received and established a plan for using Malta as a training base for Russian naval officers. As late as 1769, Grand Master Pinto wrote Catherine II praising his Russian volunteers, who had served their apprenticeship and whose imminent departure he considered a matter for regret.[6] When Catherine faced war with Sweden, she in turn requested an experienced naval officer from the knights' armada to help prepare the Baltic fleet. The Bailli Giulio Count Litta was sent. He returned to St. Petersburg shortly before Catherine's death as the knights' negotiating agent and remained to become the main figure in Paul's dealings with the order.[7]

Any active relationship between Russia and the knights involved great power politics. From the time of their establishment on Malta under a charter granted by Charles V, the knights viewed themselves as Christian Europe's defense against the Turks and Moslem raiders from the Barbary coast. By the eighteenth century, however, the order's center of political and economic gravity had shifted from the Habsburgs to the Bourbons, from Spain to France. Since French Mediterranean policy was built on alliance with the Ottoman Empire, the knights' crusade against the Turks became an embarrassment, and a truce was arranged between the Sublime Porte and the order in 1722-1723. This truce was severely tested in 1760 when Christian slaves mutinied, stole the ship on which they were incarcerated, and took refuge on Malta. The knights returned the vessel, however, and the threatened war was avoided.[8] Catherine's expansionist policies in the Black Sea and the eastern Mediterranean led her to seek the knights' aid, and in May 1769 a Russian squadron appeared at Valletta. Though friendly, Grand Master Pinto avoided committing the order to support Russia against the Turks, and his successors, Ximenes and Rohan, continued the knights' now traditional neutrality. This was in the face of considerable Russian pressure generated by an abrasive new chargé d'affaires, Count Psaro, who arrived in Valletta in 1784 and remained until 1788. Psaro apparently won some officials to a Russian viewpoint, but Grand Master Rohan remained unmoved.[9]

What had happened during the eighteenth century was that balance of power politics in general, and French influence in particular, had destroyed the knights' military raison d'être. Their operations were limited to campaigns against the Barbary pirates, and even those stopped when the Turks protested after the Algiers campaign in 1784.[10] Given their aristocratic heritage, one would have thought that the French Revolution would have created a natural field of action, but this was not the case because the knights were dependent on France and did not dare to take a stand. In 1788, of a total income for the order amounting to 3,156,719 livres tournois, over 40 percent, that is 1,392,974 livres, was collected from holdings in France. When the Estates General began their sittings in 1789, Grand Master Rohan anticipated a threat to the order's financial heart. Thus while claiming status as a sovereign power to protect the order's property, he affirmed a neutral policy in international affairs. These tactics worked during the Revolution's moderate phase, but as moderation gave way to terror, the knights' fragile legal defenses were swept away, their lands were confiscated, and though French knights escaped the general anathema pronounced against aristocrats, the economic base in France was destroyed forever, and the knights faced a fiscal crisis.[11]

Even though the French holdings were gone by 1793, the order continued to maintain its nervous neutrality. One reason was to avoid giving any state, but especially France, an excuse to attack the island. The less obvious reason was that a substantial number of French knights refused to fight against France, and by far the largest number of knights active in the order were French. Apart from this division, which grew worse with the passage of time, there was great hostility to the knights among the native population of Malta, and this condition also grew more dangerous. By the time that Bonaparte's agents went to work in 1797, there was no shortage of support for them in both the citadel and the town.[12]

By nearly every standard, the Knights of Malta had become an anachronism by the last decade of the eighteenth century, a society that had long since outlived its original purpose, and one whose leaders were reduced to fighting grimly, and largely unheroically, simply to survive. The immediate problem was financial. But it was also becoming important to find political support for the order both to compensate for what had been lost and to preserve what now was threatened in Germany and Italy.[13] It was this need that drew Rohan's attention to eastern Europe. The Grand Priory of Poland, whose six commanderies had only been established in 1775-1776, was organizationally in disorder and had paid only a fraction of the dues that it owed the order's treasury. What made the Polish problem suddenly acute was the second partition, carried out in 1793, which left the whole of the priory's lands in the Russian zone.

The bequest on which the Polish priory was built had been made by the Ostrog family in Volhynia in 1618, but when the line died out in 1673 the will was challenged in a suit that dragged on for over one hundred years. In 1772 the first partition of Poland took part of the Ostrog inheritance into Russia, and in 1773 the order sent the Bailli Michel, Marquis de Sagramoso, a Veronese who knew Russia well, to arrange a settlement. Sagramoso had visited Russia in 1748. He was received by the Empress Elizabeth, and he met both Catherine and the Grand Duke Peter. On his return visit, Catherine received him graciously and showed every indication of favoring the knights' suit. Sagramoso ended by negotiating two treaties, one in 1775 and the other in 1776, by which Poland permitted a grand priory to be established, while the order abandoned its claims to the territory that Russia took. The Polish priory, however, never achieved full status, remaining a loose association without formal representation at Malta. The Russian seizure of the lands belonging to the Polish priory raised the basic question of whose subjects the tenants on those properties were, and who could claim the rents they paid. Litta's task in 1796 was to convince Catherine that she should permit the Knights of Malta to collect their dues from the Polish commanderies.[14]

Giulio Litta had been a popular hero at Catherine's court in 1788 and 1789, when he was twice decorated for his courage and initiative.[15] Moreover, Grand Master Rohan had deep confidence in Litta, remarking shortly before dying that Litta was one of only two people who were sufficiently capable and informed to lead the knights in such troubled times.[16] Litta knew the Russian court well enough to know where power lay, and he early established entrée to the empress's inner circle through Count Zubov. Though he knew Paul personally, and though Paul later repeatedly declared his warm regard for Litta's family, especially his father who had entertained Paul and Mariia Fedorovna in 1782, there is no suggestion of any close relationship until after Catherine died.[17] Paul was careful to the point of punctiliousness about trespassing on Catherine's political preserves, and as their relations were deeply strained in the last year of her life, the grand duke spent most of his time at Gatchina rather than at court. There was no secret about Litta's mission, however, and Paul was undoubtedly informed.[18]

Whatever his abilities and standing with the empress, Litta made no progress whatsoever. Catherine's enthusiasm for the knights seemed entirely to have disappeared. She was inclined to argue that the order's neutrality was over-partial to French interests, and Litta's task became harder when news arrived that the knights had sent an accredited representative to Paris, thereby appearing to recognize the republican regime. That this happened when Catherine was preparing to give military support to Austria made a bad situation worse, while a Maltese assault on a vessel flying the Russian flag added to Litta's troubles.[19] Twenty years earlier Catherine had had to give up nothing to be cooperative; it was the knights who relinquished their claim. Now the positions were reversed, and Catherine saw no reason to be magnanimous. Nor did the religious climate favor the knights' cause. Giulio Litta's brother, Lorenzo, who was Archbishop of Thebes and the recently appointed papal nuncio for Poland, had come to Warsaw in 1794 ready to talk about the large Roman Catholic population in Russia's new western territories. Catherine flatly refused to have him come to St. Petersburg, while any negotiations were entirely out of the question.[20]

By the fall of 1796, Giulio Litta was in despair and ready to be recalled. His mission had made no progress, and French forces had overrun his family estates in Lombardy.[21] The news from Valletta was discouraging, and morale there had reached its nadir. As Doublet wrote during these days: "Nothing succeeds with us . . . nothing, I repeat, succeeds with us here. This security, or rather this state of apathy, to my mind inconceivable, disheartens me. A continual change of front, a complete indecision, chimerical fears and hopes equally chimerical—such is our pitiable and unhappy policy."[22]

Matters were at this point when Catherine suffered her stroke on 5/16 November and died the following day. Paul arrived from Gatchina on the evening of 5 November, and the fortunes of the Knights of Malta began to turn around. In a letter to Grand Master Rohan dated the day that Catherine died, Litta stated: "I have reason to believe, in view of the new Sovereign's sense of equity and his disposition to deal promptly with affairs, that the claims of the Order of Malta will obtain their due justice."[23] The hoped-for consummation did not, however, occur at once. Paul and his helpers had exploded into a perfect frenzy of activity, firing decrees in every direction and revealing what seemed to be a fixed determination to solve all Russia's problems, real or imaginary, before the new year.[24] Indeed, given the times, it was a measure of the great importance that Paul attached to the Maltese claims that he not only dealt with them, but that the entire settlement was completed within two months of Catherine's death. And it might have come even sooner. Alexander Kurakin, who handled Paul's most important business, was forced twice to put off meeting Litta, and it was not until 12/23 December that they had the chance to talk at length. Even then Kurakin had no plan to offer, though Litta reported that his intentions were favorable and that a good effect could be expected soon.[25] One week later Litta's report to Malta was rhapsodic over Paul's personal qualities, his sympathy for the order, and the friendship Prince Kurakin had shown. Kurakin had given Litta a confidential preview of Paul's plan to confirm and expand the priory's holdings while taking steps to regularize its income. Though he did not say so directly, it was clear that the tsar intended to establish the priory in Russia under his own guidance. It was also clear that what was projected was really a new priory that would absorb the old one and considerably enlarge it.[26] This news led Litta to suggest that the order would need a permanent minister in St. Petersburg to oversee the new establishment. Without a minister to maintain connections with Malta, the priory's business would be neglected, abuses would go unchecked, its holdings would be dissipated, and in the end, like its Polish predecessor, it would cease to be an asset to the order. Litta proposed himself for the post. He was on the spot, he understood the situation, and he would like to stay in Russia. He pointed out with engaging frankness that others could be found to perform this duty, but that "the particular circumstances in which I find myself, and the loss of a great part of my fortune since the French invasion of Italy, has reduced my means and leaves me no other choice than that of findng a peaceful retreat."[27]

The convention was completed and signed on 4/15 January 1797.[28] Litta claimed that he had followed his instructions faithfully, that there was nothing in the convention that contradicted the order's constitution or could embarrass it politically.[29] Paul's generosity was certainly as advertised, and while he might believe that the previous reign had bankrupted the empire, his dispositions for the Russian priory were munificent. The tsar accepted all past dues owed by the Polish priory to the treasury at Malta as legitimate claims on Russia and set up the machinery to discharge them. As expected, he proposed that the moribund Grand Priory of Poland be moved to St. Petersburg and enlarged from six to ten commanderies. He pledged himself personally to oversee and protect this transformed foundation, and he established an annual budget for the priory of 300,000 Polish florins (99,000 rubles), which was guaranteed by the Russian treasury.[30] The priory was to be renamed the Grand Priory of Russia. Only the tsar's Roman Catholic subjects would be eligible to enter and to serve, however, and Paul was adamant that no commandery could be held by other than a Russian subject.[31] Interestingly enough, the first commandery proposed for the grand master to ratify was for Giulio Count Litta.[32]

It appears certain that Paul initiated and defined the substance of this settlement, and that he did so both to show his commitment to the order and Russia's common footing with other European monarchies. When reporting Paul's intentions, Litta made the point that "it was the intention of His Majesty, the Emperor, that the Order of Malta be established here in such a way as to accord to it in Russia the same luster and consideration it enjoys on the lands of other powers."[33] In fact, Paul's ambition for his Russian priory went further, for he hoped to see a Russian *langue* created, and he considered Litta's suggestion that the Russian priory be affiliated with the Anglo-Bavarian *langue* beneath Russia's dignity. Litta remained resolute on the point, however, and the question was handled for the time being by leaving it open.[34] For the rest, Paul promised to protect the religious freedom of the Catholic knights and to observe the order's traditions, constitution, and regulations.[35]

Litta forwarded the signed convention with the remark that it should serve as an example to other Christian monarchs, showing "how worthy it is for them to support our existence and our splendor, and how much it is to their interest to assure by our conservation that of all the Nobility of Europe which is, and which will always be, the best support for thrones and monarchies."[36] In this case, the monarch deserved to be rewarded, and after describing Paul at length and in the most flattering terms, Litta suggested that an appropriate gift would be an ancient cross of Malta, preferably one that had belonged to one of the order's great grand masters: de l'Isle-Adam, la Vallete, or d'Aubusson. He thought that such a cross could probably be found, and with a certain sly ingenuousness remarked that "I am entirely certain one will be found, above all if one searches with the full intention of finding it. Your Excellency knows better than I that it is faith that produces miracles." But if Litta knew what would please Paul, he also knew what might anger him, and he warned that ratification should be swift and without quibble or qualification.[37]

Rapid ratification was one condition that could not be met. Litta's dispatches were intercepted by the French, and a further copy had to be forwarded. That document finally arrived in Valletta on 14 July (N.S.) 1797. Grand Master Rohan had died the previous day, and the knights were engaged in electing his successor. Only three days were permitted to elapse from the death of one grand master to the election of another, and Ferdinand Hompesch, Bailli of the German priory, was chosen on 16 July.[38] The new grand master and the sacred council did not approve the convention until 7 August. When they did so, however, they not only accepted the tsar's proposals unanimously and enthusiastically, but they made a special effort to show their gratitude by formally declaring Paul I a protector of the Knights of Malta. This step, it should be noted, gave the tsar a standing with the order that he had not sought, though he was delighted to receive it. Count Litta was named ambassador extraordinary and was charged with presenting Paul his new title, the requested cross of Malta, and a ceremonial coat of arms.[39]

Paul's penchant for dramatic ceremonials brought wry comments and bitter complaints throughout his reign. At the time of his coronation the court master of ceremonies appeared to be the most important official in the government, and once the Knights of Malta were established in St. Petersburg, they offered new excuses for ceremonial occasions. Paul used ceremonial to dramatize the glories of his monarchy. His guide here was Louis XIV, and like his model, he thoroughly enjoyed the drama of his duties.[40] The ceremonies attending the presentation of the knights' convention were elaborate, extended, and indicative of the importance Paul attached to the occasion. Litta left the capital to meet the couriers from Malta and then entered the city at the head of a cortège of thirty carriages filled with Russian nobles. The presentation proper took place on Sunday, 29 November/10 December 1797. Paul appeared in the costume of the order, standing alone on a raised platform beside a table on which his orb and scepter lay. Grouped behind him were the leading members of his government, the clergy, and the court nobility. The diplomatic corps did not attend. Litta made a stirring speech; the tsar personally knighted his two eldest sons; the empress received the grand cross of the order; and lesser honors were distributed to members of the court and the administration. The Prince de Condé was named grand prior of the Russian grand priory, and Litta was to remain in St. Petersburg as Paul's adviser on Maltese affairs.[41]

This reception marked the end of the first phase of Paul's relations with the Knights of Malta. The order had formally accepted a Russian grand priory; Paul had been given the ceremonial title of protector; the order had solved its complicated Polish problem and was the beneficiary in a favorable financial settlement with the promise of more to come; and Count Litta, the knights' ambassador in Russia, was firmly established in the tsar's personal favor. There is no reason to think that Grand Master Rohan would have rejected the agreement Paul proposed to Litta. But Rohan had doubted that any good could come from an association with the tsar, and he had warned Doublet that he saw only the most dangerous consequences if the knights drew too close to Russia. Rohan feared arousing French jealousy or apprehension, and it is therefore unlikely that he would have approved offering Paul the protector's title. The remainder of the settlement was politically innocuous, though Bonaparte used the financial terms to justify confiscating the Italian priories' dues for the use of the French army.[42]

On Paul's side, there is no reason to think that he intended anything more than he proposed. What he did reflected his long-standing conviction that the order was valuable in itself and worthy of support. A priory in Russia was a link with the European monarchical tradition and a means to support Europe's aristocratic heritage. At this stage, the backing and encouragement that Paul gave the Knights of Malta were exactly analogous to his free-handed reception of the French émigrés, his subsidy for the future Louis XVIII, or his later offer of asylum to Pope Pius VI. Litta may have wanted Paul to be more active in the order, but Paul focused his personal energies on the Russian priory. Like the European monarchs he admired, Paul gave the order a distinguished place in his society and became involved in its development. His generosity seemed literally limitless. He gave the priory sumptuous housing and a chapel, proposed to build a church, and richly endowed the chaplain's post. The last-named went to the papal nuncio, Lorenzo Litta, whom the tsar had invited to his coronation and then permitted to come to St. Petersburg to carry on his work.[43] But however much Paul gave the knights, he was careful to maintain the established rules and reservations. The Russian priory remained only for Roman Catholics, and Paul showed no disposition to change that provision. He seemed entirely satisfied to be a generous friend and firm supporter, and this attitude held until Bonaparte seized Malta, closed the knights' headquarters, and dispersed the membership to the far corners of Europe.

On 12 June (N.S.) 1798, Malta surrendered to Napoleon Bonaparte with hardly a shot fired.[44] The news reached St. Petersburg early in July, but nearly six weeks passed before there was any reaction. Then, on 26 August/6 September, the Russian priory set off a political bomb. Protesting in the strongest possible terms, it leveled a burning indictment of incompetence, cowardice, and treason against Ferdinand Hompesch, grand master of the order. Nor did the manifesto stop with charges. In a long supporting document, the charges were buttressed with detailed information purporting to originate with eyewitnesses of impeccable credentials.[45] Having stated the charges and provided the proofs, the Russian priory concluded that "the truth has revealed to us Ferdinand Hompesch accused and convicted of improvidence, cowardice, and treachery." In light of this conviction, the manifesto continued, "WE, Knights of the Grand Priory of Russia and others present in St. Petersburg regard Ferdinand Hompesch as disqualified from the rank to which we elevated him, and by virtue of our own rules, we consider ourselves absolved from the obedience which we would [otherwise] owe him as our Chief." The St. Petersburg group invited their colleagues in the other grand priories and *langues* of Europe to join them in a course "which honor renders indispensable, and from which we cannot abstain without sharing the opprobrium which Ferdinand Hompesch, St.Tropèz, and others have justly merited." So far as the future went, the Russian priory declared that it threw itself "into the arms of our August and Sovereign PROTECTOR Paul I" on whom it called to make known his will, which it promised to obey, and "to extend his generous protection over all the members of our Order who, in these unhappy circumstances, remain faithful to the unchanging foundation of our institution, RELIGION and Honor."[46]

This outburst was absolutely without parallel. Only the Grand Priory of Spain responded to the fall of Malta with anything like comparable speed, but its memorial commiserated with the unfortunate Hompesch while taking Bonaparte to task for aggression and the violation of neutral rights.[47] Francis II of Austria and the German Empire, who like Paul was a designated protector of the order, made no move at all, but his government permitted Hompesch to go into exile in Trieste. Neither Bavaria nor Prussia protested, but after the Russian priory declared its position, a very carefully worded statement from the imperial German priory expressed sorrow that the island had fallen and suggested the desirability of investigating the Russian charges.[48] Even Hompesch himself was unprepared to defend his surrender of the island. The memorials that he wrote and circulated before the Russian charges reached him emphasized that Malta, as a matter of policy, had been undefended, and that Bonaparte had quite literally stolen a territory whose neutrality was universally recognized. The moral onus was on France, Bonaparte had fabricated an excuse to invade, and the knights had had no choice except surrender. The Russian charges were as unexpected as they were unique, and when Hompesch attempted to answer them in a direct appeal to the tsar, he was obviously deeply confused and uncertain.[49]

At this point it would be well to look more closely at the origin of the protest, and to remember that, whatever else the Russian priory was, it most assuredly was not Russian. Russian Orthodox nobles were not eligible for membership, and even those Polish Catholics who held commanderies were under investigation to determine whether their appointments were legitimate.[50] Paul had no official status in the priory. His only office was an honorary one, and there was no one in his government eligible for a priory post. The Knights of Malta was a religious-military order; the men who became knights had to meet stringent genealogical standards, and they took an oath of chastity as well as poverty.[51] The total number of knights in 1789 was not above fifteen hundred.[52] How many were actually in St. Petersburg in the summer of 1798 is almost impossible to tell, but the only names that turn up regularly as participants in the priory's affairs are Condé, who, though grand prior, was absent most of the time; Maisonneuve, who kept the priory's annals; O'Hara, who succeeded Count Psaro as Russian minister to Malta; and Giulio Litta. Several more knights were in Condé's army, while some members of the diplomatic community and representatives of other priories were later co-opted for ceremonial occasions to hold ritual offices. None of these, however, had any direct part in condemning Hompesch.[53] The Russian grand priory was actually a handful of émigrés who clustered around Giulio Litta and enjoyed the tsar's protection. Their political philosophy tended toward the more extreme side of the emigration, pandering to Paul's vision of himself as the protector of Europe's traditional heritage. Maisonneuve, for example, asserted that Russia was the only place in Europe where someone who accepted the order's fundamental values could feel free to speak, while his nearly hallucinatory vision of Russia as the asylum for kings and the shield of monarchy deserves to be quoted:

> But there is still on earth one place where misfortune finds a certain refuge, where honor can be expressed with pride, where its language is understood, where it meets with constant and unchanging support: it is the Empire of Russia. There, a good people,

> religious, submissive to the laws, hard-working, toughened by useful labor and the rigor of the seasons; a numerous and invincible army; victorious fleets battling over the two seas with their brave allies, the English; an enlightened nobility, valorous, hospitable, and faithful to its Prince; [and] Councils full of wisdom and enlightenment, compose a state unshakable on its foundations.[54]

For Maisonneuve, it was only Russia's power plus the good will and determination of its prince that made it possible for the Russian priory to speak out trenchantly against those who had betrayed the order.[55]

Giulio Litta had the able support of his brother, the papal nuncio, in carrying on the priory's affairs, and between them the brothers embodied an immense authority. As a high official and accredited representative of the Knights of Malta, Giulio Litta was without a peer in the Russian Empire, and his knowledge of the order's institutions, procedures, and precedents gave him a special and very powerful influence with the tsar. Lorenzo Litta, as papal nuncio and an experienced Vatican politician, carried similar weight for other questions related to the Church. The presence of these men and the interlocking interests that they held go far toward explaining the Russian priory's actions and how Paul could actually believe that it was possible for him to become grand master.

Litta's dominance over the knights' affairs in St. Petersburg strongly suggests that the protest and declaration were essentially his work. Contemporaries believed this to be the case, and they regularly identified Litta as the prime mover in both the protest and Paul's later election.[56] The tsar's own role is more cloudy, but remembering his long interest in the knights, his alacrity in establishing the Russian priory, and his willingness to support the victims of French aggression, there is no difficulty in seeing his active sympathy for the knights and even his eagerness to be more fully involved. How well he was informed about what was happening is another question that we will try to answer by a careful reconstruction of events. There is no direct evidence to help us here.[57]

It will be recalled that several weeks elapsed between the time that the news of Malta's fall reached St. Petersburg and the day that the Russian priory issued its declaration. The reason for the delay appears to be that it took that long for evidence injurious to Hompesch to filter into Russia. This suggests in turn that it may have been that information which inspired Giulio Litta to attempt his coup. This impression gains strength from the fact that the first reports to reach St. Petersburg are not mentioned in the protest, though they were brought by an eyewitness who was also Russia's minister to Malta, the Chevalier O'Hara. O'Hara's correspondence has disappeared, but there are fragments of two letters written to Ferdinand Hompesch in 1798, one in the summer and the other in the fall, which indicate that O'Hara sympathized with Hompesch and believed that it was the grand master who had been betrayed. O'Hara said that he had made a full report to the tsar, but there is no subsequent mention of it anywhere. Whether O'Hara's reports actually reached Paul, or whether, as is more likely, they were submitted to Litta and suppressed, we do not know.[58]

The Russian priory's case rested on a letter allegedly written by the grand prior of Champagne, the Bailli de Tigné, the oldest and most respected of the knights still in Malta when the island fell. A second, though less important, source was a letter from the current marshal of the order, the Bailli de Loras.[59] While de Loras was a participant, his evidence was neither so precise nor so damning as that ascribed to de Tigné. In fact, without de Tigné's letter, there would hardly be a case at all. The problem is that de Tigné later denied having written the letter, and he entirely rejected the evidence that it contained.[60]

The argument that de Tigné's letter was a forgery is persuasive. The document in question is very long, covers a wide range of subjects, and leaves the impression of a man of enormous vitality rushing from the council chamber to the battlements to the beaches. None of this, however, could be true because at the time he was supposed to have written it, de Tigné was desperately ill and not expected to live. Visitors were turned away from his door, and he had received the last rites. There was quite literally no way that he could have participated in the scenes he supposedly described, nor was it possible that he could have dictated, much less written, the letter to which his name was put. As it happened, de Tigné recovered, and though he knew his name and alleged letter had been cited against Hompesch, he claimed to believe that events had passed beyond the point where his denials would have influenced them. When, however, he saw his letter published in *Le moniteur universel*, he took a notarized oath to the effect that he had not written it, and that he repudiated its contents.[61] The letter was addressed to Litta, and this suggests that Litta was the source. Even Litta, however, could not have manufactured the facts presented. The charges are too specific and show knowledge of events that did in fact happen. What Litta may have done was to use de Tigné's name to give weight to information that had come to him from a number of sources.

Giulio Litta's motives for initiating the deposition of Ferdinand Hompesch appear to have been a mixture of personal interest and commitment to larger principles. Litta professed an aristocratic ideology that portrayed contemporary monarchies as deficient in their will to support the institutions of traditional nobility.[62] He was committed to his order, and he had served it well, but he was also aware that he had to make provision for his own future. We have already recorded his request for an appointment as minister to Russia and his assertion that he was seriously considering settling there permanently. That determination grew stronger, and early in 1798 he requested a papal dispensation to free him from his religious vows so that he could marry. His intended was one of Potemkin's "nieces," the widow of Count Skavronskii, who was young, attractive, and very rich. Paul supported the request, and it was granted in August of 1798.[63] Malta's fall thus came at a critical time in Litta's life, and actually opened an opportunity for him. Committed to living in Russia, and given Paul's consuming interest in the knights, there was an obvious conjunction of interests. With the order's headquarters in St. Petersburg, and with the tsar as the order's head, Litta could expect to flourish. Events had made it abundantly clear that no other court in Europe offered a similar haven or opportunity. Hompesch was weak and lacked energy, and it seemed that he was going to permit the order to dissolve. In St. Petersburg, however, there was a commitment to the knights and the will to implement it. Finally, to make Paul grand master would involve the tsar personally and irrevocably with the order. The risks involved were small in comparison with what might be won.[64]

Lorenzo Litta was in a different and in some ways more difficult position. His mission in Russia was to arrange a new relationship between the tsar's government and the Vatican.[65] He believed his brother was in large part responsible for the favors Paul had shown him, and he was entirely pleased with his chaplain's appointment to the Russian priory—which meant a stipend and a comfortable apartment. The touchstone of Paul's generosity, however, and the best hope for the nuncio's continued good reception, lay in papal approval of Paul's relations with the Knights of Malta.[66] And until Bonaparte seized the island, there was no problem. But when the question of deposing Hompesch and advancing Paul arose, Litta should have begun to fear for his mission. If his negotiations were to be successful—and they were progressing more slowly than he had hoped—he would have to avoid any confrontation between the tsar and the pope, or between Paul and himself. Lorenzo Litta considered the Knights of Malta an issue of secondary importance that endangered the success of his mission. He was willing to make almost any concession to preserve his negotiating position, and this led him to support his brother. To have done otherwise would have meant telling Paul directly that there were limits to what he could legitimately do, and that there was a real possibility that the pope would disapprove. Whether rightly or wrongly, Lorenzo Litta appeared to believe that this was too dangerous a position to take, and so his influence was exerted to support the idea that the pope's attitude on what was happening in Russia was fundamentally approving.[67]

There was much to support Lorenzo Litta's policy of avoidance, for despite the outcry that went up later, there were no serious legal or religious questions about the relations between Paul and the Knights of Malta until the tsar's election as grand master. Paul's decree of 10/21 September approved the Russian priory's deposition of Hompesch, but it also stressed the tsar's determination to maintain the order's constitution while taking it under his active protection. His point that St. Petersburg had become the temporary headquarters for the knights could be interpreted, under the circumstances, as a simple recognition of fact.[68] Moreover, there was every reason for the Church to be cooperative. Diplomatic relations between Russia and the papacy were on the best footing ever, and there were high hopes in Rome that Litta's negotiations would create a new and very favorable situation.[69] The Russian priory's condemnation of Hompesch in no way chilled these good relations. Giulio Litta reported immediately to the pope on the Russian priory's actions, sending copies of the protest, the declaration, and, when it became available, the tsar's *ukaz*.[70] The pope's reply, dated 6/17 October, and a letter to the papal nuncio from the papal secretary, Odescalchi, dated two days later, were warmly sympathetic, and the pope's letter accepted the fact that there was an actionable case against Hompesch.[71] By coincidence, the pope had had a request from Hompesch that arrived at the same time as Litta's letter. The grand master asked that certain funds held for the order's use be released to him. The pope refused, informed Hompesch that he was suspended from his functions until the charges against him had been investigated, and then told Litta what he had done.[72]

The pope's response to the priory's act of deposition, however, was to point out that no priory had the authority unilaterally to depose a grand master and that "one would have to await the judgment of the other *langues* to verify whether the said Hompesch was guilty or not of the crimes of which the priory accused him." The pope also suggested that since Hompesch had been suspended, an acceptable member of the Russian priory should be appointed to act as grand master until the charges could be investigated.[73] And without having seen Paul's decree, the pope affirmed that St. Petersburg was, in his eyes, the temporary headquarters for the order. Odescalchi underlined this point by explaining that it was the pope's high opinion of the Russian priory that led him to propose the arrangements he suggested, and he pointed out almost apologetically that "for reasons of conformity, it is still necessary to know the opinions of the other *langues*."[74]

Despite diplomatic language and a clear disposition to favor the Russian priory, there is no possible question about the pope's views on the priory's competence to depose Hompesch. The priory could only bring charges. In light of the concessions made to the St. Petersburg group, however, this was a very soft rebuff and under normal circumstances would have left a comfortable margin for discussion and negotiation. It was obviously the pope's intention to avoid pressuring Russia when Litta's mission was going well, and Odescalchi once more reminded the nuncio of the high hopes the Church held for those negotiations.[75] There is not the slightest indication that anyone dreamed the Russian action was preparatory to offering Paul the grand mastership, and subsequent letters from the pope and from Odescalchi confirm this fact. Pius VI vacillated on the substance of the Russian charges, coming close at one point to affirming them himself and then in a subsequent letter stating that "to charge and to prove" were entirely different matters, with the obvious implication that the Russian priory had only charged. By that time, however, the pope was receiving pressure from Hompesch's supporters in Vienna, Munich, and Madrid, and the tone of his correspondence with Hompesch himself was changing.[76] There was, however, no vacillation over the legality of the Russian action. The pope was firmly committed to the position that the decision to depose required action by the entire order.

Though Pius and Odescalchi wrote at least three more letters in November that dealt with the knights' affairs, the October letters were the most important, and they probably did not reach St. Petersburg before the Russian priory offered Paul the grand mastership on 27 October/7 November 1798.[77] The letters may well have arrived by the time Paul announced his acceptance on 2/13 November, and we have positive evidence that the pope's letter was public knowledge by 19/30 November and that it was read into the order's records on 22 November/3 December.[78] The first formal response to the pope came in a long letter from Lorenzo Litta, dated 26 November/7 December, which also reported, more or less in passing, that Paul had been offered and had accepted the grand mastership.[79] The letters of 3, 5, and 16 November are never mentioned in the correspondence from St. Petersburg. If it could be shown that the pope's first letter arrived before 27 October/7 November, then it would be possible to claim that Paul and the Littas were waiting for papal approval before moving to election. As this seems unlikely, it appears that the Littas convinced Paul that the pope would probably approve, and that the election could take place. A third possibility, that Paul was prepared simply to ignore the pope's views, is hard to maintain in the light of Litta's later interpretation of the pope's position, Paul's reaction against Litta for that interpretation, and the tsar's strenuous efforts to win papal approval in 1800-1801.[80]

It is now clear how the Littas handled their problem. When Lorenzo Litta wrote Odescalchi on 26 November/7 December, he took up the pope's letter of 6/17 October and Odescalchi's covering letter. That correspondence, Litta pointed out, had brought great pleasure to everyone interested in the knights' affairs, and there was general agreement that the other *langues* should approve the Russian priory's actions. He also reported that the tsar had seen the letter, was satisfied with it, and had ordered that it be read publicly at an open session of the priory on 22 November/3 December.[81] This meeting was just one week before Paul's formal investiture. The pope was interpreted in St. Petersburg as accepting the Russian priory's case but saying that, for form's sake, it was important to have the agreement of the rest of the order. This, of course, was not at all what the pope said, and it was certainly not what he intended; but it was what St. Petersburg believed. Joseph de Maisonneuve reported in his chronicle, though without expanding on the point, that the pope had approved all the Russian priory's actions, including, presumably, Paul's election as grand master.[82] This, of course, was an exaggeration of the rather more qualified position that Litta took. However, in a letter dated 19/30 November 1798 the well-informed Swedish minister, Curt von Stedingk, reported to his government that the Bailli de Litta had received a letter from the pope "in which he approves all the measures taken by the Priory of Russia against the Grand Master; and he exhorts at the same time the Knights to choose among themselves one of their number who can replace the Grand Master. It would appear certain that the Emperor, at the prayers of the Priory of Russia, will accept the position of Grand Master, and we have already seen him in recent days taking on the functions of the Order in Russia."[83]

At the earliest, Paul first learned in late February or early March that the pope would not ratify his election, that is, nearly three months after he had accepted.[84] When he did find out, he blamed the papal nuncio for failing to warn him, though Giulio Litta caught the first edge of the imperial anger, was stripped of his title as the grand master's lieutenant, and was exiled to his new wife's estates.[85] Even so, Paul's reaction was rather mild. Though he withdrew the concessions to the Church that were under discussion, reaffirmed the traditional Russian stance on religious administration, and expelled Lorenzo Litta from the country, the tsar showed no animus toward Pius VI or the Vatican. He simply froze their relationship until such time as the question of the grand mastership could be resolved in his favor.[86] Whatever had gone before, Paul was now convinced he had a right to the election, and he turned to the problem of winning approval from the uncommitted priories. It is easy to say that, on the face of it, Paul was ineligible and should have realized that he could not accept the grand mastership. This has been the common view, and many contemporaries, including the Russian chancellor, Prince Bezborodko, believed it.[87] There was, however, a strong contrary opinion that argued from expediency and that held that, whatever might have been true in the past, it was now advantageous for the Church, for the knights, and for monarchical society that Paul be confirmed as grand master. This opinion was expressed in Rome as well as in St. Petersburg.[88]

Within this context, it seems quite clear that Giulio and Lorenzo Litta not only made the case that the order and all Europe needed Paul, but that the pope's general disposition was favorable, and that he had already in effect validated the Russian priory's decision. The combination of the Littas' standing and credentials goes far to explain how Paul thought that he might accept the proffered title. Once the Littas' role is put in perspective, the argument from the crisis of the times, especially for one of Paul's political persuasions, becomes compelling. In addition, while we may see the Russian priory as Giulio Litta's tool, it did claim a company of European nobles of unquestioned pedigree and rank who, theoretically at any rate, represented the best of the old regime, and who now appeared to be pleading with the tsar to act. The petition they addressed to Paul on 27 October/7 November 1798, called on him to preserve an ancient and valorous society, and thus to take one more stand against the enemies of good order, right morals, and true monarchy. Since the appeal undoubtedly was Litta's work, and said precisely what was necessary for Paul to justify his actions, we will quote a portion of it:

> Considering the disastrous situation of our Order, its total lack of means, the loss of its residence and its sovereignty, the dispersion of its members who are wandering without a leader or a place of meeting, the dangers that multiply around it, and finally the projects for its total ruin;
>
> Wishing and needing to employ every means that God has given us to prevent the destruction of an Order as ancient as it is illustrious, that unites the elite of the nobility and has done so much of service to Christianity; of an Order whose institutions have been founded on those sound principles that are the best support for legitimate authority; and to assure it its preservation and its future existence . . . .
>
> Understanding the impossibility in which the dispersion of our Order places us to follow in present circumstances the ancient forms and usages prescribed by the Constitutions and Statutes of our Order, but wishing at the same time to assure to it in the choice of the Successor to d'Aubusson, de l'Isle-Adam, and de la Vallette the dignity and power inherent in the Sovereignty of our Order. We . . . proclaim His Imperial Majesty . . . Paul I Grand Master of the Order of St. John of Jerusalem.[89]

Paul's response exactly mirrored the petition and repeated his commitment to preserve the order's institutions while disclaiming any territorial ambition:

> WE accept the title of Grand Master of this Order, and renew on this occasion the solemn promises which WE have made previously . . . not only to preserve forever intact all the institutions and privileges of this illustrious Order both in regard to the free exercise of religion and the different relationships resulting therefrom for the Knights of the Roman faith, and for the jurisdiction of the Order whose seat WE fix in OUR Imperial Residence; but also that WE will never cease in the future to employ OUR solicitude for the Order's growth and for its re-establishment . . . . WE pretend in no way in OUR quality of EMPEROR of all the Russias to any right or advantage carrying threat or prejudice to other Powers, OUR friends; but on the contrary, WE pledge OURSELVES with a special satisfaction to contribute in these times to all measures which reaffirm OUR friendly ties with them.[90]

Paul's election radically altered the way his relations with the Knights of Malta could be viewed in Catholic Europe. Up to this point, there had been a common interest in favoring Paul. The tsar had received nothing but encouragement for his policies toward the Knights of Malta, and in Rome the Catholic hierarchy considered the schismatic tsar a more reliable source of support than many traditional Catholic states.[91] All this changed when Paul accepted the grand mastership, and the pope in particular had to face the necessity for taking a firm stand. During January, he redefined and hardened his position. Then, after a silence of nearly two months, he informed his nuncio in St. Petersburg that the actions of the Russian priory were completely unacceptable. This protest was not sent directly to the imperial government, however, and Odescalchi suggested in his covering letter that, when Litta had the opportunity, and could do so with the least damage to his negotiations, he should bring this position to the tsar's attention. That, of course, was ingenuous. The letter was in cipher, but the papal memorandum was not. The packet was delivered to the papal nuncio with the seal broken. The memorandum had obviously been read.[92] The Russian government was thus informed of the pope's position without a formal notification, and while this meant the end of Litta's mission, it also made it possible for relations to be maintained. It appears that Pius VI actually chose the least disruptive way to inform Paul of his disapproval, and this was entirely consistent with the way the autocracy and the papacy had maintained relations since Catherine's death.[93]

If Paul had stopped short of the grand mastership a new chapter in political and religious history might well have been written, and as matters turned out, it was actually the murderers on 11 March 1801 who wrote the end to this story, and not the pope. But the question that now demands an answer is not how Paul could have come to accept the grand mastership, for that should be relatively clear, but rather why it was important for him to accept that title. Paul's own explanation appears in a letter to the pope written in December 1798, in which he repeated the arguments of his acceptance decree and added the idea that accepting the grand mastership was the next logical step in his developing campaign against French aggression. Paul also indicated that he would further strengthen the order for the struggle by opening it to his Russian nobility.[94] His appeal to the European nobility similarly emphasized the preservation, strengthening, and reestablishment of the order, and he also argued that by so doing, he would "render the most signal service to the Universe."[95]

If we cut through the rhetoric and ignore the implications of that last-quoted phrase, these declarations form a consistent pattern both in themselves and in relation to all Paul's previous statements on the knights and their affairs. Yet, in an important sense, all this begs the issue, for a moment's reflection reveals that by no means everything mentioned in Paul's decrees, or for that matter in the petitions of the order, required the tsar to become grand master in order to fulfill them. Indeed, the pope's proposal for choosing a member of the Russian priory to stand in for Hompesch was both a concession to Russia and an entirely practical solution to the order's problems. Paul, acting as protector, could give precisely the same military and financial aid that he proposed to give as grand master; St. Petersburg could be the order's headquarters and a rallying ground for the European nobility under Paul's protection; and if the tsar wanted to crusade against the Revolution, he would be no less effective as protector than he would be as grand master. In fact, he would have been much more effective since his grand mastership alienated Bavaria, momentarily divided Russia and the Vatican, and nearly destroyed the alliance with Austria.[96] Finally, if we discount the chivalric bombast to argue that Paul was really interested in Malta for reasons of *Realpolitik*, and that he was looking for ways to establish an independent Russian presence in the Mediterranean, we still do not have a motive for the grand mastership. His protectorate gave him as much leverage as any title would, and the real problem was one of fleets, negotiations and landing parties, and diplomacy and war.

One remaining alternative is to claim that Paul was simply afflicted with delusions of grandeur, and that it was to satisfy such a delusion that he accepted the grand mastership. There is a considerable element of truth here. The ceremonials, titles, and iconography of the knights were powerfully attractive and satisfying to the tsar. But there, of course, was the rub. As the knights' protector, Paul already had enjoyed a unique recognition, had wielded and worn the symbols of the great grand masters of the past, and had basked in the approval his generosity and concern had won him. Would the grand mastership mean so much more to him than what he had already had? There is no evidence that Paul showed much interest in the title (as separate from the symbols belonging to it) before June 1798, and even after that date we find no expressed interest until the fall. Although we have argued that Giulio Litta saw the grand mastership as the end product for his machinations, Paul was very cautious on the question. His reply to the priory's overthrow of Hompesch shows the tsar accepting a temporary leader's role and announcing the same comprehensive program of support that he announced later. Paul was infatuated with the Knights of Malta, but his infatuation did not seem to require the grand mastership to satisfy it. Indeed, it was only after Paul had accepted the Russian priory's offer that he became single-minded about the title, and then what he demanded was recognition and validation, something that was quite different from seeking the title in the first place.

The answer to our conundrum seems to lie in Paul's remark to the pope that, as grand master, he intended to strengthen the order by opening it to the Russian nobility. Since the Russian priory was limited to Roman Catholics, the nearest Paul could come to making it functional in Russian terms was to distribute honors to the members of his family and court. So long as Russia was Orthodox and the order Catholic, it would be impossible for the Russian nobility to participate directly. Since a protector of the order had no function in legislating the order's rules, there was relatively little Paul could do about this. It was true that there were non-Catholic priories in the Knights of Malta, but the religious and political problems involved in legislating an Orthodox priory through normal channels would have been simply overwhelming. If Paul were the grand master, however, and were served by a sacred council of his own choosing, he would be in a position to rule on the eligibility question, and the problem would solve itself. Opening the order to the Russian nobility would add greatly to the numerical strength of the Knights of Malta, but it would also mean that the balance of numbers would tilt toward Russia in much the same way that it had inclined toward France in the seventeenth and eighteenth centuries. Moreover, with Russian subjects holding the numerical balance, there could be no question about the tsar's control. Other priories could do as they wished; they would always be a minority and separate from the Russian center. The order would become entirely dependent on Paul, and no group could effectively challenge him. This gives a slightly different meaning to his assertion that he intended to build "so that the edifice will endure for a long time on a solid foundation" provided by "the institution of benefices for the use of our nobles of Russia."[97] But this point brings up a related idea. If the presence of the Russian nobility strengthened Paul's control over the order, the order also gave the tsar an instrument for indoctrinating that nobility, and the potential for an ideological nexus between tsar and nobles such as Russia had never had before.

Absolute monarchy as Paul conceived it required a devoted and loyal serving aristocracy. The nobility was the monarchy's most important class, its ruling class, which, when undisciplined or misled by false philosophy, was also the state's most dangerous class.[98] Self-sacrifice and a sense of duty were basic elements in Paul's version of aristocracy, but he considered the Russian aristocracy, particularly in consequence of the immoralities practiced in Catherine's reign, to be disorderly, self-centered, and a threat to stability. The Knights of Malta could be a vehicle for educating the nobility to values supportive of the tsar's political vision. Thus, at his installation as grand master on 29 November/10 December, Paul's first formal act was to create a second Russian priory that was open to all nobles regardless of their religious faith.[99] This priory was simply enormous, comprising ninety-eight commanderies as against the original Russian priory's ten, but it had to be large to accommodate the whole of the eligible Russian aristocracy. This group was to be subjected to the discipline of an order whose "laws and statutes . . . inspire love of virtue, contribute to strong morals, strengthen the bonds of subordination, and offer a powerful remedy against thoughtless love of novelty and unbridled license in thinking."[100] Indeed, Paul saw the Knights of Malta as "a means for states to increase strength, security, and glory," which in Russia "will offer to OUR faithful nobility a further motive to stimulate the love of glory . . . and the practice of actions useful to the Fatherland, and agreeable to its sovereign."[101]

If the Knights of Malta had become important to Paul's view of himself, they were also important for his vision of Russia. Opening the knights' ranks to the Orthodox nobility and flooding the order with his own subjects was only possible if Paul became grand master. But from that position, and commanding his own subjects, over whom his authority was absolute, Paul could provide the base for a powerful and revived institution with which to defend monarchy and traditional values. Russia was to be the center, the new homeland, a stable fortress in a world of threatening change. And behind those parapets, the Knights of Malta would provide an organizational center and an ideological form with which to shape the Russian nobility to the contours of Paul's own particular version of absolutism, and thus prepare them for the struggle in which they would have to play a leading role. In Russia, the Knights of Malta would become the centerpiece in a reformed and newly powerful monarchical society.

Paul's grand mastership most commonly has been considered a disaster, not because he destroyed the order, or even substantially damaged its traditions, but because his preoccupation with Malta disrupted the interests of his allies and broke up a promising negotiation with Rome.[102] Members of Paul's administration found it difficult to take his commitment to the order seriously, while the tsar's withdrawal from the Second Coalition, his break with England, his abandoning of Louis XVIII, and his new friendship with Bonaparte seemed to demonstrate that his ideological assertions were either cant or raving. Since the disposition of Malta was an important factor in what happened, Paul's insistence on the grand mastership appeared doubly disordering and a caricature of his former arguments for maintaining the knights' traditions intact and of his disclaimers of any territorial ambitions.[103]

To review all these issues, and especially the melancholy history of the Second Coalition, would go far beyond the purpose of this paper. It is appropriate, however, to comment briefly on what happened between the end of 1798 and Paul's death in 1801 that bore on the Knights of Malta. And the first point to stress is that, given the importance Paul attached to the knights and to foreign recognition for his grand mastership, his policies achieved a near total success. At the time the Russian priory elected him, it was already clear that Bavaria and Spain were opposed; the Bohemian priory, the most important in Austria, was skeptical; Hompesch had reasserted his rights and was pressuring both the pope and the German emperor to support him; and in February, a month before sending St. Petersburg his message rejecting the Russian priory's action, the pope had told Hompesch that he would not approve Paul's election.[104] Nine months later, the position was entirely different. Under heavy political pressure, Bavaria executed a *volte face* and accepted Paul; Francis II forced Hompesch to resign as grand master and eventually expelled him from Trieste; and a special deputation from the Bohemian priory waited on Paul to present a formal acceptance of the tsar's grand mastership.[105] The Protestant states made no trouble, though England was evasive about returning Malta should the island be recovered. That attitude led directly to Russia's break with England in 1800. By the end of 1799, however, and in accordance with the Litta interpretation of Pius VI's position, the Russian government sent an official circular to all the foreign ministries recording the fact that the priories, commanderies, and *langues* "who were free to decide" had approved Paul's election as grand master. The tsar took this as definitive and considered the matter settled.[106]

No immediate attempt was made to approach the pope, and the Church's affairs in Russia reverted to their status on Paul's accession, though the tsar remained favorably disposed to Catholic interests.[107] Pius VI died in the summer of 1799 and there was some thought that Paul might attempt to "protect" the election of a successor, but those fears proved groundless, and Pius VII was duly chosen, consecrated, and installed.[108] The tsar was determined not to negotiate with the papacy, however, until the pope recognized him as grand master. On his side, Pius VII was unwilling to approve the election of a married schismatic who had never taken orders to be head of the Knights of Malta. One possible solution was to secularize the order, which would make acceptance of Paul, if not his formal recognition, much easier, but this was only a possibility. In St. Petersburg, the shadowy but influential Jesuit, Father Gruber, and the Neapolitan minister, Serra Capriola, continued to work on Paul's pro-Catholic sympathies while protecting the Church's interests against self-interested local potentates.[109]

A year later, after the Second Coalition had dissolved, relations with the papacy sprang to life again. The first tentative proposals came from Rome, but then the initiative seems to have passed to Paul.The intermediary was the representative of Naples.[110] Though determined to have papal recognition, Paul refused to accept the Vatican view that he himself was actually the issue. And he ignored the fact that his marriage and his secular status were as much barriers to papal recognition as his faith. It was the religious issue that dominated his thinking and led him to minimize his differences with Rome. In the course of a long discussion with Serra Capriola, Paul expressed incredulity at the Vatican position, and remarked pettishly that he was, after all, a Christian. On another occasion he was heard to say, with every evidence of conviction, that in his heart he was a Catholic.[111] It is also this period that gives us the tradition that Paul was privately converted to Catholicism. That story, in the light of Paul's lifelong inclination toward Rome, as well as his hopes for papal ratification of his election, is by no means unbelievable. And it gains credibility from Father Gruber's personal influence with Paul. But no direct evidence has ever appeared, though Pope Benedict XV is supposed to have said that the proofs were in the Vatican archives.[112]

There is, however, positive evidence that communications were reestablished between Paul and the Vatican in the winter of 1800-1801 with warm interest on both sides. Unfortunately we can only speculate about what those contacts really meant, since they reached a critical stage on 7 March 1801, and four days later Paul was dead. With his death the Malta question, and the religious issues depending on it, snapped back like an overwound spring, though Alexander retained a diplomatic interest in Malta, while the imperial household continued to support the Orthodox priory until 1917.

The last burst of activity between Paul and the papacy has given rise to the argument that the tsar was prepared to institute proceedings that would have led to reunifying the eastern and western Churches. Father Rouët de Journel, whose brilliant work on the Litta and Benvenuti missions has established the basic documentation, argues strongly for this position.[113] Valentin Graf Zubow, who caught only a part of Rouët de Journel's argument, and in fact did not use his massive documentary compilations, embellished it with a kind of medievalism to arrive at a wholly romantic interpretation.[114] Since everything here is speculation, there is not much purpose in extending the argument other than to note that the documents Rouët de Journel published on Paul's conversations with Serra Capriola show no more than the tsar's willingness to reopen the negotiations broken off with Lorenzo Litta. Specifically, Serra Capriola reported that Paul proposed negotiations through the good offices of the Neapolitan king; that the tsar would accept the pope as supreme head of the Catholic Church, and that he would even recognize the pope as "the first bishop of Christendom." The pope, on his side, would recognize Paul as grand master of the Knights of Malta.[115]

Paul never denied, of course, that the pope was the spiritual head of the Catholic Church, and there is no question about his pro-Catholic leanings. Indeed, Paul was far more sympathetic to Rome than any of his ministers, and Litta's mission had actually been made more difficult by resistance within the tsar's administration.[116] The basic issue between Rome and the tsar, however, was sovereignty, and, more narrowly, administrative competence. The weakness in Rouët de Journel's treatment of the Litta mission is a too optimistic view of what the nuncio could expect from Russia. Paul was willing to grant the Church's spiritual independence. The problem was that even Paul defined "spiritual" very narrowly and insisted that the Church, as an institution, was entirely subordinate to secular authority. So far did this secular supremacy go that papal bulls were subject to censorship, while issues connected with divorce and marriage were treated through the civil administration. The question was not "caesaropapism," as the Latin hierarchy liked to describe it, but rather that in Russia the secular authority had gained absolute control over the ecclesiastical. If Paul were indeed a Catholic in 1801, and had he lived to rule longer, he would have been a strong Gallican Catholic who, for all practical purposes, could accept no effective limit on his secular authority. He was, after all, the autocrat and tsar of all the Russias. There is not the slightest indication that he intended to retrench on that position. Past performance indicated that even if the pope recognized Paul as grand master, there were well-defined limits on what the tsar could and would do for the Catholic religious establishment in Russia. One is tempted to conclude that if a reunification of the Churches had actually occurred, it would have been on Russian rather than on Roman principles.[117]

Though a synthesis of East and West does not appear to be a justifiable reading of the story, Paul's relations with the Knights of Malta do give rise to other tentative conclusions or speculations. The first of these is to note the extraordinary degree to which the tsar defined himself and his functions in Western cultural terms. He saw nothing anomalous in leading a Latin crusading order, he ignored the schism institutionalized in Russian Orthodoxy, and he offered the Knights of Malta as a model for the Russian nobility. In none of his statements on defending traditional society is there the slightest appreciation for, or even reference to, Russia's native heritage, and, in fact, the only Russian ruler Paul could be said to have admired was his grandfather, Peter the Great.

Paul appears to have been entirely Europeanized, but as a European he looked backward rather than ahead. The group whose cultural and historical vocabulary was closest to his own was the French emigration, and that brings us to another point. Though we have regularly met such terms as *knightly* or *chivalric* in the course of this study, it should be quite clear that the tradition in which Paul believed had little to do with the medieval world. His religious attitudes, which were broadly tolerant, belonged to the late seventeenth and eighteenth centuries, while his political and social values derived from the sixteenth and seventeenth centuries. That was also the age of glory for the Knights of Malta, and it was the status the knights enjoyed in that period that Paul was determined to restore. Paul tended to see the present as having declined from a golden age, and he regularly measured current realities against the previously existing ideal. Thus his most strenuous efforts aimed at preserving the valued remains while reestablishing or reconstructing what had been lost. Here the Knights of Malta form a nearly perfect paradigm for Paul's outlook: his every statement referred to the order's former glory and to his own commitment to restore it to those conditions. Nor was this only rhetoric. Paul saw himself as an absolute monarch in the great tradition, and the Knights of Malta were to play a role in his court similar to the one they had had in the great courts of the past. Maisonneuve reflected on precisely this point when he described how Paul knighted his sons, interpreting the scene as a return to those golden days of Henry IV and Charles V when the first gentlemen of every royal realm were members of the Knights of Malta.[118] And the paradigm holds in another sense, for Paul's voyage into the past required a radical transformation of what the Knights of Malta had become. Though we have only the outline, the Russified version of the order bore no more resemblance to the knights of the sixteenth century than the nineteenth-century Russian autocracy bore to Charles V's vast realms. What Paul might have done, had he lived to carry out his plans, would have been to give the knights a modern base from which to confront the nineteenth-century world. In effect, from the order's perspective, Paul's schemes amounted to a program of modernization. Yet if he had been successful in using the knights as a model or instrument of indoctrination for Russia's aristocracy, they would have then served as an instrument to reinforce the barriers against change, and a weapon to fight the corrosive influences of modernity.

Paul was committed to preserving traditional political and social values. He saw the world in hierarchies, he feared change, and he showed no inclination toward even a gradual evolutionary view. His emphasis throughout was on restoring and perfecting a universally valid sociopolitical system that could only grow in the sense of completing or fulfilling itself. Structural transformation meant the perversion or destruction of the system. Perhaps the contemporary closest to Paul in his view of political culture was Napoleon Bonaparte, whose careful reconstruction of a traditional social hierarchy to support his version of imperial absolutism produced a modernized and infinitely elaborated edition of the great monarchies of the preceding two centuries. Bonaparte, however, had his own extraordinary charisma combined with the ideological fervor carried over from the Revolution on which to build a positive consensus. Russia lacked this energizing drive, while Paul possessed a sort of negative charisma that shrank his real accomplishments and generated a debilitating, and often entirely deserved, contempt. Paul's competence was small when compared with Bonaparte's many-sided genius, and it was further reduced by emotional instability, while Russia, both culturally and economically, was clearly less developed than was France. These differences, however, are obvious. It might be more fruitful to consider Bonaparte's empire as embodying in organizational and even moral terms what Paul was dreaming about. But dream and reality were far apart in Paul's Russia, and never farther than between his vision and what he actually accomplished.

Like so many other projects Paul undertook, his plans for the Knights of Malta collapsed into a welter of inconsequence.[119] The tsar became enmeshed in the details of establishing his new priory, distributing honors and offices, and providing funding, while on the diplomatic scene first the recognition issue and then the disposition of the island engaged his energies. The first, as we have seen, was satisfactorily resolved, while the second was part of a move toward reconciliation with France, the results of which were never to be known. Beyond the circle where Paul's personal influence could be felt, the order had little effect. The tsar's enthusiasm generated no discernible response among the nobility, and Paul himself showed no indication that he could use the order effectively. Neither Ivan IV's *oprichnina* nor the Bolshevik party are acceptable analogues for Paul's knights; they were neither an internal police force, nor a paramilitary political organization, and most certainly had no vanguard role in society at large. But these conceptions are doubtless too modern to apply to a sixteenth-century ideal implemented at the opening of the nineteenth century. The anachronisms possible are endless. Even the order's character as a monastic-military society was entirely bowdlerized once Paul began to integrate it into his system, and this would have had the inevitable effect of diluting whatever moral force the traditional forms of the institution might have possessed. Yet there always seems to be some kernel of value hidden in the ruins of Paul's perverse and macerated programs. His thought that the Russian autocracy lacked the rich tradition of supporting and reinforcing institutions that bolstered Western monarchical society showed an interesting political perception, especially in the Russian context; the idea that the Knights of Malta might educate the Russian nobility to its moral responsibilities and thus strengthen the autocracy suggests insight into a critical problem in political culture; but there the matter ends. Whatever Paul's intentions, the Knights of Malta in Russia became, in fact, one more embellishment for the court, and, when all was said and done, a cultural-historical anomaly of the first magnitude.

NOTES

1 For background on Paul, his personality, and the character of his reign, see E. S. Shumigorskii, *Imperator Pavel I: zhizn' i tsarstvovanie* (St. Petersburg, 1907); Pierre Morane, *Paul I de Russie avant l'avènement, 1754-1796* (Paris, 1907); Dmitrii F. Kobeko, *Der Cäsarewitsch Pawel Petrowitsch, 1754-1796* (Berlin, 1886); Valentin Graf Zubow, *Zar Paul I: Mensch und Schicksal* (Stuttgart, 1964). The best monograph on Paul's reign is M. V. Klochkov, *Ocherki pravitel'stvennoi deiatel'nosti vremeni Pavla I* (Petrograd, 1916). Chapter 1 reviews the historical tradition. For a particularly valuable recent contribution on Paul's education see David L. Ransel, *The Politics of Catherinian Russia: The Panin Party* (New Haven and London, 1975), pp. 213, 222-223, 282-283, and especially pp. 287-289. For a recent view of Paul based on reports by men who worked with him, see Roderick E. McGrew, "A Political Portrait of Paul I from the Austrian and English Diplomatic Archives," *Jahrbücher für Geschichte Osteuropas*, Band 18 (n.s.), Heft 4 (Dec. 1970), 503-529.

2 The general diplomatic issues are well discussed in Comte Michel de Pierredon, *Histoire politique de l'ordre souverain de Jérusalem (Ordre de Malte) de 1789 à 1955*, I (Paris, 1956), chapters 3-10, pp. 23-218. Pierredon, though by no means flawless, is the best and most reliable historian on the recent political history of the order, and his book contains an excellent selection of documents for the period of Paul I. With special reference to Russia, see Norman E. Saul, *Russia and the Mediterranean, 1797-1807* (Chicago, 1970). Saul's notes and bibliography are an excellent guide. The Vatican aspect was particularly important. See Paul Pierling, *La Russie et le Saint Siège: études diplomatiques*, 5 vols. (Paris, 1912), especially V, iii-iv, 177-334. The most important work on this subject is M. J. Rouët de Journel, S.J., *Nonciatures de Russie d'après des documents authentiques: Nonciature de Litta, (1797-1799), Studi e Testi*, 167 (Vatican City, 1943) and *Interim de Benvenuti, (1799-1803), Studi e Testi*, 194 (Vatican City, 1957). Rouët de Journel's introductions to the documents in these volumes are fine historical essays. The documents themselves are the best published sources we have on Russo-papal relations at the end of the eighteenth century, and they include material of the first importance for Paul's relations with the Knights of Malta. Pierredon uses Rouët de Journel's material, but on religious questions Rouët de Journel is superior; in the periods covered he supplants Pierling.

3 On Paul's interest in chivalry and the Knights of Malta, see Shumigorskii, *Pavel I*, pp. 17-18, 107; Kobeko, *Pawel Petrowitsch*, pp. 133-134; Zubow, *Zar Paul I*, pp. 24-25. The history that Paul studied was l'Abbé de Vertot, *Histoire des Chevaliers Hospitaliers de S. Jean de Jérusalem, appellés depuis Chevaliers de Rhodes, et aujourd'hui Chevaliers de Malthe*, with the first edition at Paris in 1726. The version Paul probably used was the fourth (1755). That edition was in thirteen books of narration to 1568, a chronological summary in one book to 1725, and a fifteenth book that summarized the governing institutions and procedures of the knights. There is no substantive difference between the first and fourth editions. The history is a straightforward political and military account that pointedly excludes supernatural events and miracles. Romantic as the subject matter may be, the tone of the book is dispassionate and even objective. The work went through fourteen editions with the last appearing in 1853. Pierredon considers it "more distinguished for the elegance of its style than for its historical accuracy" (*Histoire politique*, I, xi). His standard is a twentieth-century one. The book is impressive and was one of the most popular in its time.

4 *Joseph de Maisonneuve, Annales historiques de l'ordre de St. Jean de Jérusalem depuis l'année 1725 jusqu'au moment présent* (St. Petersburg, 1799), pp. 44-45. Maisonneuve had been chamberlain for Louis XVI and was named minister plenipotentiary for the Knights of Malta in Warsaw and Berlin. He was chargé d'affaires for the order in St. Petersburg during Paul's reign, and his *Annales historiques,* which was published by the imperial press, may be considered an official account. On Maisonneuve see Pierredon, *Histoire politique,* I, 65, n. 1. For the view of Paul and the Knights of Malta as it was presented within the imperial family, see Baron F. I. Brunov [Brunnow] "Aperçu des principales transactions du cabinet de Russie sous les règnes de Catherine II, Paul I, et Alexandre I," *Sbornik IRIO,* XXXI (1881), 197-416, and especially 233-239. This essay was written in 1838 for the Grand Duke Alexander Nikolaevich. The portion on Paul stresses the role that Paul hoped the knights could play in resisting Revolutionary influences. An annotation by Nicholas I (n. 1, p. 234) indicates that for the first time he understood his father's idea. See also Baron Michel de Taube, *L'empereur Paul I de Russie, grand maître de l'ordre de Malte, et son "Grand Prieuré Russe" de l'ordre de St. Jean de Jérusalem* (Paris, 1955) and "Le tsar Paul I et l'Ordre de Malte en Russie," *Revue d'histoire moderne,* V (1930), 161-177, and especially 167-168, 171.

5 See A. A. Aliab'ev, "Snosheniia Rossii s Mal'tiiskim Ordenom do 1789 g.," *Sbornik Moskovskago glavnago arkhiva Ministerstva inostrannykh del,* V (1893), 175-218; Giuseppi Greppi, *Un Gentiluomo milanese, guerriero-diplomatico: 1763-1839; Appunti biografici sul Bali Conte Giulio Litta-Visconti Arese* (Milano, 1896), chapters 2 and 3; Claire-Elaine Engel, *L'Ordre de de Malte en Mediterranée,* 1530-1798 (Monaco, 1957), pp. 192-197, and *Histoire de l'Ordre de Malte* (Geneva, Paris, Munich, 1968), pp. 260-293. Engel has useful material, but both books should be used with extreme care. In the 1968 volume, for example, which is much the better of the two, the author insists on Paul's death occurring on 3 Mar. 1800 (see p. 308).

6 Aliab'ev, "Snosheniia Rossii," pp. 175-178; Greppi, *Giulio Litta,* pp. 6-19; Engel, *L'Ordre de Malte en Mediterranée,* pp. 192-193.

7 Greppi, *Giulio Litta,* pp. 45-86. See also A. F. Bychkov, comp., "Depeshi Grafa Litty: poslannika Mal'tiiskago ordena v Peterburge: pisannyia v kontse 1796 i nachale 1797 goda," *Sbornik IRIO,* II (St. Petersburg, 1868), 175-218. See especially the introductory essay, pp. 164-185.

8 Pierredon, *Histoire politique,* I, xxx-xxxiv. Pierredon stresses the period after 1789, but his introduction is a good summary essay on the order's dilemmas before the Revolution. Cf. Engel, *L'Ordre de Malte en Mediterranée,* and *Histoire* for expanded coverage of the pre-1789 situation.

9 Aliab'ev, "Snosheniia Rossii," pp. 179-218; Greppi, *Giulio Litta,* pp. 19-40; Engel, *L'Ordre de Malte en Mediterranée,* pp. 193-198, and *Histoire,* pp. 260-293. See also Norman Saul, *Russia and the Mediterranean,* introduction and chapter I.

10 Pierredon, *Histoire politique,* I, xxxiv.

11 This summary is based on Pierredon, *Histoire politique,* I, 1-67. Appropriate documents are published at the end of the volume. See also Frederick W. Ryan, *The House of the Temple: A Story of Malta and its Knights in the French Revolution* (London, 1930).

12 Pierredon, *Histoire politique,* I, 36-42, 68-213.

13 *Ibid.*

14 *Ibid.,* pp. 55-56; "Depeshi Litty"; Greppi, *Giulio Litta,* p. 86; Engel, *Histoire,* pp. 260-293.

15 Greppi, *Giulio Litta,* pp. 50-86; "Depeshi Litty," pp. 164-166.

16 The remark was made to Ovide Doublet, second secretary in the French Department at Malta from 1781-1798. Doublet recorded it in his diary, and Ryan, *House of the Temple,* p. 245, quotes it.

17 Greppi, *Giulio Litta,* pp. 87-89. Greppi cites some of his material as being from Litta's autobiography. Paul's references to Litta's family are reported in Litta's letters to Grand Master Rohan. See "Depeshi Litty," No. 61, 7/18 Jan. 1797, p. 226. Greppi also uses this correspondence.

18 On Paul's isolation from court, see McGrew, "A Political Portrait," pp. 504-510. For Paul's Gatchina world, Kobeko, *Pawel Petrowitsch,* pp. 213-214, 224-230. See also James Harris, First Earl of Malmesbury, *Diaries and Correspondence,* I (London, 1845), 212-213, 227-228, 234-241; II, 18-19.

19 Greppi, *Giulio Litta,* pp. 87-92; Pierredon, *Histoire politique,* I, 55-56.

20 Rouët de Journel, *Litta,* pp. vi, vii-viii.

21 Greppi, *Giulio Litta,* pp. 89-91.

22 Quoted in Ryan, *House of the Temple,* p. 242.

23 "Depeshi Litty," No. 51, 6/17 Nov. 1796, p. 188.

24 McGrew, "Political Portrait," pp. 511-515 for Paul's first days.

25 "Depeshi Litty," No. 56, 2/13 Dec. 1796; No. 57, 12/23 Dec., pp. 190-192. Cf. Greppi, *Giulio Litta,* pp. 94-96.

26 "Depeshi Litty," No. 59, 19/30 Dec. 1796, pp. 199-201.

27 *Ibid.,* pp. 201-205; the quote is on pp. 204-205.

28 "Convention entre Sa Majesté Impériale de toutes les Russies et l'Ordre Souverain de Malte et Son Altesse Eminentissime Monseigneur le Grand Maître," Maisonneuve, *Annales historiques,* pp. 48-71. Cf. *Polnoe sobranie zakonov,* Series I, 30 vols. (St. Petersburg, 1830), No. 17708, 4 Jan. 1797.

29 "Depeshi Litty," No. 61, 7/18 Jan. 1797, pp. 209-237. Litta began this report in a triumphant vein: "I have finally finished very happily, and indeed even better than we could hope, the affairs of the Order of Malta in the North, and I flatter myself to have entirely fulfilled all the objects of the mission to which the orders of Your Eminent Highness called me." Cf. Greppi,

Giulio Litta, pp. 98-99, where the point is stressed that the agreements conformed to the order's rules, but that it remained to the order to accept them. If the order did not, the agreement was void.

30 "Convention," *passim.* Cf. "Depeshi Litty," No. 61, *passim.*

31 "Convention," 4th separate article, pp. 76-77. Cf. "Depeshi Litty," No. 61, pp. 222-224.

32 "Depeshi Litty," No. 62, 25 Jan./5 Feb. 1797, pp. 240-241, where Litta reports the tsar's recommendation as an exception to the rule and declares how gratified he is at Paul's high regard for him. He then emphasizes how important it is to Paul that the Russian priory is only for Russian subjects. *Ibid.,* pp. 241-242.

33 *Ibid.,* No. 59, 9/30 Dec. 1796, p. 201.

34 *Ibid.,* No. 61, 7/18 Jan. 1797, pp. 218-221. Greppi considered this point to be particularly important. Greppi, *Giulio Litta,* p. 100. A "langue" or "tongue" was the largest regional grouping in the knights' administrative structure. There were eight *langues* at the time of the French Revolution. Priories and commanderies were subordinate to *langues,* and commanderies were divisions of priories. Paul was seeking a much more elevated status for the Russian priory by requesting its organization as a *langue*.

35 "Convention," especially preamble, p. 49, and articles XI and XII, p. 58.

36 "Depeshi Litty," No. 61, 7/18 Jan. 1797, p. 210.

37 *Ibid.,* pp. 230-231, 232-233.

38 Greppi, *Giulio Litta,* pp. 104-105; Engle, *Histoire,* p. 293.

39 Greppi, *Giulio Litta,* pp. 106-107; Engel, *Histoire,* p. 294, is especially critical. Cf. Engel, *L'Ordre de Malte en Mediterranée,* p. 270. Pierredon, though showing a generally low opinion of Hompesch, gives much less weight to the convention than to the general political situation and the decline of the order. See Pierredon, *Histoire politique,* I, chapters 3-9.

40 On ceremonial and the reaction to it, McGrew, "Political Portrait," pp. 515-517. The disgust was general in the diplomatic community.

41 Maisonneuve, *Annales historiques,* pp. 94-105, describes the ceremonies and quotes the speeches. Cf. Greppi, *Giulio Litta,* pp. 108-112.

42 Ryan, *House of the Temple,* pp. 244-245.

43 Rouët de Journel, *Litta,* pp. vii-xii, xxvi-xxviii. Rouët de Journel thought the "flood of gold" Paul poured over the knights was corrupting and a factor in the Littas' failures.

44 See Pierredon, *Histoire politique,* I, 140-194, for a detailed account of the events with supporting documents. Pierredon gives the official French account, Ferdinand Hompesch's account, and accounts provided by knights who supported the order. This is by far the best and most complete description available.

45 See "Protestation du Grand Prieuré de Russie" and "Manifeste du Grand Prieuré de Russie," Maisonneuve, *Annales historiques,* pp. 170-174, 174-190. Reprinted as Nos. L and LI in Pierredon, *Histoire politique,* I, 339-340, 341-349. Maisonneuve is Pierredon's source. The imperial press published a collection of documents entitled *Actes du chapitre du Grand Prieuré de Russie* (St. Petersburg, 1798). This includes the "Protestation," and "Manifeste," plus Paul's *ukaz* of 10/21 Sept. 1798; the proclamation of Paul as grand master, 27 Oct./7 Nov. 1798; Paul's acceptance, 13/24 Nov. 1798; Paul's decree in Latin, which established St. Petersburg as the headquarters for the knights, 21 Dec. 1798/1 Jan. 1799. This pamphlet, which I have seen nowhere else, is filed in the correspondence of Pius VI with Giulio Litta. Archivio Vaticano, Nunziature Polonia-Russia, No. 344/I, Folio 89, Pius VI to Bali Giulio Conte Litta, Firenze 5 Nov. 1798.

46 "Manifeste," Maisonneuve, *Annales historiques,* p. 188. Paul-Julien de Suffren-Saint-Tropèz, bailli and grand croix of the order, was accused of abandoning his post in the face of the French attack. Saint-Tropèz's brother had been the order's ambassador to Paris.

47 Pierredon, *Histoire politique,* I, 221. The Grand Priory of Castille and Leon reaffirmed its oath to the order and its support of the grand master on 13 Sept. (N.S.) 1798. It did not yet know of the Russian protest.

48 Pierredon, *Histoire politique,* I, No. LVII, "Adhésion du Vénerable Grand Prieuré d'Allemagne," 23 Oct. 1798, pp. 361-362. The document is reprinted from Maisonneuve, who used it to show German support for the Russian position. This was a conscious misreading of it. The intention of the German priory was to avoid conflict, and it wanted the charges investigated. This is very clear from an unpublished manuscript memo, "Considerant [*sic*] du vénble chapitre du Grand Prieuré d'Allemagne," and a copy of the covering letter to Giulio Litta which explained the priory's position at length and was "an invitation to him, Bailli de Litta, to recommend as far as possible, the observance of our Statutes." The document that Maisonneuve published appears

to be abbreviated; the doubts are less apparent, and the proposed letter to Litta, which was quite pointed, does not appear. See Archivio Vaticano, Polonia-Russia, No. 344/VI, untitled folio, 26 Maggio-2 Ottobre 1802 [*sic*: 1798-1802]. This would seem to indicate that Litta and Maisonneuve manipulated evidence entering the priory. See below, especially part III.

49 Pierredon, *Histoire politique,* I, gives several of the Hompesch efforts at exculpation. See No. XLVIII, Hompesch to Francis II, 28 July 1798; No. XLIX, Manifesto to the Emperors of Austria and Russia, 28 July 1798, pp. 336-338, 335-336; No. IL, Hompesch to Colloredo, 29 July 1798, pp. 338-339; No. LIII, Manifesto of Protest against Bonaparte, pp. 349-351; No. LVIII, Hompesch to Paul I, protesting the Russian priory's August actions, 30 Oct. 1798, pp. 363-364. None of the published letters give Hompesch's position in detail. This appears in a very long memo to the King of Sweden. The memo is accompanied by a "Progetto di Protesta . . . contre la presa di Malta fatta dall' Armata Francese." The covering letter is dated 28 July 1798 from Trieste. The object of these accounts is to demonstrate French bad faith and to prove that the order had taken no steps that could be interpreted as belligerent. It starts from the assumption that Malta was unprepared and seeks to demonstrate that the fortress stayed that way. The angle of approach could hardly have been more different from that of the Russian priory. See Stockholm Riksarkivet, Diplomatica Italica, Vol. 47, Malteser Ordens: Originalbrev. A similar account is filed in the Vatican. See Archivio Vaticano, Polonia-Russia, No. 344/Add/vi (Undesignated Folio).

50 "Depeshi Litty," No. 61, 7/18 Jan. 1797, pp. 222-223.

51 The rules of membership and the regulations governing the order should have been known to Paul from Vertot's history, the last volume of which is a structural description and rehearsal of the rules. For a modern summary, see Pierredon, *Histoire politique,* I, chapter 1. The oath of the order is given on p. 12. See also Reuben Cohen, *The Knights of Malta, 1523-1798* (New York, 1920), pp. 30-43.

52 Claire-Elaine Engel, *The Knights of Malta: A Gallery of Portraits* (New York, 1963), p. 184.

53 There is no list of the priory's members before Paul became grand master. Maisonneuve records those members supporting the priory's actions, but in every case they were away and expressed their opinions after the fact, usually writing from Condé's field headquarters. See *Annales historiques,* p. 194 and annexes 1-4. In a special report in March 1799, Stedingk commented that Paul's selection as grand master owed to a group of five or six knights "who are found here, but of whom none could have a voice in the chapter since not one of them has taken vows." Stockholm Riksarkivet, Diplomatica Muscovitica 460, Stedingk au roi, 18/29 Mar. 1799 (hereafter Dip. Musc.).

54 Maisonneuve, *Annales historiques*, pp. 168-169.

55 *Ibid.,* p. 170.

56 This opinion was unanimous. See Stockholm Riksarkivet, Dip. Musc. 460, Stedingk au roi, 18/29 Mar. 1799; Public Record Office, London (hereafter PRO), FO 65/42, No. 13, 13 Mar. 1799. Whitworth's conclusions on the Malta affair and the relevant dispatches are summarized in McGrew, "Political Portrait," p. 522 and n. 53. Whitworth believed that Paul offered himself as protector, but that Litta urged him to go farther. Paul already of course had been officially designated as protector. See also l'Abbé J. F. Georgel, *Mémoires pour servir à l'histoire des événemens de la fin du dix-huitième siècle depuis 1760 jusqu'en 1806-1810,* VI (Paris, 1818), 188-189. Georgel was in Petersburg in 1799. Recording the events concerning the Knights of Malta, he placed the full responsibility for Hompesch's deposition and Paul's election on Giulio Litta. Pierredon, *Histoire politique,* I, 218-219, quotes Georgel but argues that Litta had the idea of elevating Paul when, in the course of his address to the throne (29 Nov./10 Dec. 1797), Litta called on Paul "to place himself at the head of this institution." This goes too far. The context of the speech (reproduced in Maisonneuve, *Annales historiques,* p. 98) makes it clear that what Pierredon quotes is one phrase in a grandiose rhetorical flourish that did no more than underline the order's *offer* of a protectorate and urge Paul to accept it as offered.

57 The diplomatic reports cited above all tend to minimize Paul's personal initiatives. The opposite view, for which there is no evidence at all, namely that Paul took the initiative and dragged Litta with him, appears in Engel, *L'Ordre de Malte en Mediterranée,* pp. 265-270. When Engel used Rouët de Journel's documents, however, she shifted her position to emphasize Litta's role. See *Histoire,* pp. 301-302. Shumigorskii, *Pavel I,* pp. 145-148, discusses Paul's predilection for the order and his reactions to the priory's proposals. But Shumigorskii is more concerned with

the significance of Paul's acceptance: that he combined his interest in chivalric values, the defense of traditional institutions, and his religious world view into an ideological basis for the campaign against France. Zubow's emphasis is similar, but it stresses the mystical-religious aspect, and especially the reunion of the Churches. Paul's behavior becomes more comprehensible when we look at it in relation to the Littas' interests and policies. For additional comments on this question, see N. K. Schilder, *Imperator Pavel I* (St. Petersburg, 1907), p. 398; and the same author's *Histoire anecdotique de Paul I* (Paris, 1899), pp. 126 and 148. See also Kazimierz Waliszewski, *Le fils de la grande Catherine: Paul I, empereur de Russie 1754-1801,* 3rd ed. (Paris, 1912), pp. 333-335. The point is developed in detail in parts III and IV of this essay.

58 Pierredon, *Histoire politique,* I, 214-215, cites the fragments of O'Hara's letter from Chevalier C. J. de Meyer-Knonau, *Révolution de Malte en 1798* (Trieste, 1799), p. 120. Meyer-Knonau was with Hompesch and had access to his correspondence. Pierredon shows the book to be in the Bibliothèque nationale: K. 3612. The first letter was dated 4 Aug. 1798; the second, 20 Sept. 1798. O'Hara appears in Doublet's memoirs as an impetuous, romantic, and slightly giddy young man of warm enthusiasms and strong attachments. That he wrote Hompesch a friendly letter after Hompesch had been anathematized by the Russian priory, and just one day before Paul approved that action, indicates a robust individualism. O'Hara's subsequent career is obscure. For a colorful incident involving O'Hara, see Ryan, *The House of the Temple,* pp. 321-322. One would expect that O'Hara's reports and letters would be in the archives of the Knights of Malta in Leningrad. Dom, later Cardinal, Pitra was permitted to see the order's Petersburg archives in 1859/60, but found nothing. Pierredon was not permitted to see them, and the material Rouët de Journel received is routine.

59 De Loras apparently was a friend of Count Psaro, the Russian chargé d'affaires on Malta, and he was associated as well with the Neapolitan party. Engel refers to him as an agent. See *Histoire,* p. 261.

60 The following argument is based on Pierredon, *Histoire politique,* I, 215-217. Pierredon follows Meyer-Knonau. De Tigné's letter as it appeared in *Le moniteur universel,* 12 Brumaire, l'An VII (2 Nov. 1798) and 13 Brumaire, l'An VII (3 Nov. 1798), pp. 171, 175-176, is reprinted as No. LIV, pp. 351-359 in Pierredon, *Histoire politique,* I. Cf. "Manifeste du Grand Prieuré de Russie," Maisonneuve, *Annales historiques,* pp. 174-190.

61 De Tigné's denials were notarized on 3 Oct. 1800. The document appears in Pierredon, *Histoire politique,* I, No. LXXIX, pp. 395-397.

62 See "Depeshi Litty," No. 61, 7/18 Jan. 1797, p. 210; Greppi, *Giulio Litta,* pp. 111-112, 128.

63 Greppi, *Giulio Litta,* pp. 141-142.

64 Pierredon, *Histoire politique,* I, 218-219, argues very strongly that Litta's "gamble" was prompted by self-interest. Stedingk's indictment is even stronger: Litta pushed Paul into grand mastership to protect his own position at court. Stockholm Riksarkivet, Dip. Musc. 460, Stedingk au roi, 18/29 Mar. 1799. Only Greppi, *Giulio Litta,* pp. 128-129, stresses the point that Litta saw Paul as the only person who could restore the pope to Rome and the knights to Malta.

65 Rouët de Journel, *Litta,* p. vi.

66 *Ibid.,* pp. viii, xii, xxvi-xxx, xxxiii-xxxiv.

67 *Ibid.,* p. iv, discusses the conflict. Lorenzo Litta, in a long review of his Russian mission, noted that the question of the Knights of Malta disrupted his efforts but never expressed the view that he might or should have handled the problem differently. See Litta to Odescalchi, Vienna, 17 Aug. 1799, Rouët de Journel, *Litta,* No. 191, pp. 394-402. Litta also wrote a history of the Malta crisis in St. Petersburg in which he regretted the papal decision not to recognize Paul as grand master, and in a cipher letter to Cardinal Antonelli in Venice (28 Jan. 1800), he pointed out that the interests of thousands of Roman Catholics were needlessly sacrificed over the Malta question. Archivio Vaticano, Polonia-Russia, No. 344/VI: untitled, unnumbered folio with "38 Litta (?)" on cover. See part III of this essay.

68 *Ukaz,* 10/21 Sept. 1798, Maisonneuve, *Annales historiques,* pp. 192-193.

69 For the Catholic approach to negotiating with Russia, see Litta au ministère impériale, Moscow, 17/28 Apr. 1797 and especially the enclosed "Mémoire" of the same date, Rouët de Journel, *Litta,* Nos. 20 and 21, pp. 33-44. For Pius VI's appeal to Paul, *ibid.,* No. 87, 29 Mar. 1798, pp. 189-195 and especially 194-195. See also Pius to Litta, 31 Mar. 1798, *ibid.,* No. 89, pp. 197-199; Litta to Pius VI, 19/30 Mar. 1798, *ibid.,* No. 88, pp. 195-197 conveys the tsar's offer of asylum. See also Rouët de Journel, *Litta,* pp. xxxi-xxxii.

70 Archivio Vaticano, Polonia-Russia, 344/I Folio 89, Pius VI to (G.) Litta, 17 Oct. (N.S.) 1798, and *ibid.,* 5 Nov. (N.S.) 1798. Litta's enclosures and copies of the pope's replies are here. The letter itself is missing.

71 Pierredon, *Histoire politique,* I, No. LV, Pius VI to Bailli Litta, 17 Oct. (N.S.) 1798, pp. 359-360; LVI, Odescalchi to Msgr. Litta, 20 Oct. (N.S.) 1798, pp. 360-361; Rouët de Journel, *Litta,* No. 126, p. 269.

72 Pius VI to Bailli Litta, Pierredon, *Histoire politique,* I, No. LV, p. 359.

73 *Ibid.*

74 Odescalchi to Msgr. Litta, Pierredon, *Histoire politique,* I, No. LVI, p. 360.

75 *Ibid.,* pp. 360-361.

76 See Pius VI to Bailli Litta, Pierredon, *Histoire politique,* I, No. LX, 5 Nov. (N.S.) 1798, pp. 365-366 and No. LXII, Pius VI to Bailli Litta, 16 Nov. (N.S.) 1798, p. 368. Odescalchi wrote Hompesch on 9 Nov. 1799 that the pope would never accept the acts committed by the Russian priory. Pierredon, *Histoire politique,* I, No. LXXI, p. 380. This letter may be the source of the first news Paul had; it would have been "leaked."

77 See above n. 71. See also Odescalchi to Msgr. Litta, Pierredon, *Histoire politique,* I, No. LIX, 3 Nov. (N.S.) 1798, pp. 364-365. Rouët de Journel, *Litta,* No. 127, p. 270. Since there was no urgency, the pope's letter probably followed a normal routing through Vienna and required from four to six weeks. The priory's offer to Paul is in Maisonneuve, *Annales historiques,* pp. 197-200; Pierredon, *Histoire politique,* I, No. LXI, pp. 366-367. Paul's acceptance is in Maisonneuve, *Annales historiques,* pp. 201-203; Pierredon, *Histoire politique,* LXIII, pp. 368-369.

78 Curt von Stedingk mentions the pope's letter in a dispatch dated 19/30 Nov. 1798, Stockholm Riksarkivet, Dip. Musc. 459, Stedingk au roi. Litta mentions in his dispatch of 26 Nov./7 Dec. 1798 that the letter was to be read and recorded in the archives. Litta to Odescalchi, Pierredon, *Histoire politique,* I, No. LXIV, p. 370. See below. An extract of the protocol for the 22 Nov./3 Dec. meeting of the Russian priory records that the letter was read into the record, and that the Chapter was "deeply moved." Archivio Vaticano, Polonia-Russia, No. 344/VI (Untitled) 26 Maggio-2 Ottobre 1802 [*sic:* 1798-1802].

79 Litta to Odescalchi, 26 Nov./7 Dec. 1798, Pierredon, *Histoire politique,* I, No. LXIV, pp. 369-372.

80 See part IV. See also M. J. Rouët de Journel, S.J., "Paul I de Russie et l'union des églises: documents inédits," *Revue d'histoire ecclésiastique,* LIV, No. 4 (1959), 838-863.

81 L. Litta to Odescalchi, Pierredon, *Histoire politique,* I, No. LXIV, p. 370.

82 Maisonneuve, *Annales historiques,* p. 196.

83 Stockholm Riksarkivet, Dip. Musc. 459, Stedingk au roi, 19/30 Nov. 1798.

84 L. Litta to Odescalchi, 8/19 Mar. 1799, Pierredon, *Histoire politique,* I, No. LXXIV, pp. 389-392; Rouët de Journel, *Litta,* No. 179, pp. 362-364. The rumor was told to Litta by Prince Bezborodko in a private interview on 3/14 Mar. In a cipher message sent 25 Feb./8 Mar., L. Litta had already asked for his recall, explaining that his work would soon be finished, and that his brother's position, to which his own was tied, was becoming precarious. He laid the blame on court intrigues. Rouët de Journel, *Litta,* No. 172, p. 349.

85 Greppi, *Giulio Litta,* pp. 128-130; Rouët de Journel, *Litta,* pp. lviii-lxix; Pierredon, *Histoire politique,* I, 230-235.

86 Rouët de Journel, *Litta,* pp. lxii-lxiii and Rouët de Journel, *Benvenuti,* pp. viii-xi. Giulio Litta spent the rest of his life in Russia, a respected member of society. Greppi, *Giulio Litta,* pp. 141-142 and ff.

87 See, for example, Engel, *Histoire,* p. 305. This is also Pierredon's view and, though more gently stated, Rouët de Journel's. Bezborodko's opinion was stated obliquely in his conversation with Lorenzo Litta on Mar. 3/14 (see above n. 84) and much more strongly to the Austrian ambassador, Count Cobenzl. On 10 Dec. 1798 Cobenzl reported a private conversation with Bezborodko in which "he [Bezborodko] perfectly agreed with me that everything being done here relative to the Order of Malta was absolutely illegal, and that if the Emperor had any interest in being charged with this Grand magistracy, he ought to have limited himself to being Protector of the Order while working to maintain it and to restore it to its former state." Haus-, Hof-, und Staatsarchiv, Vienna (hereafter HHSA), Russland II Berichte, Carton 89, No. 65, apostille 5, 10 Dec. 1798, Cobenzl to Thugut.

88 The Catholic case for Paul has not been widely documented in published materials except in those of persons like Maisonneuve who were part of his entourage. There is, however, a substantial case, and a considerable body of unpublished data. See, for example, "Motifs à

proposer à engager le Cour de Rome de reconnaitre Paul I comme Grand-Maître de l'Ordre hospitalier et militaire de St. Jean . . .," Archivio Vaticano, Polonia-Russia, No. 344/VI, Folio 88; see also Folio "Malte" for Monsignore de Pietro's collection of pro and con opinions on Paul's grand mastership. Lorenzo Litta remained certain that, for practical reasons, Paul should have been recognized. See his letter to Cardinal Antonelli cited above, n. 72. See also "Lettres de Msgr. Fr. de Bernis, Archevêque de Albi," which contains three letters from Petersburg supporting Paul. The first, dated 10 Feb. 1800, is almost certainly by Father Gruber. The "Lettre" folio is also in Polonia-Russia, No. 344/VI. For a modern defense of Paul I, very partisan in tone but well argued, see Baron Michel de Taube, *L'Empereur Paul I.*

89 "Proclamation," Maisonneuve, *Annales historiques,* pp. 197-199.

90 *Ibid.,* pp. 201-203.

91 Pius VI to Paul I, 29 Mar. (N.S.) 1798, Rouët de Journel, *Litta,* No. 87, pp. 189-195; Odescalchi to Litta, 31 Mar. (N.S.) 1798, Rouët de Journel, *Litta,* No. 89, pp. 197-199.

92 Rouët de Journel, *Litta,* pp. lix-lx; Odescalchi to Litta, 16 Mar. 1799, No. 175, pp. 350-353 and "Pro Memoria," pp. 354-357. Pierredon, *Histoire politique,* I, 230-235.

93 Both Rouët de Journel and Pierredon develop this argument. It seems entirely reasonable.

94 Paul I to Pius VI, 14/25 Dec. 1798, Pierredon, *Histoire politique,* I, No. LXVIII, pp. 375-377; Rouët de Journel, *Litta,* No. 146, pp. 299-301.

95 "Appel de . . . Paul I," Pierredon, *Histoire politique,* I, No. LXIX, pp. 377-379; Maisonneuve, *Annales historiques,* pp. 257-261.

96 Schilder, *Pavel I,* pp. 404-424; Waliszewski, *Paul I,* pp. 336-338. See also McGrew, "Political Portrait," pp. 518-525.

97 Paul I to Pius VI, Pierredon, *Histoire politique,* I, No. LXVIII, p. 376.

98 Paul remarked to Stedingk that the main difference between southern and northern Europe was that in the south the people were rebellious and the nobility loyal, while in the north, and especially in Russia and Sweden, the nobility threatened the stability of monarchs while the people were reliable. See Stockholm Riksarkivet, Dip. Musc. 464, Stedingk au roi, 30 Mar./11 Apr. 1800. Paul flatly denied that the nobility had any special privilege vis-à-vis the crown; he also believed that nobles had special responsibilities toward society. V. O. Kliuchevskii saw this as indicating a modern conception of a society as a collective whole rather than a hierarchy of special corporate bodies with exclusive rights inhering in the aristocracy. See *Kurs russkoi istorii,* 5 vols. in *Sochineniia* (Moscow, 1956-1959), V, 236-237; notes to lecture LXXXII, pp. 437-441. See also Ransel, *Panin Party,* pp. 205-225. In my view, Paul believed in a disciplined, loyal nobility that acted as society's elite in a very traditional social hierarchy. See Roderick E. McGrew, "The Politics of Absolutism: Paul I and the Bank of Assistance for the Nobility," *Canadian-American Slavic Studies,* VII (Spring 1973), 15-38. See especially pp. 36-37 and n. 49. (The essay is reprinted in this collection.)

99 "Paul I of Russia, *ukaz*: 29 Nov./10 Dec. 1798" (British Museum Pamphlet filed under Paul I). Cf. *Polnoe sobranie zakonov,* Series I, XXV, No. 18766, 29 Nov. 1798.

100 "Appel de . . . Paul I," Pierredon, *Histoire politique,* I, No. LXIX, 21 Dec./1 Jan. 1799, pp. 379-383; especially p. 382.

101 "Appel de . . . Paul I," *ibid.;* "Ukaz," pp. 1-2.

102 This view was held by both Rouët de Journel and Pierredon; quite naturally it dominated the reports of contemporary diplomats, including Cobenzl, Whitworth, and Stedingk. It also fits with the idea that the last two years of Paul's life showed increasing irrationality. I have no quarrel with any of this.

103 Shumigorskii, *Pavel I,* pp. 148, 178-179; Aleksandr Trachevskii, ed., "Diplomaticheskiia snosheniia Rossii s Frantsiei v epokhu Napoleona I," I: *1800-1802, Sbornik* IRIO, LXX (1890). See especially part II of the Introduction, pp. xv and ff. Paul's letter to Bonaparte, 18/30 Dec. 1800, uses a rhetoric similar to that which we have been reading, though now the focus is on "returning peace and calm to the world," while wishing to discuss "neither the rights of nor the principles of different governments." The letter begins, however, by saying that "It is the duty of those on whom God has placed the power to govern peoples to think and be concerned about their well-being." The shift from the old order to Napoleon was not as dramatic ideologically as it was practically, for Paul, though an absolutist, saw the possibility for corrupt men to ruin sound institutions, and sound men to repair corrupt ones. This seems to have been one underlying rationale in his approach to Napoleon.

104 The news of Bavaria's opposition came at the same time as Paul's induction and created a "disagreeable incident" in which the Bavarian minister was expelled from St. Petersburg.

Litta to Odescalchi, Pierredon, *Histoire politique,* I, No. LXVI, pp. 374 ff. The most complete review of the Bavarian incident is a part of Stedingk's long report sent by special courier (to avoid Paul's secret service) describing events in St. Petersburg in late 1798 and early 1799. The report covers twelve folio pages, four sides each, and is perhaps the best and most thoughtful available commentary on Paul's court by a contemporary. See Stockholm Riksarkivet, Dip. Musc. 460, 18/29 Mar. 1799, Stedingk au roi. Stedingk notes that in addition to Bavaria, Portugal, Spain, and Austria were either reluctant or opposed, and that Paul suspected Prussia of opposition and so pressured the Prussian representative for a positive stand. Cf. PRO, FO 65/42, No. 13, Whitworth to Grenville, 13 Mar. (N.S.) 1799; HHSA, Russ. II Ber. 89, No. 65, apostille 5, Cobenzl to Thugut, 10 Dec. 1798; No. 67, 18 Dec. 1798; *ibid.,* 91, No. 36, apostille 14, Cobenzl to Thugut, 17 Mar. 1799.

105 On the terms of Bavaria's capitulation, Archivio Vaticano Polonia-Russia, No. 344/VI, Folio 26 Maggio-2 Ottobre 1802 [*sic*: 1798-1802], preliminary convention and secret convention between the Elector of Bavaria-Palatinate and the Order of the Knights of Malta. The preliminary agreement was dated 6 July 1799, and the convention was signed by Paul as grand master on 29 July 1799. Baron Flachslander stresses in his covering letter that there was no choice but to accept, and that to do so was required by "The interest of the Church, perhaps that of the Order." Archbishop Albi agreed strongly. Austria's situation was especially difficult, as Paul forced the Austrian government to abandon Hompesch (see Pierredon, *Histoire politique,* I, Nos. LXXVI and LXXVII, pp. 393-394, for Francis II's curt order and Hompesch's resignation) and the Bohemian priory to recognize his grand mastership. Cobenzl played the central role. See HHSA, Russ. II Ber. 91, No. 42, Cobenzl to Thugut, 11 June 1799; *ibid.,* 92, No. 49, apostille 1, 3 July 1799. On the Bohemian priory's deputation to St. Petersburg and Paul's refusal to accept an address as protector, No. 60, 9 Apr. 1799. On the Bohemian priory's complete surrender to Paul, No. 61, 13 Aug. 1799; No. 62, 16 Aug. 1799. Cobenzl also believed that Paul declared war on Spain primarily because of Malta. *Ibid.,* 92, No. 57, 31 July 1799. Stedingk's report confirmed this opinion. Stockholm Riksarkivet, Dip. Musc. 460, 24 July/4 Aug. 1799.

106 A circular signed by Rostopchin and Panin, dated 20/31 Dec. 1799, announced that since Paul had been accepted by a plurality of the *langues* of the order, "the Imperial Residence of St. Petersburg will be the Seat and Capital of the Sovereign Order of St. John of Jerusalem." Stockholm Riksarkivet, Dip. Musc. 464: enclosure, Stedingk au roi, 3 Jan. 1800. See also "Motifs à proposer . . . ," Polonia-Russia, Archivio Vaticano No. 344/VI, Folio 88, where the acceptance by nearly every *langue* and priory of Paul as grand master, and by most of the governments in Europe, is offered as a basic reason for the papacy to recognize him, too.

107 See Rouët de Journel, *Benvenuti,* pp. viii-x, xii-xiii, No. 2, Benvenuti to Litta, 10/21 Aug. 1799; No. 4, Benvenuti to Consalvo, 9 Mar. 1800 and 18 May 1800. See also Litta to Cardinal Antonelli, 17 Aug. 1799, Archivio Vaticano, Polonia-Russia, No. 344/23.

108 Benvenuti to Litta, 10 Aug. 1799, Rouët de Journel, *Benvenuti,* No. 2, p. 6. See also Cardinal Albani to Benvenuti, 18 Jan. 1800, Archivio Vaticano, Polonia-Russia, No. 344/IV: "Benvenuti."

109 Rouët de Journel, *Benvenuti, passim,* is our best quide here. See n. 113 below.

110 Benvenuti to Consalvi, 5 July 1800, Rouët de Journel, *Benvenuti,* No. 9, pp. 17-22; 27 Aug. 1800, No. 12, p. 27. The tsar's prerequisite for receiving another nuncio was recognition as grand master.

111 Rouët de Journel, *Benvenuti,* p. xiii for Paul's refusal to understand the religious grounds for papal opposition; his remark that "at heart I am a Catholic" was made to Father Gruber and was reported to Benvenuti. See Benvenuti to Consalvi, 30 Nov. 1800, Rouët de Journel, *Benvenuti,* No. 25, pp. 56-57.

112 De Taube, *L'Empereur Paul I,* uses the point as one justification for accepting Paul as grand master.

113 See Rouët de Journel, *Benvenuti,* pp. x-xvi and especially Rouët de Journel, "Paul I et l'union des églises," pp. 838-863. The negotiations were under way when Paul died. See also Polonia-Russia: No. 344/II, Folio 103, for two letters from the Russian minister in Naples to the papal secretary of state dated 7 Mar. 1801, which deal with the question of recognition for the grand mastership in exchange for negotiations in Russia over Catholic subjects. A messenger was sent.

114 See Rouët de Journel, "Paul I et l'union des églises," pp. 838-863; Rouët de Journel, "L'Imperatore Paolo I e la Reunione delle Chiese," *La Civiltà Cattolica,* III (1959), 604-614. The latter is the summary article that Zubow, *Zar Paul I,* pp. 41-46, cites.

115 Rouët de Journel, "Paul I et l'union des églises," pp. 839-844.

116 An excellent summary statement of the Russian view was given to Lorenzo Litta by Count Kochubei after the negotiations broke off in the spring of 1799. See Rouët de Journel,

Litta, "Note ministérielle," annex to No. 184, Litta to Odescalchi, 22 Apr./3 May 1799, pp. 381-382. Point 2 refers to the "supremacy of the Roman pontiff" being limited to the spiritual realm, while the first point stressed the subordination of the Church to the civil authority. Paul showed no disposition to change these principles. This explains why Litta's task was so difficult and why the agreements he was finally offered were so unsatisfactory.

117 See Rouët de Journel, *Litta, passim.* This excellent collection of documents makes a detailed analysis of the respective Russian and papal positions possible. One weakness is the underrepresentation of Vatican documents opposed to Litta's mission. Litta himself may have been over-optimistic about what could be achieved. This subject deserves further specialized study.

118 Maisonneuve, *Annales historiques,* p. 86.

119 A review of the legislation enacted for the Knights of Malta in 1799 and 1800 reveals that it dealt entirely with formal organizational issues. The legislation clearly broadened the order from what it had been. The entire list of decrees, eight in number, is given in I. K. Antoshevskii, *Derzhavnyi orden Sviatago Ioanna Ierusalimskago imenuemyi Mal'tiiskim v Rossii* (St. Petersburg, 1914), pp. 11-12. The last decree was registered 10 Oct. (O.S.) 1800.

5

WAS PAUL BONAPARTE'S FOOL?: THE EVIDENCE OF NEGLECTED ARCHIVES

Hugh Ragsdale

Bonaparte's courting of Paul I has long been a familiar story. The first consul flattered the emperor, sent him fulsome letters, liberated several thousand Russian prisoners of war, and offered to restore Malta to the Order of St. John. Paul seemed to reciprocate obligingly by breaking relations with Austria and England, expelling Louis XVIII from his asylum at Mitau, forming the League of Armed Neutrality, and sending a plenipotentiary to Paris to negotiate an alliance that was apparently spoiled only by the emperor's violent death. The benefits to Bonaparte were enormous. According to all appearances, Paul was Bonaparte's fool. The English, the Austrians, and, for a time, the French certainly thought so. Western historians have agreed with them.

Adolphe Thiers's judgment is typical: "When these diverse communications [offer of the prisoners and Malta] arrived in St. Petersburg, they produced their inevitable effect. Paul I was vividly impressed, and he surrendered himself from that time without reservation to admiration for the First Consul . . . . Paul I, the furious enemy of France, became her friend, her ally, against the powers of the former coalition."[1] Kazimierz Waliszewski, the most widely read biographer of Paul, concurs: "The First Consul himself sent a personal appeal to the Czar, in which Caesar addressing Don Quixote made good use of the information he had been able to collect about the character of his eccentric correspondent . . . . Don Quixote rushed into the path which he was expected to take with an ardour beyond the most sanguine calculations."[2] Geoffrey Bruun sums it up succinctly: "Bonaparte . . . in less than a year had seduced the tsar with flattery and laid the promising basis for a Franco-Russian union."[3]

This misunderstanding of Paul's relations with the French is the product of the peculiar selection of sources on which it is based. These are primarily the great, and easily accessible, diplomatic archives of western Europe: the Quai d'Orsay, the Public Record Office, and—to a lesser extent—the Vienna Staatsarchiv. And these materials are, in this case, all poorly informed. A mere moment's reflection shows why, for Paul had, during the period of his alleged cooperation with Bonaparte, broken diplomatic relations with Austria and

England and not yet established relations with France. Not one of the great powers whose papers have attracted most historians' attention had an agent in St. Petersburg. Hence their information on Paul's policy was based exclusively on appearances. Thus Bonaparte was able first to believe, and later, when he discovered the contrary, to persuade Vienna and London, that a Franco-Russian alliance against them was imminent.

What we need to set the record straight, then, is more reliable sources, and the Russian ones ought to be considered first. The printed Russian sources are significant and readily accessible but not very abundant, and they do not provide a careful and authoritative record of Paul's policy.[4]

What of the manuscript sources? Unfortunately, foreign scholars in the Soviet Union are still denied access to these, so it is impossible to judge directly how much unpublished information on Paul's foreign policy the Soviet archives contain. Indirectly, it is possible to make a well-informed estimate, for several Russian historians have used these materials.[5] There are two pertinent conclusions to be drawn from their works. The first is that the recent publications do not produce new material on Franco-Russian relations[6] but tell us essentially the same story told by Miliutin and Trachevskii long ago. The second is that though historians' views of Paul and his mental condition and his political ability differ considerably—and some, especially Miliutin, see him not as fool but as hero—only Stanislavskaia recounts the difficulties of Paul's relations with Bonaparte. And none of them provide a convincing alternative explanation of Paul's policy to contradict the common conception of him as Bonaparte's fool.

Do we have, then, in published form, all or virtually all the Russian documentation on Paul's foreign policy? It is not possible that Paul and his ministers formulated their foreign policy and transacted their diplomatic business largely in conversations among themselves and in interviews with the diplomatic corps, that Paul's obscure aims and ideas during these mysterious months were thus never committed to paper, and hence that the archives do not contain a satisfactory record of his foreign policy? We cannot be sure without seeing the Soviet archives, but it seems at least possible.

Fortunately, if Russian diplomatic history is among the most difficult areas for foreigners to research in the Soviet Union, it is one on which we can get first-rate manuscript sources elsewhere. What follows here is the result of an experiment to see if additional light could be shed on the meager published Russian records by using the neglected diplomatic correspondence of powers with which Paul *did* maintain relations throughout the period in question. The materials chosen are in this case Swedish, Prussian, and Danish.

Paul had astonished Europe in 1796 by denouncing Catherine's aggression and announcing his own pacific intentions. He proclaimed loud and long that Russia stood in need of recuperation, reform, and prosperity, and therefore of peace. He recalled the corps of troops sent to campaign against the

Persians in the Caucasus. He withdrew the squadron operating with the British in the Channel. He decided not to send the promised army corps to join the coalition against France.

When, a few months later, in the summer of 1797, the Austrians appealed to him for support against Bonaparte, Paul offered instead his mediation of the conflict. He tried to persuade Prussia to associate herself with the proposed mediation. But Bonaparte forced Vienna to sign Campoformio before Paul's plan matured. The course of French aggression in the Low Countries, Italy, and Switzerland followed—and Bonaparte himself took Malta and the Ionian Islands and landed in Egypt.

Paul was offended and threatened. He formed an alliance with the Turks, and together they prepared to drive the French out of the Ionian Islands and Malta. He soon allied with Austria, England, and Naples to complete the formation of the Second Coalition. His war aims at that time were specific and clear: to obtain the cooperation of the Prussians; to protect Naples from the French; to return France to her pre-Revolutionary frontiers; to prevent the aggrandizement of Austria; to restore the king of Sardinia.

Paul soon found the imperial pretensions of his Austrian ally as little to his taste as those of the French. As the Austrian and Russian armies pushed the French out of Italy, Paul naturally expected the restoration of the old monarchies there. The Austrians refused, and it soon turned out that they themselves had designs on France's former Italian satellites. Offended now by his own ally, he decided to withdraw from the coalition. Characteristically, he issued a manifesto to explain why.

He had gone to war, he said, to protect the equilibrium of Europe from the threat of the French. But he discovered in the course of the war that the Austrians were using Russian troops for their own imperialist purposes. He did not intend to tolerate in Austria what he combated in France. "The Emperor Paul covets nothing but the general welfare; honor is his only guide . . . . The Emperor does not lose from sight the general well-being; and when the time comes, he is ready to take up arms again." He assured the little powers of Europe that he had not forgotten them.[7]

The war then continued without Russian participation. Paul rejoiced at the victory of Bonaparte over the Austrians at Marengo (14 June 1800). The perfidy of Vienna had thus gotten its due. Even before Marengo, reports circulated all over Europe that Paul was an admirer of Bonaparte. In fact, he seems to have counted on Bonaparte to discipline the Revolution. Discipline, or restraint and control of the political process, is just what Paul anticipated for France—as for Russia and the world. Paul's attitude toward the first consul was, however, tentative and skeptical even while it was hopeful. He remained attentive to the work of the new government of France and reserved judgment until he had seen more of it.

When the Danish ambassador, Rosenkrantz, arrived at his new post in St. Petersburg in July 1800, he found that Paul had withdrawn from the capital to his estate at Gatchina and that he exhibited some distaste for the diplomatic corps and for foreign affairs in general. It was hard, for example, in mid-summer to arrange an audience with him at all.[8] Presumably, Russian foreign policy was undergoing a readjustment if not a thorough reappraisal.

By late summer, new developments began to emerge. The first was a kind of involuntary axiomatic reflex of Russian policy, that is, after a disappointment with one of the German powers, a move closer to the other. On 28 July, Russia and Prussia signed a defensive alliance in St. Petersburg. It was a carefully hedged and qualified agreement, conspicuously innocuous. It did, however, invite the accession of Sweden, Denmark, Saxony, Hanover, Hesse-Cassell, and the Ottoman Porte.[9] At the same time, Paul ordered Vice-Chancellor Nikita Petrovich Panin, former ambassador in Berlin, to press for a joint Russo-Prussian armed mediation between the belligerents.[10] It soon became apparent that this was Paul's now dominant idea and that the defensive alliance was but a prelude to it. The Prussian ambassador in St. Petersburg reported that the overtures of the French had been badly received, that they had in fact provoked the proposed joint armed mediation, as the Russian court remained as suspicious of the ambition of the French as of that of the Austrians.[11] The principles that Paul sought to sustain through the proposed armed neutrality were spelled out: "that France not abuse too much the preponderance that she has acquired in Italy; to contain within just limits the designs of Austria; to preserve the political existence of the Kings of Naples and of Sardinia; to save all that it is possible to save in Germany; and to use . . . our combined mediation for a general, stable, and permanent peace that would put an end to the plagues of humanity and guarantee in the future the security of nations."[12]

In August and September, Paul stationed two large armies on his western frontier and put them through extensive maneuvers. The Prussians were invited to take similar measures on their side of the frontier.[13] The Russians explained these measures to the Scandinavian ambassadors exactly as they had to the Prussian ambassador, Lusi.

Baron Stedingk reported to the Swedish court that they were the result of the overtures of the French. "The assembly of the two Russian armies on the frontiers of the dominions of Austria . . . has the visible purpose of imposing [Russo-Prussian mediation] on the court of Vienna and of preventing it from disposing on its own, or in concert with France, of the states of Italy and the Empire."[14] At the same time, the Russian ambassador in Stockholm, Baron Budberg, explained to Chancellor Ehrenheim that the object of the mediation was "to contain the ambitions of Austria and France and to preserve the integrity of the German constitution."[15]

Rosenkrantz received similar explanations. According to Panin, Paul thought that mediation was the "sole means of preventing the balance between the different powers of Europe and their respective independence from being entirely destroyed." He hoped that the Prussian treaty of 28 July would lead to an association of northern European powers that would prevent an agreement between France and Austria to subjugate their neighbors.[16]

Unfortunately for the Russians, the Prussians obviously took a different view of the ambiguous treaty, and in October they refused to participate in the mediation project. This part of Paul's plans thus came to nothing, but it tells us a good deal about what he was thinking. And he was obviously not thinking of allying with France.

In the meantime, the deterioration of Russian relations with England and constant conflicts between the English navy and the neutrals raised the prospect of a new League of Armed Neutrality. It is obvious how much advantage the French derived from the Armed Neutrality, but they were not responsible for its formation. In fact, it was Rosenkrantz who brought up the idea in the first place. He complained to Panin about the Russians' recent neglect of their formerly cherished principles of neutral trade. He asked if they intended to give up these principles. Panin said no, that he in particular did not want to diminish his uncle's[17] glory in that way. Russia had not supported neutral trade in the recent war, he candidly explained, because it would have damaged the coalition, meaning England, and benefited France.[18]

At this point, an incident precipitated a crisis. On 25 July the Danish frigate *Freja,* convoying Danish merchantmen into French ports, was summoned by a British squadron in the Channel to submit to search. Captain Krabbe of the *Freja* refused. A battle followed, and the Danes had to yield to superior force. They were taken into an English port, and the Danish ministry protested. A long dispute ensued, followed by a convention in which the English agreed to release the convoy and the Danes to suspend convoys temporarily, while the settlement of the principles at issue was deferred to a future conference.[19] The convention was a flimsy truce, and even while it was being negotiated, several things happened that aggravated the crisis.

First, the Danes proposed to London to let Paul mediate the dispute, and the English refused.[20] Simultaneously, both Denmark and Sweden appealed to Paul for support of neutral rights.[21] Paul responded to the appeals of the Swedes and Danes by inviting them to join him and the court of Prussia in reestablishing the Armed Neutrality.[22] The northern powers responded enthusiastically. According to the Danish chancellor, "This declaration fulfills the hopes and realizes the wishes of the King .... His Majesty ... sincerely applauds ... the resolution of His Imperial Majesty to restore the principles of the armed neutrality."[23] Stedingk reported to Panin that the declaration "was accepted by His Majesty [the King of Sweden] with ready applause and complete conformity of sentiment."[24] The development of the League of Armed Neutrality was thus attributable to Swedish and Danish initiative, and in the early fall of 1800, it was an association of equals. The Prussians agreed to join it in October,[25] and the treaties were signed in December.

At this point, the Malta crisis intervened. It had been agreed, when the Second Coalition was formed, that Malta should be occupied and garrisoned jointly by the English, the Russians, and the Neapolitans. The English had given the Russians the most explicit assurances on this point until the very last moment. In fact, when the French surrendered, the English, alarmed by the growing evidence of Russian hostility, excluded the Russians and their Neapolitan allies and raised the English flag alone. Paul was of course furious, and he reacted accordingly. He laid down an embargo on English trade, confiscated English ships and goods, and exiled English sailors under guard to various parts of Russia.[26]

This episode had a sudden and drastic effect upon Paul's view of the Armed Neutrality, and the change was evident in the new tone with which he addressed his Baltic protégés. Rosenkrantz was especially struck by a note of 29 October warning that Paul "would take . . . any unwillingness to respond to his intentions [in defense of Baltic trade] as a sign of lack of earnestness on the part of His Danish Majesty to pay back a loyal and faithful ally."[27] At this point, the initiative in the Armed Neutrality changed hands completely. Whereas previously we found the northern neutrals imploring Paul to protect them, we now find Paul directing them by intimidation to help him punish England recklessly and remorselessly. They were in an unenviable position, for they could not desert Paul without falling defenselessly between two fires. Rosenkrantz concluded that the fall of Malta turned a league for the protection of neutral trade into a league for a despot's revenge, and he deplored the "confounding" of the two issues. Ironically, it was the Swedes and the Danes who had first urged Paul to invoke some of the measures that they were now reluctant to imitate. In September, Rosenkrantz told Rostopchin that "a measure even more effective [than mobilizing the fleet] would be to place an embargo on all the English ships in the ports of Russia."[28] A few days later, Stedingk told Paul personally that "the most damaging war for the English was one made against their stock exchange."[29]

Having taken this advice on his own coasts, Paul insisted that his allies follow his example. When they procrastinated, he lost his temper. He delivered an ultimatum to Prussia demanding the occupation of Hanover and the closure of the Elbe and the Weser to English trade, and another to Denmark demanding the occupation and closure of the port of Hamburg.[30] Both powers promptly complied.[31]

This evidence suggests that Paul's use of the Armed Neutrality to pursue a vendetta against England owed everything to developments at Malta, to the suggestions of Stedingk and Rosenkrantz, and to his irascible temperament—and nothing to the inspiration of the French. There is no good evidence to the contrary. Paul was capable of formulating a policy toward either England or France independently of his policy toward the other country. He could be either the friend or the enemy of both—or of all the world—at once.

By this time the Russians were preparing a response to the gestures of the French. It seems desirable to establish the reaction of three persons, Rostopchin, Panin, and Paul. Panin's aversion to the French advances is well known and well documented.[32] Rostopchin's attitude should logically reflect his famous memorandum favoring a Franco-Russian alliance based on the partition of the Ottoman Empire.[33] This is, in fact, the case. In conversations with both Rosenkrantz and Stedingk, he warmly approved cooperation with the French.[34]

Only Paul's reaction contradicts our expectations. He was by no means deluded and intoxicated by Bonaparte's flattery. Paul agreed to accept the liberation of the Russian prisoners *sur parole,* that is, on the condition that Bonaparte impose on them the oath never to fight the French again. Rosenkrantz explained to Bernstorff: "You see, Monsieur, that this response was dictated by the Emperor's distaste for the gratuitous favors of the French government." As for the offer of Malta, Rostopchin told Rosenkrantz that Paul regarded it as illusory, since it could not be unknown to Bonaparte that the island was on the point of surrendering. The Russan government would, Rostopchin said, deal with the French government in the interest of its allies, but Paul suspected that the French were merely fishing for Russian recognition of their new government. Paul would cooperate with Bonaparte on certain clearly defined conditions, and Bonaparte's reaction to these conditions would determine what came of his overtures.[35]

These conditions were embodied in the official Russian response to Bonaparte, written by Rostopchin on 8 October:

> His Imperial Majesty of All the Russias ... has ordered me to inform the First Consul that concord with my Master can be established only by the fulfillment of his desires:
>
> 1. The return of the island of Malta ... to the Order of St. John . . . .
>
> 2. The reestablishment of the King of Sardinia in his dominions . . . .
>
> 3. The integrity of the dominions of the King of the Two Sicilies . . . .
>
> 4. Of those of the Elector of Bavaria, and
>
> 5. Of those of the Duke of Württemberg.[36]

This was an extraordinary diplomatic, or undiplomatic, document. It was not addressed to anyone but was simply forwarded to Paris through Berlin. It was not in the least conciliatory. It did not even observe the forms of diplomatic courtesy. There was not a suggestion in it of joining in Bonaparte's conquests or despoiling the Ottoman Empire. It stood rigidly for equilibrium and status quo.

The French responded on 20 October. Instead of accepting Paul's terms, Talleyrand proposed terms of his own, much like those of the treaty of Lunéville some months later, specifically French annexation of Savoy and the left bank of the Rhine and indemnification of Bavaria and Württemberg by secularizations in the empire. Paul found this reply unsatisfactory. He demanded a categorical acceptance of his conditions. The ambassadors of the two powers in Berlin, Citizen Beurnonville and Baron Kriudener, continued their contacts and talked in a desultory fashion throughout the fall of 1800. When the French grew impatient and Beurnonville complained of the dilatory response of the Russians, Kriudener explained to him candidly that when the French government accepted Paul's terms fully and explicitly and in writing, serious negotiations could begin at once.[37]

Paul stood his ground on this point stubbornly, and the reluctant reaction of the French soon noticeably aggravated his suspicions of them. After an interview with Rostopchin on 5 December, Rosenkrantz reported that Talleyrand's unsatisfactory reply to Paul's conditions had been very badly received: Talleyrand had said nothing about Malta and refused to restore the king of Sardinia.

> I understood from the language of the Principal Minister that his August Sovereign has no intention of signing any act or convention whatever with plenipotentiaries of the current chief of the French government until he fulfills ... the conditions attached by His Imperial Majesty to the reconciliation of His Empire with France .... Count Rastopsin remarked to me very judiciously that until then they had nothing to offer Bonaparte.[38]

A conference with Rostopchin on 13 December was equally definite. Paul was "persuaded that Bonaparte is not in good faith." The first consul's evident designs on Germany, Rosenkrantz said:

> have reawakened in His Imperial Majesty the strong repugnance that He has not ceased to have against any measure by which He would contribute to the consolidation of the authority of the Chief of the French nation .... [Rostopchin] maintained that it would not accord with the dignity of the Emperor to seek the friendship of Bonaparte, who, until now has not offered any security, any proof of [his] sincerity.[39]

In mid-December, then, Paul's attitude toward Bonaparte was demonstrably contrary to all we have been taught about it.

In December and January, the French continued to find the Austrian negotiating position intractable, even after the battle of Hohenlinden. They apparently decided to humor Paul's pretensions and to give all possible appearances of accepting his view of European politics. In any case, Talleyrand, in a curious and suspicious change of heart, suddenly reported that the French accepted the same Russian conditions that they had rejected in October. On 21 December, Talleyrand wrote that Paul's terms "seemed just and suitable in every particular and the First Consul adopts them."[40] On the same day, Bonaparte himself addressed a letter to Paul:

> I want to see the two strongest nations in the world promptly and irrevocably united. I have tried in vain for the past twelve months to bring peace and tranquillity to Europe; I have not succeeded, and the fighting continues without cause, so it would seem, at the

> sole instigation of English policy. Twenty-four hours after Your Majesty has charged someone enjoying His confidence and privy to His desires with special and full powers, the continent and the seas will be at peace. For when England, the Emperor of Germany and all the other powers are convinced that the wills as well as the forces of our two great nations reach for the same end, their arms will fall from their hands, and the current generation will bless Your Imperial Majesty for having arrested the horrors of war and the discords of factions. If these sentiments are shared by Your Imperial Majesty, as the loyalty and the largess of His character lead me to think, I believe that it would be suitable . . . that Europe discover simultaneously the ordering of the borders of the states, that peace is signed between France and Russia, and the reciprocal engagements that they have contracted for pacifying all the states. This strong, frank, and loyal guidance will offend certain cabinets, but it will unite the approbation of all the peoples and that of posterity.[41]

At the same time Paul's attitude to the French underwent a modest change. On 29 December, he wrote a letter to Bonaparte:

> *Monsieur le Premier Consul.* It is the duty of those to whom God has given the power of governing peoples to occupy themselves with their welfare. To this end, I propose to You that we concert between ourselves the means of putting an end to the ills which have desolated all of Europe these past eleven years. I do not speak of, nor do I want to discuss, either the rights of man or the principles of different governments . . . [but] to restore to the world the peace and calm which it so much needs . . . . I am ready to listen and to treat with You . . . I invite You to join me in reestablishing the general peace, which, if we want it, can scarcely elude us.[42]

This letter represents an obvious change of intent, and hence it raises two important questions. First, why did Paul change his mind? Second, what was the nature of the change, or how much did he change his mind?

The change itself can be dated relatively definitely. It took place some time between Rosenkrantz's 13 December interview with Rostopchin and the date of the letter itself, 29 December. This makes it possible to eliminate one potential influence. Paul's change of heart was not caused by the arrival of Bonaparte's letter and Talleyrand's acceptance of Paul's conditions, for these were written on 21 December. A fast trip between the two capitals required twelve to fifteen days, and this was not the season for fast trips in northern Europe. Thus the French documents could not have arrived before Paul wrote to Bonaparte. Paul first acknowledged Bonaparte's letter when he wrote the first consul a second time, on 14 January.[43]

As to the reason for the change, the most distinct persuasion that Paul was subjected to during these sixteen days was that of Rosenkrantz. Rosenkrantz was becoming increasingly alarmed by the violently Anglophobe drift of Russian policy. He feared that Denmark alone would pay the price of

Paul's posturing and concluded that Russia must ally with France, probably in the desperate hope of overawing the English and dissuading them from attacking the neutrals. And he tried to convince the Russians of his views. As early as 12 November, he spoke thus to Panin:

> If the Emperor is bound to quarrel openly with England and [if] Denmark and Sweden must act in concert with Russia, His Imperial Majesty must join . . . those powers that are at war with England . . . not in order to destroy England, but to lead her back to equitable principles . . . . Only urgent necessity could bring me to insist upon the Emperor's joining the chiefs of the French government; because without such a union—and the cooperation of Prussia, who must be persuaded to occupy Hanover and to close, together with Denmark, the Elbe and the Weser—to demand of us to risk being treated as an enemy by the English would be to destroy us to no purpose and without any hope of attaining a reasonable political objective.

Panin—who must have hoped not—responded that circumstances might force the formation of just such a system. Tatishchev, Panin's assistant, said that an alliance with France was quite possible if Bonaparte accepted Paul's conditions.[44] But Panin, as a devoted Anglophile, is unlikely to have encouraged such views even if he repeated them. In any case, he was dismissed from his post soon after this conversation, and Rosenkrantz took up the same subject with Rostopchin—on 13 December, the same day he received from Rostopchin such a dubious report of the prospects of Paul's cooperation with the French.

> I showed him that by the vigorous measures that have been taken here against the navigation and the commerce of Great Britain, Russia has committed in fact acts of hostility against this power, with which Bonaparte, as head of the French government, is at war; that consequently when once Russia pulls in the same harness with France, since she acts against the same enemy, it would only be natural to cooperate together . . . against a common enemy, which England certainly is.

Rostopchin, who must have been delighted to hear his own sentiments repeated, promised to give Paul a faithful account of these views.[45]

We do not have direct evidence that it was this intercession that changed Paul's mind, but it is our best clue.

Now, what was the nature of the change? First, it is worth remarking that Paul's letter to Bonaparte is by no means an unreserved commitment. In fact, it is, apart from the symbolic significance of a letter from the proud Emperor of All the Russias to a parvenu usurper, a conspicuously guarded and tentative gesture in which Paul's scruples show up like sensitive sores. It tells us little that is specific. The document that provides the details that the letter lacks is Paul's instruction to his plenipotentiary Stepan A. Kolychev, who was designated to go to Paris to negotiate with Bonaparte.

Paul proposed the "abasement of the house of Austria . . . , persuaded that the peace of the rest of Europe depends on it." He accepted the Rhine as the border of France with the understanding that the German princes who suffered losses there should be compensated from the hereditary lands of the Habsburgs. He proposed the integrity of the territory of Naples and the indemnification of Sardinia, Bavaria, and Württemberg at the expense of the ecclesiastical states in the empire. He demanded a formal guarantee of the return of the island of Malta. The French, he said, must withdraw all their troops from Egypt. He requested consideration for the pope, and he said that when these conditions were met, he was ready to recognize the French Republic.[46]

If we compare the five conditions of 8 October with the instructions of 30 December, we find that Paul had made some significant concessions. He was now willing to see France annex the left bank of the Rhine, which meant that he had to accept the principle of indemnification for Bavaria and Württemberg instead of their territorial integrity. He would also make concessions of Sardinian territory to France in return for proper indemnification, but he still insisted on the territorial integrity of Naples. He now allowed significant constitutional changes in the German Empire, approving indemnification of princes dispossessed on the left bank of the Rhine by the secularization of ecclesiastical estates.

On the other hand, he was still rather haughty. He invited France first to fulfill his conditions, after which he promised to recognize the republic. He explicitly required the return of Egypt to the Ottoman Empire. We may conclude, therefore, that the spirit of these instructions is still much closer to the five conditions of 8 October than to Rostopchin's scheme of Ottoman partition and French alliance. Kolychev's instructions, in spite of important territorial changes and considerable French annexations, did not represent a revolution in the European balance of power. It is impossible, for example, to derive the principles of Tilsit from these instructions. Paul still stood stubbornly for multinational equilibrium.

When Kolychev arrived in Paris, his relations with the French government could scarcely have been more difficult and less harmonious. Kolychev himself bristled with hostility and paraded condescension. Even before the beginning of the negotiations, his dispatches leave hardly any doubt about the outcome.

> I am generally dubious about the success of my mission. There is here a measureless ambition since the abasement of Austria[47] and our rupture with England . . . . I strongly doubt that we have anything good to expect from France; . . . they seek to embroil us with all the world . . . . I beg you, *M. le comte* [Rostopchin], to withdraw me from here as soon as possible; I see everything in the blackest colors, and I am sick of it . . . . I would never become

> accustomed to the kind of people who govern here; I would never trust them . . . . Their intention is to embarrass us and to subjugate Europe; finally, they know that they can accomplish this only by encumbering us.[48]

Kolychev was convinced that Bonaparte was deceiving Russia, using her entirely for his own ends. He made no effort to compromise conflicts, and he behaved in the most disagreeable fashion. What he and Talleyrand found to dispute was almost everything. Talleyrand invited him to sign peace with France first, after which he offered to discuss details of a general European peace. But Kolychev was not so simple as that. As he saw it, peace with Russia was to be France's reward for agreeing to all of Paul's wishes. Therefore the terms of the general pacification would have to be negotiated first; then these and the reconciliation of France and Russia could be signed simultaneously. Kolychev raised the question of Egypt. Talleyrand refused even to discuss it. Kolychev objected to Bonaparte's unilateral meddling in the affairs of Italy in a spirit contrary to Paul's stipulations and the promise Talleyrand had given on 21 December. The French had sent troops into Naples, Russia's ally, and they proposed to occupy Neapolitan ports in order to reinforce their army in Egypt. They would give no assurances about the restoration of the king of Sardinia now. Though they had clearly violated in Italy their previous promises, Bonaparte and Talleyrand were nevertheless shocked at Kolychev's truculence. They charged him with misrepresenting Paul's intentions, and virtually accused him of attempting, on his own authority, to thwart these intentions.[49] In fact, though he was undoubtedly guilty of personal spitefulness, he was only following Paul's orders.

Late in March, Bonaparte resorted to another Russian in Paris, General Sprengporten, the commissar sent to arrange the release of the Russian prisoners. He invited Sprengporten to dinner and made an earnest appeal:

> I offer to sign a peace, which no one desires more sincerely than I, in conformity with the five points established by His Majesty himself . . . . I will sign it whenever he wants; but regarding Egypt, that is a matter entirely apart. . . . This colony is the prize of the purest blood of France, useful besides for a thousand connections to the arts, to the commerce of the two nations, to humanity at large. It is the only possession through which France may one day be able to counterbalance the enormous maritime power of the English in the Indies. I have little to refuse your Emperor; but if he will consider these great interests, I believe that he will see that his and ours are the same. Can the Turks . . . oppose us? We shall arrange things as we like and share the reciprocal advantages of a lucrative commerce upon a sea from which the English can and must be excluded, or where they will enjoy only such privileges as we want to accord them: they enjoy enough power in the world . . . . If the English want war, we will give it to them . . . . You will not remain indifferent, I hope, to this quarrel. You have as much interest as we in humbling their domain.[50]

Bonaparte—like the rest of western Europe—was still under the illusion that Paul was wedded to that classic Russian imperialist design of Peter I and Catherine II. The Testament of Peter the Great was, after all, a French document.

Contemporaries and historians have alike been deceived: the alliance was forestalled not by Paul's death but by irreconcilable disagreements.

Paul may or may not have been a fool, but he was not Bonaparte's fool. He clung stubbornly to the foreign policy principles that he had so idealistically enunciated at the beginning of his reign. When he departed from his preferred policy of peace to enter the Second Coalition, he did so, he said, to contain the imperialist threat of the French. When he left that coalition, he did so, he said, in protest against the similar pretensions of the Austrians, and, later, the English. When he began talks with Bonaparte—reluctantly—it was not to share with him, as the French encouraged Paul to think, the dominion of Europe, but to constrain the Austrians and to persuade the French to constrain themselves. Paul chose his allies with an easy indiscriminacy that both his contemporaries and ours have found quite confusing. In fact, he did not prefer one ally or the other or one country or the other. It was matter of principles that he preferred, and he was willing to work with antique monarchies or unholy canailles if only his ally shared the touchstone of his policy: the principles of autocracy and justice. Legitimacy he cared nothing for. He was prepared to suggest to Bonaparte, if and when Bonaparte accepted Paul's conditions for a general peace in Europe, that he make the crown of France hereditary in his family.[51]

We can imagine what Paul meant by autocracy; we can witness how he exemplified it. What he meant by justice is more complicated. But Paul thought that he understood what justice was, and he thought that he understood how to attain it, and he must have believed that the conscientious application of his concept of justice would achieve, both in Russia and in Europe, social harmony and political equilibrium of the sort required for the well-being of insecure and fear-ridden monarchs such as himself. Here we probably have the best clue to a better appreciation of his much misunderstood dealings with Bonaparte.

This essay is intended primarily to suggest an answer to problems of interpreting the foreign policy of Tsar Paul, but it raises other questions of perhaps more general concern. Do the Russian archives contain nothing of the important documentation that can be adduced from the Swedish, Prussian, and Danish records on the problem of Paul's foreign policy—or, conceivably on a multitude of other historical issues? If they do not, why not? If they do, why is there so little of it represented in Russian historical literature?

NOTES

1 *Histoire du Consulat et de l'Empire,* II (Paris, 1845), 93.

2 *Paul the First of Russia* (Philadelphia, 1913), pp. 359-360.

3 *Europe and the French Imperium* (New York, 1938), p. 43. A similar view is found in other reputable works, including classics, e.g., Albert Sorel, *L'Europe et la Révolution française,* VI (Paris, n.d.); John Holland Rose, *The Life of Napoleon I,* 2 vols. (New York, 1901-1902); Edouard Driault, *La politique extérieure du Premier consul* (Paris, 1910); Harold C. Deutsch, *The Genesis of Napoleonic Imperialism* (Cambridge, Mass., 1938).

4 The official correspondence—carried on in the absence of regular diplomatic relations largely through Prussian channels—was published in A. A. Trachevskii, ed., "Diplomaticheskiia snosheniia Rossii s Frantsiei v epokhu Napoleona I," *Sbornik IRIO,* LXX (St. Petersburg, 1890). It is quite spare. Much of the private correspondence of Chancellor F. V. Rostopchin is in the *Arkhiv kniazia Vorontsova,* 40 vols. (Moscow, 1870-1895). Vice-Chancellor N. P. Panin's papers are in Alexander Brückner, ed., *Materialy dlia zhizneopisaniia Grafa N. P. Panina,* 7 vols. (St. Petersburg, 1888-1892). Neither correspondence is very informative on the subject of this study.

5 Over 100 years ago the trusted civil servant of Alexander II, D. A. Miliutin, produced a formidable study of Paul, *Istoriia voiny 1799 g. v tsarstvovanie Imperatora Pavla I,* 5 vols. (St. Petersburg, 1852-1853). Miliutin was painstaking and thorough. The war of 1799 provided him the focal point for a study of war and diplomacy throughout Paul's reign. During the 1890s, A. A. Trachevskii published the collection of documents cited above, "Diplomaticheskiia snosheniia." Soon afterwards, two major biographies appeared: N. K. Schilder, *Imperator Pavel I: istoriko-biograficheskii ocherk* (St. Petersburg, 1901) and E. S. Shumigorskii, *Imperator Pavel I: zhizn' i tsarstvovanie* (St. Petersburg, 1907). A. M. Stanislavskaia has published the most authoritative Soviet account of Paul's diplomacy, *Russko-angliiskie otnosheniia i problemy Sredizemnomor'ia, 1798-1807* (Moscow, 1962). Though focused especially on England and the Mediterranean, the whole subject is inextricably bound up with Franco-Russian relations, and Stanislavskaia's work, like Miliutin's, is much more broadly cast than the title suggests. A. Z. Manfred, in his article "Poiski soiuza s Rossiei, 1800-1801," *Istoriia SSSR,* 1971, No. 4, 38-59, and in his biography *Napoleon Bonapart* (Moscow, 1971), went through the same materials again. Even though it is reviewed in Soviet journals, Manfred neglected the recent English-language scholarship (of Norman Saul, Roderick McGrew, and myself) which Stanislavskaia, V. G. Sirotkin, and other Soviet scholars follow.

6 Stanislavskaia, *Russko-angliiskie otnosheniia,* does, however, cite significant new documentation on Russo-Turkish relations.

7 Miliutin, *Istoriia voiny 1799 g.,* V, 312-320.

8 Rosenkrantz to Chancellor Bernstorff, 1 July, 22 July 1800; Copenhagen Rigsarkivet, Departement for udenrigske Anliggender, Rusland II, Depecher. (State Archive, Department of Foreign Affairs, Russia II, Dispatches. Hereafter abbreviated according to standard Danish archival practice: Rigsarkivet, Dpt. f. u. A. Rusland II, Depecher.) Division II, Depecher, contains dispatches incoming from ambassadors abroad, and Division I, Ordrer [see note 23 below], contains orders and instructions outgoing to ambassadors from the court. Pagination and numbering of documents is sometimes multiple and complex, and the easiest way to locate a document is by date. I have put "Copenhagen" before "Rigsarkivet" to help distinguish it from the confusingly similar spelling of the corresponding Swedish institution, also cited here, "Stockholm Riksarkivet.")

9 F. F. Martens, ed., *Recueil des traités et conventions conclus par la Russie avec les puissances étrangères,* VI (St. Petersburg, 1883), 271-283.

10 Brückner, ed., *Materialy Panina,* V, 426-434, 471-474.

11 Lusi to court, 6/18 July 1800; Deutsches Zentralarchiv, Historische Abteilung II, Merseburg (DDR), Ministerium für auswärtige Angelegenheiten, AA I Rep. 4 Nr. 487.

12 Haugwitz, chancellor, to Lusi, 12 Aug. 1800; *ibid.*

13 Lusi to court, 22 Aug./3 Sept. 1800; *ibid. M. I. Kutuzov; sbornik dokumentov,* I (Moscow, 1950), Nos. 809-812.

14 Stedingk to Chancellor Ehrenheim, 28 Aug., 30 Aug. 1800; Stockholm Riksarkivet, Ur Muscovitica 464: samtliga handlingar från och med 1/6 1800 till och med 31/12 1800: Ambassadoren Friherre C. Stedingks depescher. (State Archive, Muscovy Affairs 464: Complete Proceedings from and including 1 June 1800 to and including 31 Dec. 1800: Ambassador Baron C. Stedingk's dispatches. Documents are easily located by date.)

15 Ehrenheim to Stedingk, 12 Sept. 1800; Stockholm Riksarkivet, Ur Muscovitica 499: Brev från Kungl. Majestät, Sept. 1800-Sept. 1801.

16 Rosenkrantz to Bernstorff, 16 July, 28 July, 23 Aug., 30 Sept. 1800; Copenhagen Rigsarkivet, Dpt. f. u. A. Rusland II, Depecher.

17 Nikita Ivanovich Panin, Catherine's foreign minister at the time of the formation of the first League of Armed Neutrality, 1780.

18 Rosenkrantz to Bernstorff, 19 July, 25 July, 1 Aug., 23 Aug. 1800; Copenhagen Rigsarkivet, Dpt. f. u. A. Rusland II, Depecher.

19 Convention of 29 Aug. 1800; *Danske Tractater efter 1800, første Samling: Politiske Tractater,* I (Copenhagen, 1877), 1.

20 Bernstorff to Whitworth, 26 Aug. 1800; Georg Friedrich von Martens, ed., *Supplément à Recueil des principaux traités . . . des puissances et états de l'Europe,* II (Göttingen, 1839), 336.

21 Rosenkrantz to Panin (copy), 20 Aug. 1800; Copenhagen Rigsarkivet, Dpt. f. u. A. Rusland II, Depecher. Gustavus Adolphus IV to Paul, 20 Aug. 1800; Miliutin, *Istoriia voiny 1799 g.,* V, 495.

22 James Brown Scott, ed., *The Armed Neutralities of 1780 and 1800: A Collection of Official Documents* (New York, 1919), pp. 489-492.

23 Bernstorff to Rosenkrantz, 19 Sept. 1800; Copenhagen Rigsarkivet, Gesandtskabarkivet Rusland I, Ordrer. (Legation Records, Russia I, Instructions.)

24 Stedingk to Panin (copy), 26 Sept. 1800; Stockholm Riksarkivet, Ur Muscovitica 464.

25 Kriudener to Panin, 23 Oct. 1800; Brückner, ed., *Materialy . . . Panina,* V, 487.

26 For documentation, see my article, "A Continental System in 1801: Paul I and Bonaparte," *Journal of Modern History,* XLII (Mar. 1970), 70-89.

27 Rosenkrantz to Bernstorff, 29 Oct. 1800; Copenhagen Rigsarkivet, Dpt. f. u. A. Rusland II, Depecher.

28 Same to same, 4 Sept. 1800; *ibid.*

29 Stedingk to Ehrenheim, 15 Sept. 1800; Stockholm Riksarkivet, Ur Muscovitica 464.

30 Lowendal (replaced Rosenkrantz) to Bernstorff, 7 Mar. 1801; Copenhagen Rigsarkivet, Dpt. f. u. A. Rusland II, Depecher.

31 Documentation cited in Ragsdale, "A Continental System in 1801."

32 Brückner, ed., *Materialy Panina,* V, 419.

33 *Russkii arkhiv,* 1878, I, 103-110.

34 Stedingk to Ehrenheim, 14 Oct. 1800; Stockholm Riksarkivet, Ur Muscovitica 464. Rosenkrantz to Bernstorff, 15, 18 Oct. 1800; Copenhagen Rigsarkivet, Dpt. f. u. A. Rusland II, Depecher.

35 Rosenkrantz to Bernstorff, 30 Aug., 31 Oct. 1800; Copenhagen Rigsarkivet, Dpt. f. u. A. Rusland II, Depecher.

36 Trachevskii, ed., "Diplomaticheskiia snosheniia," pp. 10-11.

37 Miliutin, *Istoriia voiny 1799 g.,* V, 268, 499-500. Archives des Affaires étrangères, Paris, Correspondance politique, Prusse 228, No. 87.

38 Rosenkrantz to Bernstorff, 5 Dec. 1800; Copenhagen Rigsarkivet, Dpt. f. u. A. Rusland II, Depecher.

39 13 Dec. 1800; *ibid.*

40 Trachevskii, ed., "Diplomaticheskiia snosheniia," p. 26.

41 *Correspondance de Napoléon I,* VI (Paris, 1861), No. 5232.

42 Archives des Affaires étrangères, Paris, Correspondance politique, Russie, Supplément 17.

43 *Ibid.*

44 Rosenkrantz to Bernstorff, 12 Nov. 1800; Copenhagen Rigsarkivet, Dpt. f. u. A. Rusland II, Depecher.

45 13 Dec. 1800; *ibid.*

46 *Russkii arkhiv,* 1874, II, cols. 961-964.

47 The peace of Lunéville, 9 Feb. 1801.

48 Trachevskii, ed., "Diplomaticheskiia snosheniia," pp. 43-44.

49 *Ibid.,* pp. 45-113.

50 *Ibid.,* pp. 93-94.

51 *Russkii arkhiv,* 1874, II, col. 965.

III
INTERNAL AFFAIRS

6

PAUL I AND THE MILITARIZATION OF GOVERNMENT

John L. H. Keep

The Emperor Paul, leaving his palace one day, ordered a sergeant on guard duty to board his sled, saying, "Climb in, lieutenant." The man protested, "Sire, I am but a sergeant." Paul replied: "Climb in, captain." Three days later the newly commissioned officer, by now a lieutenant colonel, caused the emperor some offense and found himself reduced to the ranks as suddenly as he had risen from them.[1]

The story must, alas, be dismissed as apocryphal, if only because Paul, for all his well-known arbitrariness, showed the utmost solicitude for that rigid hierarchy of rank (*chin*) that was the heart and soul of imperial Russian officialdom. We have cited it because it illustrates the wealth of myth that for too long has impeded serious historical research into the reign of this unhappy emperor. Throughout the nineteenth century Herzen's view of Paul as "the poet and dialectician of autocracy," who substituted "an orgy of cruelty, pain and brutality" for his mother's sensuality,[2] set the tone for journalists, memoir-writers and belletrists, whether in Russia or abroad. Not until 1916 was an attempt made to probe more deeply into the subject. In that year Mikhail Vasilevich Klochkov published a magisterial study on certain aspects of the Pauline administration, based on a conscientious study of printed and archival sources.[3] But Klochkov's approach was old-fashionedly institutional—he stood in the tradition of the "historical-juridical school"—and such liberal critics as Baron S. A. Korf justly took him to task for the apologetic tendency evident in his work.[4] Korf himself embodied the tradition of Russian *obshchestvennost'*—those privileged elements in society who sought to defend the autonomous rights of corporate and local institutions against encroachment by the central government. He saw Paul's repression of the nobles' assemblies and elective offices, granted them by Catherine, as a precedent for the later Romanovs' contemptuous treatment of the *zemstvo* and the *Duma*.

Neither viewpoint can be considered adequate today. However, modern historians have as yet barely come to grips with the problem of Paul's handling of state affairs. Soviet writers have shown relatively little interest in administrative questions[5] and for this period have tended to adopt and embroider the stock arguments of prerevolutionary "bourgeois" historiography. In the West Professor Marc Raeff, stimulated by Max Weber's concept of the "rationalizing" function of the modern bureaucratic state, since developed by historians like Otto Hintze and Gerhard Ritter with special reference to Prussia, has investigated parallel developments in Russia and has done much to illuminate the social and psychological ambiguities of the *dvorianstvo,* the service class.[6] Hans-Joachim Torke, in a recent analysis of Russian officialdom under Alexander I and Nicholas I, has argued plausibly that the bureaucratic abuses rendered so familiar by the literature of the period are largely attributable to the tyranny of the Table of Ranks, the weakness of the legal system, and the immaturity of the country's general social development: notably, the lack of those estates of the realm (*Stände*) that elsewhere resisted the pretensions of the centralized absolutist state.[7]

It was in Paul's reign that Russia first experienced the excesses of bureaucratic rule that were to become so characteristic of the age of Nicholas I. In this sense it deserves to be regarded as a formative period, not a mere aberration. This point was noted by Kliuchevskii and later by Pokrovskii.[8] However, neither of these eminent historians pursued the line of inquiry that this insight opened up. At the time when they were writing it seemed enough to say that Paul's reign marked a widening of the breach between "government" and "society," dramatically expressed in the coup d'état of 11 March 1801—simultaneously the last of the "palace revolutions" and a prelude to the Decembrist revolt. Today we may go further, and assert that Paul's reign witnessed three interrelated processes:

First, the allocation to the military establishment of definite responsibilities in civil administration;

Second, a shift in the locus of executive power away from the aristocratic elite to professional administrators;

Third, a change in the ethos of the public service best expressed by the term *militarization.*

We shall speak here of *the militarization of government* as a convenient shorthand term for what was in effect an attempt to achieve greater rationality in the functioning of the administrative machine—a task that preoccupied all the rulers of pre-Reform Russia, from Peter I and Catherine II to Nicholas I.

By way of introduction we may note that Paul's policies of "militarization" implied the conscious adoption of a foreign model. As many contemporaries noted, he greatly admired Frederick the Great of Prussia, in this regard resembling his putative father, Peter III, with whom it became a veritable obsession. Paul hoped to copy Frederick's achievement in building a *Polizeistaat* or "regulated state" in the eighteenth-century understanding of this term: that is to say, he sought to centralize real decision-making power in the autocratic sovereign, whose will was to be law; to demarcate clearly administrative responsibilities among officials within a hierarchical structure dedicated to the pursuit of efficiency, strict discipline, and economy in the use of resources; and to harness all his subjects' energies, within the limits technically possible at the time, to the achievement of certain state-approved tasks.

It was a stern and narrow concept of government that left no place for the autonomous individual or social group. Duty, rather than freedom, was to be its watchword. To the modern mind, such an ideal seems inadequate, indeed utopian; but it was one that exercised a strong appeal upon contemporaries all over Europe. (Even the great skeptic Voltaire was not impervious to it.)

Now Russia, one might suggest, was in different ways both peculiarly fitted and peculiarly unfitted for experiments in "Prussianism." On the one hand, the idea of a "service state" had deep roots in the country's history; it had been reinforced by the Petrine reforms, and only slightly weakened by those of Catherine. On the other hand, the Russian elite differed from that of Prussia (or Sweden or France) in its cultural pattern and social ethos. It was more other-worldly, easy-going, and individualistic. Its members' principal affinities were to the family group, or even to the locality of residence, rather than to the noble estate (*soslovie*) as such—which after all barely existed in Russia, since corporate institutions were to be found only on the local level. Their political loyalty was given to the autocrat, not to the state, an abstraction they as yet but dimly comprehended; they served in the hope of winning personal advancement, or from economic necessity, not in order to accomplish some distant ideal. The *dvorianstvo* was unpromising material with which to forge a second Prussia. No wonder the attempt failed! Indeed, the "Prussianization" of Russian life that aroused such loud complaints—especially from a later, more articulate generation—existed in men's minds rather than in real life. What offended the critics was not the realization of these goals but the aspiration to reach them. This is a point to which we shall return at the conclusion of this article.

The trouble was that in attempting to emulate foreign experience one could so easily mistake the appearance for the essence, so easily confuse form and substance. The Frederician state certainly had its harsh, cruel, and arbitrary aspects, but it had a core of rationality: the means employed bore some rough correlation to the ends in view. In the Russia of Paul this balance was not evident. Discipline became an end in itself, and the original purpose was lost sight of.

Nowhere was this more evident than in the military sphere. Frederick's concern with organizational detail had been combined with strategic flair; Paul, however, was never exposed to the test of battle—not because he lacked courage, but for reasons of high policy. Instead he was given every opportunity to indulge his naive enthusiasm for the external trappings of military glory without being forced to consider too closely the practical function that soldiers were supposed to perform. Hence what contemporaries called "the Gatchina spirit"—a preoccupation with parades and maneuvers, uniforms and equipment, awards and punishments, in short with the minutiae of army life, and a corresponding neglect of weightier matters likely to prove decisive in war: morale, professional training, technical progress, etc. True, such failings were in some degree common to all the *ancien régime* armies, including the Prussian: hence Valmy and Jena. In the Russian case they could be transcended by a brilliant commander like Suvorov, who realized that success in battle demanded more than a capacity for blind obedience. This led him into conflict with Paul, whose ideal was basically a mechanistic one: an army should move like a well-oiled timepiece, each unit responding automatically to the appropriate signal and carrying on smoothly its allotted function. His attitude was also paternalistic: just as he knew his senior officers personally, he wanted relations between officers and men to be simple and direct. This was why he insisted that commanders should report to him at frequent intervals,[9] and why he ordered units to be named after their commanders, not the areas whence they were recruited. The army seems to have strongly resisted this reactionary move, for the decree had to be repeated on several occasions and was repealed soon after his death.[10]

It should be added that some of Paul's military reforms were reasonable. He centralized the administration in the hands of the War College, which he kept under his close personal control;[11] he did a little to humanize the recruiting system, and tried to keep army strength and expenditure within specified limits. Above all he sought to suppress the venal practices that were so widespread. To this end, as well as to enforce discipline generally, he set up an auditor general's department with a hierarchy of judicial officials, some of whom were civilians; their job was to supervise the actions of the military and to hear complaints against them, in much the same way as the procuracy supervised the civilian agencies.[12]

Paul has been generally criticized for his harsh disciplinary measures, especially those taken against officers, and beyond question many of his actions were indefensible. Yet it was the means employed rather than the ends pursued that were objectionable. There was a good deal of "slack" in the army as he inherited it: officers surplus to establishment drew high salaries for a minimum of work, while others toiled for a pittance. Paul's rough justice compelled everyone, high and low, to fulfill his service obligations to the letter. This gladdened the hearts of the common soldiers, even though they knew they could not hope to rise to officer rank, since (like Frederick) Paul wanted his officer corps to consist wholly of noblemen. This was certainly reactionary; yet let us note that he also strove to make these noble officers gentlemen, in the Western sense, imbued with notions of chivalry. The introduction into Russia of the Order of St. John of Jerusalem, often seen as pure eccentricity on Paul's part, thus had its rational aspect. Its members, especially those who were officers, were expected to set a pattern for the entire gentry class.

Naturally this aim was scarcely compatible with Paul's exaggerated ideas on discipline. The tension between these objectives, one rational and the other supremely irrational, was inherent not only in his military reforms but also in his policy with regard to the state apparatus, to which we may now turn.

Our first point is that the military was given a definite role in the government of the country. The picture is at first sight a rather confused one.

Army garrisons were maintained throughout the empire—infantry in urban and cavalry in rural areas.[13] The number of men involved probably increased, at least in the first, war-free years of Paul's reign. Civil authorities faced with trouble were encouraged to invoke the assistance of these troops without going through time-wasting procedural formalities.[14] In the main centers *voennye gubernatory* (military governors), *komendanty* (commandants), and *plats-maiory* (town-majors) were appointed. As a rule, if not invariably, these were army officers. According to the statute on the administration of St. Petersburg, the military governor had ultimate responsibility for police matters, but his immediate subordinates were civilians.[15] No doubt in the provincial towns, where civilian agencies were notoriously understaffed, the military played an even greater role in urban affairs than it did in the capital cities. In practice the military governors concerned themselves with the construction of barracks, water-supply systems, and the like. One typically curt order to General Iu. V. Dolgorukii, when he took over this office in Moscow, reads as follows: "On assuming responsibility for the Catherine Palace, turn it into barracks."[16] All this reinforces the familiar impression given by memoir literature of a country suddenly placed under the heel of the jackboot.

Yet on closer inspection one finds a number of measures that can only be described as positive in intent, designed to demarcate the respective spheres of military and civilian responsibility and to protect each from encroachment by the other. Thus the Kazan' military governor was told to stop using troops to *maintain* (as distinct from building) the town's water pipeline, since this was the function of the civil police.[17] Army men in the College of Manufactures were told not to refer to themselves as regulars or to wear regular army uniform.[18] All persons with military rank in civil departments were transferred to the appropriate civilian equivalent.[19] A decree of January 1801, doubtless prompted in part by military exigencies, withdrew all NCOs and soldiers from employment in various government offices and posted them, if they were fit enough, to active service.[20] Even the construction of barracks had a healthy impact on public life, since it got the troops out of private quarters, where their violent behavior often led to conflict with civilians. This was an old problem for eighteenth-century Russian administrators, which Paul tried earnestly to alleviate. One of the functions of the military auditors was to resolve complaints by civilians against the military. The same objective probably inspired his decrees that civilian rather than military agencies should purchase cloth for uniforms, another potential source of friction,[21] and that officers and men on leave should not visit the capital cities without special permission.[22] Military men who incurred debts to civilians were made to pay. A typical order reads: "Dismiss from the service *kornet* Protopopov, of Annenkov's hussar regiment, and proceed according to the law with the suit against him by the merchant Meyer."[23]

Prior to Paul's accession there had been much confusion in the responsibilities of military and civilian functionaries, although one task of the procuracy was to ensure that office-holders did not infringe upon one another's authority. According to the statute on local government of 7 November 1775, the *namestnik* (governor general) exercised the duties of commander-in-chief; in frontier areas he might be either superior or inferior in authority to the military commander, as the sovereign directed. Similarly, urban commandants could summon military forces to maintain order in an emergency, but their rights vis-à-vis the regular chiefs of these bodies were not prescribed by law.[24]

The emperor's guiding idea, it appears, was that *voennye* and *shtatskie* should keep to their own bailiwicks, but work together amicably on state business. There was to be a kind of "peaceful coexistence" between the two parallel hierarchies. The aim is best exemplified by an ordinance of February 1798, that civil government departments and provincial governors should send only "communications" (*soobshcheniia*), not decrees (*ukazy*) to military commanders or units, since the latter were not subordinate to the former, but solely to the War College and ultimately to the emperor; each instance, whether military or civilian, was to fulfill the lawful demands of the other, since "the duty of service and mutual effort to advance the Sovereign's affairs requires them to afford [each other] every assistance and satisfaction."[25]

Admittedly, this law seemed more concerned to protect the military from civilian interference than vice versa, and in practice no doubt the men with rifles usually got the better of the bargain. But this was not Paul's intention. When Alexander I restored the old order of things, six days after his accession, he (or Count Pahlen, his chief adviser) threw out the baby with the bathwater. Two reasons for the change are given in the decree, only the first of which is plausible: the Senate, it was said, had been unable to communicate directly with the military governors on *civil* matters; if this was indeed the situation in 1801, it clearly had to be remedied. But the second argument blandly declared it "inappropriate" that military commanders should be able to send only memoranda (*vedeniia*), rather than orders, to civilian organs, and so disregarded Paul's objective of achieving equilibrium.[26] Had Alexander gone on to introduce constitutional reforms, this need not have mattered; as it was, the way was open to all manner of abuses by the military, such as those to which the Decembrists vainly drew attention. Nor did Nicholas I redress the balance. On the contrary he went much further than Paul in staffing the administration with army officers, who often fulfilled their peaceful tasks in the spirit of the barracks.[27]

This brings us to the second point: the nature of the bureaucracy. Paul's reign, we have suggested, sees a shift towards the "professionalization" of the administrative machine—a slight and temporary phenomenon, to be sure, but none the less significant for that. Under Catherine a number of officers had resigned their commissions to enter civilian life and had found their way into the administration; they had been made welcome because this was almost the only source of recruitment of officials within the service class. Paul, however, considered that all noblemen, unless physically unfit, should perform their duties in the armed forces. The logical corollary would have been to make the civilian bureaucracy a non-noble preserve. This, of course, was politically unfeasible—but Paul's government did take some hesitant steps in this direction, as we shall see in a moment.

A more limited measure that was adopted had the purpose of stemming the drift to civilian jobs by army officers who found the new harsh discipline uncongenial. It did not enforce a total ban on such transfers, but tightened the controls exercised over all appointments by the Heraldmaster's Office

(*Gerol'diia*). A department in this agency, the Judicial Desk (*Sudeiskii stol*), issued the necessary documents, among them one stating the applicant's service record and seniority in rank (*starshinstvo*); and this form was now redrafted so as to include more information.[28] In later years these personnel records were to become still fuller, although to the modern eye they look naive and perfunctory.

In the Russian official class before the Great Reforms a man's career depended on rank or social status rather than personal merit. His first appointment owed much to his family background and "connections" as well as his educational qualifications; and his gradual ascent up the hierarchical ladder, with its fourteen rungs, might well come about automatically, regardless of his actual performance, since promotion was granted after one had served a certain term in a given rank. This system was obviously harmful to state interests, but it had become so firmly entrenched that even rulers as strong-willed as Paul or Nicholas I could do little to change it. On the contrary, within a few months of his accession Paul issued an order to the effect that when making appointments strict attention should be paid to the seniority of applicants and the offices concerned (*starshinstvo mest i chinov*).[29] Later, in December 1799, he extended the service term for automatic promotion from three years to four in all the junior grades between the fourteenth and the eighth (which conferred noble rank).[30] The object of this was presumably to discourage men from pursuing this leisurely course and to make them work harder, in the hope that their exemplary service would be reported to the emperor, who would then intervene and promote them regardless of their seniority (and regardless of the decree mentioned above). It was consonant with Paul's philosophy of autocratic government that the sovereign had the sole right to confer rewards of this kind and to punish laggards. Popular legend credits him with many such interventions (as noted at the beginning of this article), but in the absence of a statistical analysis of the archival evidence it is impossible to say how frequently the normal promotion pattern was disturbed.

Another small step toward professionalism was to open up a few limited opportunities to commoners. As we have noted, in the army commoners were rigorously excluded from the officer corps,[31] but in the civil service a rather more broad-minded policy was adopted. In 1798 the Senate learned that 205 men of non-noble origin (merchants, *meshchane,* and even taxpaying peasants) had entered the ranks of officialdom, of whom 29 had reached the eighth grade. It was decided, sensibly enough, that they should be allowed to stay where they were, and that any further such cases should be judged on their individual merits.[32] Paul did not, however, dare to repeal the general prohibition on entry by commoners dating from the 1770s, and in May 1800 he forbade children of clergy to enter the civil service without his express permission.[33]

We now have some statistics on the social composition of the Russian bureaucracy in this period, unearthed and analyzed by Professor Walter Pintner. These show that of those serving in certain central government agencies in the period 1798-1800, 16.5 percent were commoners, compared with 11.5 percent for the longer period 1798-1924.[34] The figures for the provincial organs, if available, would doubtless reveal a wider breach in noble prerogatives. Michael Speranskii was only the best known of a number of *raznochintsy* who made use of this loophole to pursue a successful career in the bureaucracy—although characteristically he needed protection to overcome the tremendous disadvantages that faced those who sprang from the lower orders.

Commoners, alas, did not write memoirs; but many of them would probably have shared the feelings of N. A. Sablukov, a guards officer who "made good" in Paul's service. (Of 132 officers in his regiment in 1796, he was the only survivor in 1801.) In is words, "Promotion went extremely rapidly for those who had good nerves." In an age of general insecurity those with little to lose must often have looked forward to the prospect of making rapid gains at the expense of their privileged superiors. Life was a lottery, and one might be lucky. This feeling helps to explain Paul's popularity with the masses, or (as Sablukov puts it): "the millions, [who] greeted the Emperor with such delight on every possible occasion, so that he ascribed the nobles' coolness and apparent disaffection to their moral degeneracy and Jacobin inclinations."[35]

Thus one might say that Paul opened a window and allowed a cool draft of competition to dispel the stifling atmosphere of privilege, precedent, and protection that pervaded the official milieu. One can scarcely speak of a "democratization" of government; the emperor's views were unashamedly elitist, but he did appreciate that the martial virtues he cherished were not confined to men of noble birth—much though he may have wished it were otherwise—and he was prepared on occasion to measure a man's worth not by his rank but by his office, provided that his functions served the state interest as the emperor himself understood it.

This indicates a move, albeit a hesitant one, toward greater rationality in the conduct of state affairs. Two developments in the institutional field deserve mention in this context: the decisive role accorded to the procurator general and, in the local government sphere, the shift from elected to appointed officials.[36]

The procurator general was seen, in the Petrine tradition, as the supreme guardian of legality, and was also entrusted with some vague general authority over policy, the two functions not being clearly distinguished.[37] In practice the procurator general became an embryonic prime minister. It is true that in Paul's reign (unlike his predecessor's) the incumbent changed too frequently for consistency, and that he was entrusted with too much power, especially in regard to the Senate, without being provided with any real security against the whims of his autocratic master. Nevertheless, taken in conjunction with the ministerial reform (completed in 1802, but prepared during Paul's reign), this marked a step along the road to responsible cabinet government.

The policy of replacing elected officials by appointed ones in the provincial organs of authority[38] was inspired not by any animus against the gentry as such, but by a belief that paid officials who were entirely dependent upon the central power and who had an assured place in the bureaucratic hierarchy would be able to perform their duties in more responsible fashion than men whose allegiance was necessarily divided between their superiors and the electorate. It may of course be objected that this view was too simple, and that Russian "society" was being pressed back into the straitjacket from which Catherine had gingerly begun to free it. But it could also be argued that the officials nominated from the center represented a nucleus of professional administrators in the rural areas, the need for which was felt by Russian rulers and statesmen from Peter I to Stolypin.

Not that Paul himself saw these officials as a professional group: to him they were just his servants. But he would have surely acknowledged that they performed certain specialized functions for which they needed to be trained—and this in itself was a step forward. One of his first decrees called for restoration of the so-called "Junker schools," originally set up by Peter but closed in 1763, to prepare entrants for the civil branch of the service. These pale copies of the prestigious Cadet Corps offered a two-year program divided between general studies (*nauki obshchie*) and professionally oriented subjects (*nauki zvaniia*). Among the latter jurisprudence was to have pride of place; among the former, as distinct disciplines, were ethics (*nravouchenie*) and logic—for in the words of the decree, "logic is a science which no civil official, and especially a judge, can do without."[39] Praiseworthy sentiments: alas, in the event only one such school saw the light of day, and its performance was poor; in practice far more emphasis was placed upon general "humanities" than upon the study of jurisprudence. As Torke writes, "the principle of specialized education had not yet won a footing in the government's thinking, but instead, true to the eighteenth-century spirit, priority was given to encyclopedic knowledge."[40]

The assumption in the legislator's mind was that the graduates of this school would set an example to their colleagues, morally as well as intellectually. This brings us to the third aspect of Paul's "militarism": the struggle against corruption. He deplored this vice because it weakened the state and dishonored those who practiced it; and he made a sincere effort to eliminate it and to inculcate what one might call the "bureaucratic ethos" by measures derived from military experience. His weapons, in ascending order of priority, were exhortation, control, and discipline.

The first of several general hortatory decrees was prompted by the affair of an army doctor who was detained for two days in Saratov by a pair of locally elected civilian officials who were drunk at the time. Paul characteristically put them in the guardhouse on a diet of bread and water and then issued a philippic against such "violent and insulting behavior toward a neighbor." Officials were called upon to display "goodwill and humanity toward the people . . . , restraint and mildness, without any slacking, and continual vigilance that the established order is universally observed in each locality."[41] Naturally enough, no one took the slightest notice.

Control over official actions in eighteenth-century Russia was a task that fell to the procuracy. A creation of Peter I, its powers had since been eroded, and Paul sought to strengthen it. A steady stream of reports on illegalities and abuses of every kind flowed up though these channels to the procurator general and the emperor himself, and usually resulted in administrative or legislative action. When a member of the procuracy appeared in a local government bureau, the officials were obliged to produce forthwith the papers he requested—not least those documents relating to prisoners under detention, some of whom might have spent years in the cells before their case was heard.[42] The Senate was instructed to catch up on its arrears of business and to make its subordinate agencies do likewise.[43] Klochkov has shown that the number of cases settled in the Senate rose from 21,000 in 1797 to 44,000 in 1800—three times as many as in the last years of Catherine's reign.[44] Of course, such statistics do not tell us anything about the quality of the justice dispensed, and it is characteristic of Paul that he should adopt such a crude, numerical criterion of success, which even Klochkov, writing a century later seems to find unobjectionable.

Such action was typical of the emperor's tendency to concentrate on the externals of bureaucratic routine instead of examining the substantive decisions taken by his subordinates. He lavished decrees on such trivia as the need to submit reports regularly, to observe punctual office hours, to return promptly from leave, and the like.[45] No less than 48,000 orders were issued by the emperor in the single year 1797.[46] A reluctance to delegate power is one of the hallmarks of despotism; yet one should not forget the immense obstacles that the authorities faced in enforcing elementary discipline upon officials. For example, it was found necessary to lay down that every state agency that received a Senate ordinance should, when acknowledging the fact, specify the number of copies received: evidently some functionaries, disliking certain decrees, pretended that they had never been informed of them.[47] These petty regulations added to the atmosphere of fear and intrigue that prevailed in government circles during this period. In the hope of escaping or diverting the emperor's wrath, officials would connive with one another to conceal their misdeeds or put the blame on third parties. The humiliations and brutalities inflicted upon them they would avenge upon the populace committed to their charge, convincing themselves that such roughness accorded with the sovereign's own desires—which was by no means the case.

This *excès de zèle* by frightened functionaries sometimes took a ridiculous form. We may dismiss as apocryphal the familiar tale of St. Petersburg policemen ripping off passers-by certain articles of imported clothing deemed to have revolutionary associations. But Sablukov, a reliable witness, tells a hair-raising story about his father, a government contractor, whom the emperor dismissed and banished from the capital for failing to supply uniform cloth in the proper shade of dye. Count Pahlen, the police chief, insisted that the order be carried out immediately, on a cold winter's day, although the elderly Sablukov was confined to bed with a high temperature. When his son protested, Pahlen replied, "If one of us is to be banished, I prefer it to be he"—but promised to do what he could later. After Paul heard what had happened, he apologized.[48] The really significant point in this affair is not the emperor's arbitrariness, which so impressed the writer of the memoir, but the unimaginative and irresponsible reaction to it by a leading official.

Servility, formalism, brutality, short-sightedness, and sheer stupidity—these were the vices that disfigured the imperial bureaucracy prior to the Great Reforms and imprinted their legacy upon later generations. Of all these faults the most serious was the general indifference to consideratons of legality. In this regard Paul's efforts to cure corruption by regimentation served only to make matters worse. He was beset by the dilemma that faced all reforming autocrats: any concession to legality could not but weaken the sacred principle of unlimited autocracy. On the one hand he sincerely wished to encourage respect for the law; on the other he held as stubbornly as any Russian ruler to his sovereign prerogatives, even claiming that his own will constituted the *only* valid source of law—a notion that had no basis in fact. Paul refused to recognize that for any real improvement in public administration to occur it was imperative that officials should be free to state their opinions and to make recommendations without thereby setting themselves at personal risk. In short, Russia needed a modern corpus of administrative law or *Beamtenrecht*. Paul and his military advisers were of course still more opposed to the notion that persons outside the highest governmental circles might play some part in the policy-making process, or exercise some public control over the workings of the administrative apparatus. In his suspicious mind such ideas smacked of "Jacobinism"; indeed, it was partly in order to combat them that he embarked upon measures designed to rationalize the workings of government. Yet militarism was not enough. His reforms were doomed to failure—and may even have cost him his life.

The coup d'état of 11 March was not just a palace revolution against an anachronistic tyranny: it was a blow against the increased bureaucratization of Russian society, struck by a small group within the service class, both military and civilian, who enjoyed the tacit support of a much wider segment of elite opinion. In this respect the conspiracy anticipated that of the Decembrists a quarter-century later. The movement had some characteristics of an aristocratic *fronde*, but can scarcely be said to have been motivated by class interest. Far more significant was a nostalgia for a vanished age of easy informality. It was a protest in the name of traditional values against a particularly brutal kind of state-sponsored modernization. As such, it prepared the ground for the growth of romantic ideology in the 1830s and 1840s. In Nicholas's Russia the struggle between idealistic, individualistic romanticism and unimaginative official conservatism ended—temporarily, at least—in a victory for the latter. Nicholas held to many of his father's ideals and made a more sustained, and no doubt more balanced, attempt to put them into effect. Paul was never able to reconcile the rational and the irrational facets of his policies. Yet his reign is of the utmost significance in the history of Russia: it represented a crucial stage in the emergence of that modern Moloch, the militaristic-bureaucratic state.

NOTES

1 F. Vagts, *A History of Militarism* (New York, 1937), p. 269.

2 *My Past and Thoughts: the Memoirs of Alexander Herzen,* tr. Constance Garnett, revised by Humphrey Higgins, 4 vols. (London, 1968), pp. 255, 1521.

3 M. V. Klochkov, *Ocherki pravitel'stvennoi deiatel'nosti vremeni Pavla I* (Petrograd, 1916).

4 S. A. Korf, "Pavel I i dvorianstvo," *Golos minuvshego,* No. 7 (1913), pp. 5-18 (a review of a preliminary sketch by Klochkov).

5 An encouraging exception is N. F. Demidova, "Biurokratizatsiia gosudarstvennogo apparata absoliutizma v XVII-XVIII vv.," *Absoliutizm v Rossii (XVII-SVIII vv.): sbornki statei k 70-letiiu ... B. B. Kafengauza* (Moscow, 1964), pp. 206-242. This study is only marginally concerned with the period after 1762.

6 Marc Raeff, *Origins of the Russian Intelligentsia: the Eighteenth Century Nobility* (New York, 1966).

7 Hans-Joachim Torke, "Das russische Beamtentum in der ersten Hälfte des 19. Jahrhunderts," *Forschungen zur osteuropäischen Geschichte,* XIII (Berlin, 1967), 7-346. For a fresh and balanced picture, see Roderick E. McGrew, "A Political Portrait of Paul I from the Austrian and English Diplomatic Archives," *Jahrbücher für Geschichte Osteuropas,* XVIII (n. s.), 4 (Dec. 1970), 503-529.

8 V. O. Kliuchevskii, *Kurs russkoi istorii,* in *Sochineniia v vos'mi tomakh,* V (Moscow, 1959), 188; M. N. Pokrovskii, "Biurokratiia," *Bol'shaia sovetskaia entsiklopediia,* 1st ed., VIII (Moscow, 1927), cols. 468-480, in Roman Szporluk, ed., *Russia in World History: Selected Essays by M. N. Pokrovsky* (Ann Arbor, 1970), p. 66. Another pre-Revolutionary writer on the period, E. Shumigorskii, noted that Paul "sought to create a new instrument of governmental power, the bureaucracy, which was to stand outside class (*soslovnye*) interests and implement exactly the will of the monarch." *Imperator Pavel I* (St. Petersburg, 1907), p. 120.

9 *Polnoe sobranie zakonov Rossiiskoi imperii,* Series I, 30 vols. (St. Petersburg, 1830), No. 17865, 5 Mar. 1797.

10 *Ibid.,* Nos. 17720, 9 Jan. 1797; 18470, 8 Apr. 1798; 18725, 31 Oct. 1798; 18809, 31 Mar. 1801.

11 Cf. Klochkov, *Ocherki,* pp. 284-293, where the War College is considered in relation to the other colleges rather than to the army.

12 *Polnoe sobranie zakonov,* Nos. 17719, 9 Jan. 1797; 17757, 24 Jan. 1797; 18853, 11 Feb. 1799.

13 *Ibid.,* No. 17646, 14 Dec. 1796.

14 *Ibid.,* No. 17801, 12 Feb. 1797.

15 *Ibid.,* No. 18663, 12 Sept. 1798; for the Moscow statute, see No. 18822, 17 Jan. 1799.

16 "Pis'ma Imperatora Pavla Petrovicha k moskovskomu glavnokomanduiushchemu," *Russkii arkhiv,* 1876, I, 11 (4 May 1797).

17 *Polnoe sobranie zakonov,* No. 17878, 18 Mar. 1797.

18 *Ibid.,* No. 17817, 19 Feb. 1797; cf. No. 17951, 2 May 1797.

19 *Ibid.,* No. 17723, 11 Jan. 1797; cf. No. 17876, 11 Mar. 1797 for the special case of surveyors. A decree of 1 Feb. 1797 (No. 17777) ordered all commandants who drew their salary from civil funds to be renamed *gorodnichi* and to come under the civil authorities instead of the War College as heretofore.

20 *Ibid.,* No. 19727, 22 Jan. 1801.

21 *Ibid.,* No. 18384, 17 Jan. 1798.

22 *Ibid.,* No. 17705, Dec. 1796.

23 "Pis'ma Imperatora Pavla Petrovicha," p. 22 (Jan. 1798).

24 *Polnoe sobranie zakonov,* No. 14392, 7 Nov. 1775, articles 81, 89, 253, 264, 270.

25 *Ibid.,* No. 18400, 25 Feb. 1798.

26 *Ibid.,* No. 19796, 17 Mar. 1801).

27 Cf. Herzen, *My Past and Thoughts,* pp. 214-215, for a description of the police chief in Perm', who "belonged to a special type of military men turned officials."

28 *Polnoe sobranie zakonov,* No. 18440, 15 Mar. 1798.

29 *Ibid.,* No. 17926, 20 Apr. 1797.

30 *Ibid.,* No. 19219, 9 Dec. 1799, cited by Torke, "Das russische Beamtentum," p. 54.

31 *Ibid.,* No. 18486, 17 Apr. 1798. In Dec. 1800, the guards regiments were purged of commoners, who were transferred to the category of *odnodvortsy: Polnoe sobranie zakonov,* No. 19696, 23 Dec. 1800.

32 Torke, "Das russische Beamtentum," p. 104.

33 *Polnoe sobranie zakonov,* No. 19434, 27 May 1800; cf. Torke, "Das russische Beamtentum," p. 110.

34 Walter M. Pintner, "Social Characteristics of the Early Nineteenth-Century Russian Bureaucracy," *Slavic Review,* XXIX (Sept. 1970), 436. The assumption we make here is that the higher proportion of commoners in 1798-1800 reflected deliberate government policy, but in the absence of comparable figures from Catherine's reign it is difficult to be sure; social pressures may have been responsible.

35 "Iz zapisok N. A. Sablukova," *Russkii arkhiv,* 1869, p. 1903.

36 For details, see Klochkov, *Ocherki,* pp. 224-270.

37 *Polnoe sobranie zakonov,* No. 17652, 16 Dec. 1796. He was to show "vigilance . . . in ensuring exact fulfillment of the laws" and to watch over "the proper flow of the various affairs passing through government offices."

38 See Klochkov, *Ocherki,* pp. 434-480.

39 *Polnoe sobranie zakonov,* Nos. 17707, 1 Jan. 1797; 17733, 14 Jan. 1798; 17912, 8 Apr. 1797.

40 Torke, "Das russische Beamtentum," p. 146. Torke accepts Grech's rather improbable story that when Paul discovered that 4,500 prospective pupils had registered in place of the 50 provided for, those surplus to the norm were sent off to the army as NCOs.

41 *Polnoe sobranie zakonov,* No. 18964, 15 May 1798.

42 *Ibid.,* No. 18937, 28 Apr. 1798.

43 *Ibid.,* No. 17884, 22 Mar. 1797.

44 Klochkov, *Ocherki,* pp. 219-220.

45 E.g., *Polnoe sobranie zakonov,* Nos. 17680, 23 Dec. 1796; 17685, 26 Dec. 1796; 18648 31 Aug. 1798; 18709, 20 Oct. 1798.

46 McGrew, "Political Portrait," p. 515n.

47 *Polnoe sobranie zakonov,* No. 18357, 31 Jan. 1798.

48 "Iz zapisok Sablukova," p. 1913.

7

THE POLITICS OF ABSOLUTISM: PAUL I AND THE BANK OF ASSISTANCE FOR THE NOBILITY

Roderick E. McGrew

Paul I ascended the throne in 1796 firmly convinced that the Russian social and political system was on the brink of dissolution, that his mother's reign had been an unmitigated disaster, and that his own life was in immediate danger. He believed that only bold, decisive action could save him from his father's ugly fate and prevent a revolution in the Russian Empire. Thus during his first weeks as tsar, Paul began to overhaul the Russian system. He suspended or reversed most of Catherine's policies, issued a storm of orders that revolutionized the appearance and atmosphere of the court, and set an inner circle of trusted friends to work on plans to reestablish Russian absolutism on a firm foundation. Above all else, Paul wanted Russia to be tranquil and secure, well-ordered and prosperous. To attain these ends, he reestablished the principle of a hereditary succession, reorganized the army, attacked waste, luxury, and corruption wherever they appeared, and began a comprehensive program of rationalization and centralization in the state administration. The military style became the standard mode for court and government; subordination and a punctilious discipline were vigorously enforced; and each segment of society, from the great nobility to the peasant serfs, was confirmed and reinforced in its traditional role and status. The whole of this vast political composition centered on the tsar, who bore sole responsibility for society's welfare and whose power, in Paul's eyes at least, was absolute.[1]

Paul's program, though innovative in detail, was actually an effort to consolidate and strengthen what he conceived to be the traditional social order. He turned the immense power that he wielded as autocrat to building barriers against change, and he used every instrument at his command to enforce conformity, loyalty, obedience, and a sense of duty among his subjects. But preservation meant more than discipline. It also meant mobilizing the economic resources necessary to maintain external security and to promote domestic programs. Here Paul was true to the conservatizing psychology. Assuming that the wealth he needed was present but untapped, he developed fiscal policies whose primary purpose was to fill the imperial treasury by eliminating unnecessary expenses, improving administrative machinery, increasing taxes of all sorts, and uncovering new sources of public revenue.[2] These policies were combined with a frontal assault on inflation through withdrawing substantial quantities of assignats from circulation. Economic development played no part in these proposals, since the primary emphasis fell on rationalizing and improving the system as it existed, and Paul himself was actually hostile to the kind of innovation necessary to promote economic growth.[3]

The most important single piece of legislation in Paul's fiscal program was the creation of a new Bank of Assistance for the Nobility, which was announced on 18 December 1797.[4] Its stated purpose was to provide sufficient inexpensive credit for the landholding gentry to liquidate its outstanding debts and reestablish itself on a firm financial footing. Its further purpose, though one that was never formally articulated in the enabling legislation, was to allow the imperial treasury to recover funds previously loaned to the nobility and to open new sources of revenue for the state. But these financial considerations inevitably involved much broader issues. The Bank proposal reflected Paul's determination to stabilize and strengthen the foundations of Russian society while intensifying and consolidating the power of the tsar. It was a measure designed to reform and preserve the nobility and bind it to the crown, but it was a proposal that also recognized the interdependence of the landed class with merchants and artisans, and therefore sought to promote cooperation and the recognition of mutual responsibility in the interests of the whole society. In sum, the Auxiliary Bank was a central item in Paul's reform program that reflected both the problems and the approach to solving problems current in his reign. Therefore the circumstances under which the Bank was organized, the character of the institution itself, and the goals to which it was directed, when taken together, provide an unusual opportunity to study the values and political attitudes that characterized Russian absolutism under Emperor Paul.[5]

In the course of the eighteenth century the Russian landed gentry had developed a nearly insatiable appetite for credit and a comparable inability to repay what it owed. The most common explanation for this condition was that the nobility was wasting its substance in uncontrolled spending on superfluous and morally debilitating luxuries, all in the name of maintaining an acceptable standard of living. This explanation, however, was vastly oversimplified, and in fact masked basic social and economic realities. The domainal economy of the eighteenth and early nineteenth centuries was very low in productivity and was geared to consuming what it produced. Gentry serfholders, both small and great, shared the consumption approach of the peasants who worked their lands, while powerful cultural sanctions worked against the agricultural innovations necessary for increased productivity and an enlarged money income.[6] Yet in that same period, partly in response to cultural westernization, which created new consumer demands and partly in response to growth and diversification in the Russian economy itself, the need for money income rose sharply. And this tendency was accelerated by Catherine's inflationary money policies. Luxuries apart, most members of the gentry lacked the money income necessary to carry on their lives, and the most common means used to bridge the gap between income and expenses was credit. Pawnbrokers, moneylenders, and foreign banking houses all made loans to needy nobles, while merchants, shopkeepers, and artisans sold goods and services on credit, since the alternative was not to sell at all. The resulting indebtedness threatened the viability of the gentry as a class, posed an ever-increasing barrier to economic growth, and by the end of the eighteenth century had become a major burden on the state.[7]

The gentry's economic dilemmas brought early action by the crown. In 1729, just four years after Peter's death, the state established the *Monetnaia kontora* to help nobles redeem valuables pledged to pawnbrokers, and in 1733 this institution was authorized to make loans secured by jewelry, gold, or silver at a flat 8 percent annual rate. The need, however, far outran these limited resources, and in 1754 Empress Elizabeth capitalized the first Nobles' Bank at 750,000 rubles. This too was insufficient. The economic tides were growing stronger, the gentry was losing ground, and in the next three decades capitalization for the Nobles' Bank ballooned to 6 million rubles without satisfying the demand. The same pattern persisted in Catherine's reign. In 1786 she founded the Government Loan Bank which absorbed the Nobles' Bank and added 5 million rubles to the capital. But before this she had tried other expedients as well. The Assignat Bank, established in 1769 to issue paper money, was granted the right to make gentry loans; beginning in 1772, the Foundling Homes in St. Petersburg and Moscow were permitted to loan their idle funds; and in 1775, the charity boards of provincial governments gained loaning privileges, while the Charter of Nobility (1785) permitted the provincial Noble Assemblies to found local banks for the nobility. Credit from these public institutions continued to be cheap, costing a modest 6 to 8 percent as compared with private rates that were often three times or more as high, and the nobility borrowed to the limits of the capital available. By 1792, the Government Loan Bank alone had over 22 million rubles in outstanding loans. Other government institutions had loans in excess of that figure, while the size of the nobility's private indebtedness was at best a matter for conjecture. Repayment was very slow, new loans were used to service old debts, and as the mass of indebtedness increased, the demand for additional credit grew proportionately.[8]

The volume of gentry indebtedness was obviously a danger signal, but to a nation that was itself in desperate fiscal straits, the gentry's indebtedness to the crown was particularly important. The government, like any other creditor, suffered from the nobility's improvidence, and there seemed to be no end to the support that the nobility required. Moreover, it could be presumed that vast sums of money were passing into the hands of moneylenders, while properties were being alienated from the nobility when it was unable to pay. A scheme that could at one and the same time force the nobility to pay off the state as well as private creditors, while turning the gentry's need for credit into a source of continuing public revenues, could contribute both to economic order and the government's solvency. Moreover, to accomplish this by forcing the nobility to regularize its life, to give up luxury and ostentation for a more modest style commensurate with its income, and to recognize the binding force of obligations, would promote both stability and security. These considerations, which as we shall see were an integral part of the Bank proposals, make the Auxiliary Bank quite a different institution, both in intent and in organization, from its predecessors in the field of gentry credit. Though superficially similar, the Bank of Assistance for the Nobility marked a radical departure from accepted practices and showed a thoroughly innovative approach to a long-standing problem.

When Paul first became tsar, he appointed a committee under his procurator general, Prince Alexis Kurakin, to study fiscal reforms. The proposal for the Auxiliary Bank apparently came from this committee's work, and the draft proposals were drawn by Kurakin himself.[9] Kurakin was not, however, the man who planned and organized the Bank. This distinction belonged to a travelling Dutch financier named Robert Voud [Woot, Vut', Wood, Vout] who represented the great Amsterdam banking house of Hope and Company. This house had become the main source of credit for the Russian government during the 1790s, had made personal loans to Paul while he was still grand duke, and had given a substantial line of credit to the Polish monarchy as well. Voud initially came to Russia to get guarantees that the imperial government would honor the Polish debt. He made a favorable impression on Paul, who accepted Hope's claims on Poland as binding on Russia, and was welcomed into the so-called empress's circle where he became an intimate of Kurakin as well as a protégé of the powerful Prince Bezborodko. He was also on good terms with Baron Nicolay, another influential figure in Russian finance. The empress's circle, and Mariia Fedorovna herself, dominated domestic affairs during the first eighteen months of Paul's reign, and Voud, through admission to it, was well placed to pursue his interests. Voud advised the tsar concerning the Bank while working on it with Kurakin, and if the decree as published reflected Paul's values and showed flashes of his style, the plan's mechanics were Voud's work.[10]

Voud's role in the Bank's creation underlines the point that this institution, whatever its predecessors may have been, was intended to be much more than a simple subsidy for the serfholding gentry, while his intimate connection with the Bank undermined confidence from the start. Whatever Hope and Company's reputation was, Voud was considered to be a slippery and unscrupulous rascal, an "archswindler," as Count S. R. Vorontsov was pleased to call him. Count Dietrichstein reported a conversation at the British ambassador Whitworth's residence in which Voud, in front of a group of English and Dutch merchants, called Russia a regular Peru inhabited by apes, and asserted that any businessman who had failed to make a fortune there after two or three years could only be very stupid. On another occasion, when Voud was asked why he had organized the Bank the way he did, he replied that his house had such large claims against the Russian government that in the normal course of things there was no hope that they would ever be paid; the Bank was an attempt to supply that hope.[11] Curt von Stedingk, the Swedish ambassador to St. Petersburg, confirmed that comment and reported that the link between the Auxiliary Bank and the House of Hope was an agreement to consolidate the Polish debts into a single loan of 88,300,000 Dutch florins. This loan, according to Stedingk, was to run for thirty-two years with the stipulation that during the first twelve the Russian government would only pay the annual 5 percent interest, while in the thirteenth year, one twentieth of the principal would fall due with a similar amount due annually to the end of the contract. Funds for meeting this obligation would be drawn from the anticipated profits of the Auxiliary Bank.[12] Certainly Voud's plan was an ingenious one that involved at the least some measure of misdirection. This struck Viazzoli, the Austrian consul general for economic affairs, so forcibly that he flatly refused an appointment as court banker, reporting that the Bank was patently fraudulent, and that no honest man dared put his name to it.[13]

When we turn to the December decree in which the Bank was formally announced, however, we find no hint of high financial politics. On the contrary, the emphasis falls on the gentry's financial condition and the means for improving it. The general goals that Paul intended the Auxiliary Bank to serve were articulated in the preamble and conclusion, but they resonated as well throughout the plan's various provisions. Some of this material deserves quotation both for the rhetoric and the insight that it gives into the social values Paul intended to promote. In the preamble, Paul set out his purposes and approach as follows:

> On OUR accession to the hereditary Throne of OUR Empire of ALL the Russias, WE took a sacred oath before Almighty God unceasingly to watch over the welfare of OUR faithful subjects, to assure their tranquillity, to procure for them every means of prosperity, and to guarantee among them, in the most inviolable manner, good faith and harmony in their mutal engagements. Constantly absorbed in concerns so dear to OUR heart, WE see with the most profound sadness that a great number of noble families, groaning under the weight of debts transmitted to them from generation to generation with the inheritance of their fathers, or contracted through their own negligence, have failed to profit from the means that the Imperial Banks offer them to ease their burden; the greatest part, on the contrary, doubling the mass of its debts, has deranged the fortunes of its creditors and, unable to escape from the shameful extremity of falling into the hands of grasping usurers, multiplies the number of those deadly bloodsuckers and, what is worse still, prepares for its innocent posterity the melancholy prospect of being a prey to poverty. Profoundly distressed by these conditions, and desiring to find an immediate remedy for this unfortunate situation, while conserving in the families from generation to generation the hereditary property acquired by honorable service or by the cares of their ancestors, it pleases US . . . to give to OUR Nobility new and prompt help by the establishment of a State Bank of Assistance for the Nobility.[14]

The conclusion to the *ukaz* picks up and develops the same motifs:

> Having laid down such principles as the foundation of an establishment that owes its birth to OUR Imperial beneficence alone, WE surrender OURSELVES to the hope dear to OUR heart that OUR nobility, knowing OUR determination to save them and their descendants from the danger that menaces them, will know how to make good use of OUR benefits, will recover its properties from the hands of avid usurers, will pay all its debts, and after having thus reestablished its name in honor, will expand all the branches of its economy, and above all, curtailing in its dwellings the superfluous expenses that are the consequence of the imaginary

> needs of Luxury, will commit itself to a praiseworthy moderation and will transmit to its most distant posterity the fruits it will have collected under OUR reign.[15]

It is worth noting that at no place in either this decree or in the regulations expanding on it is there any mention of economic problems as such. Moreover, there are only two glancing references to development, while the idea of progress is entirely missing. The society envisioned is tranquil, stable, and unchanging. The gentry, freed of its burden of debt, will prosper and will bequeath a solid inheritance to its posterity, while the gentry's creditors will be secure in the knowledge that the obligations owing to them will be discharged. The tsar appears in this composition as a benevolent father who is concerned about the welfare of his erring children, and who is prepared to help them redeem their errors for their own good and for the good of the whole society. The entire decree is suffused with a high moral tone, and the implication, especially of the decree's conclusion, is that if the gentry will moderate its life style, eschew luxury, and practice thrift, it can enjoy an idyllic life, the state will be secure, and posterity will inherit prosperity and peace. Much of this was so familiar as to be clichés, especially the attacks on usury and the dangers of luxurious living. What was different was the intention developed in the Bank's technical provisions to force the nobility to meet its obligations, to behave morally, or to face the most serious consequences. As debt had become a major social problem, so the tsar seemed prepared to coerce the recalcitrant into meeting their obligations and regulating their lives.

The Bank of Assistance for the Nobility was at base a scheme for consolidating the gentry's debts while making the state its primary creditor. The Bank was so constructed that conceivably it could absorb everything the gentry owed to private as well as public lenders, though it was obviously most effective in dealing with debts from public institutions. No upper limit was set on the quantity of Bank credit available, and there was no defined capitalization. To consolidate the whole of the gentry's indebtedness required total flexibility. Kurakin had recommended the enormous sum of 100 million rubles for the Bank's capitalization, but this idea was dropped in favor of a simple statement that the Bank would be open for two years to make loans "in proportion to the needs of those who have recourse to it, and to the amount [value] of the pledged properties which will be presented to it with the necessary validating certificates."[16] And as we shall see later, the pledged properties became the Bank's capitalization. In line with the principle of consolidation, provision was made to transfer existing debts from other government lending agencies to the Auxiliary Bank, while special regulations were drawn to cover properties already mortgaged, or those sequestered to satisfy older debts.[17] Once the Bank had opened, private creditors who found that their clients were making no arrangements to pay what they owed could make a formal complaint to the Bank. If the complaint was found to be justified, the Bank was empowered to force the debtor to accept a loan large enough to meet his creditor's claim.[18]

At one blow, Paul had, theoretically, made the greatest part of the landed class debtors of the state, and the decree laid down the terms that they were expected to meet. First, the borrower was to pay a broker's fee or premium to the Bank for making the loan. This fee was initially 8 percent of the face value of the loan, but later it was reduced to 6 percent. Two percent of the premium was to be paid in circulating currency, the balance could be paid in Bank scrip, and the whole of the premium was to be deducted from the amount of the loan when it was made. Thus a noble borrowing 1,000 rubles under the 6 percent rule could pay 20 rubles in cash, 40 rubles in scrip, and receive 940 rubles. His interest, however, was then computed on the full 1,000 rubles. Presumably, if he chose to do so, he could pay the entire premium in currency, and then receive the full amount of the loan, but this was not stated explicitly. What was clear was that the premium had to be paid in advance.[19]

Once a loan was made, its recipient was committed to meet a schedule of fixed payments spread over a twenty-five year period. During the first five years, the borrower paid only interest at a rate of 6 percent per annum. Interest payments, however, in the original decree, could only be made in circulating currency; no Bank scrip was allowed, and the payments were to be made three months before the expiration of the year. In the sixth year of the loan, principal reductions began. Payments on principal could be made in Bank certificates, and the stipulated reduction was 20 rubles per 1,000 rubles loaned. The principal reductions per thousand rose arbitraily by fives from 20 rubles in the sixth year to 80 rubles in the twenty-fifth year. Reductions in principal also brought reductions in interest payments. The total annual payment of principal and interest per thousand rubles loaned varied from a low of 78 rubles 80 kopecks in the seventh year to a high of 96 rubles 20 kopecks in the fourteenth year.[20]

In a typically elliptical way, Paul commented in Article 30 that it would be hard to believe that, given the advantages the Bank made available to the nobles, anyone would fall behind in his payments. "But if, contrary to all expectations, such a case should occur," stringent measures were provided for dealing with defaulters. The borrower was allowed a ten-day grace period. If the amount due was still not paid, penalties of 1 percent for the first month, 2 percent for the second, and 3 percent for the third were to be assessed. If the due amount was still not paid, the Bank could apply to the Provincial Assembly in the *guberniia* where the mortgaged property was located to have the property taken over and managed to satisfy the amounts owing to the Bank. Once this step had been taken, the state authorities retained administration of the lands either for the full twenty-five years the loan was to run, or until the obligation was entirely discharged. During that period the owner received no income from the property, was forbidden to have any part in administering it, and was even prohibited from visiting it. When the debt was discharged, however, the property reverted to its owner. Thus a noble who refused to regularize his affairs might live in penury, but his property would not be alienated from his family, and there was no danger of its falling into nongentry hands. If the gentry was unable to protect its patrimony, the crown would do this for it while guaranteeing that its creditors would be paid. Thus society could be protected against its members' failures.[21]

Loans from the Auxiliary Bank, whether forced or voluntary, were made in a special scrip which, in the original proposal, could only be used to pay debts.[22] Though consistent with the idea of forcing debt consolidation and repayment, this provision had to be changed since the scrip created serious problems for private creditors. The original intent, however, would appear to have been to prevent borrowers from using Auxiliary Bank loans for current expenses, though the suggestion was made that loans could be used to improve the borrowers' economy.[23] The loans were secured by the borrowers' landed properties, which were described in detail on the face of the scrip.[24] The value of the lands pledged was measured by assigning a per capita valuation to the male serf population on the land. Factories and other plants were also acceptable security, but the valuation in those cases was based on previous income. By far the greatest number of loans was secured by land contracts.[25]

For loan purposes, the provinces of the empire were divided into four classifications. In Class I, the serf valuation was 75 rubles; in Class II, 65 rubles; Class III serfs were valued at 50 rubles; and in Class IV the limit was 40 rubles.[26] Though supposedly based on fertility and productivity, these valuations were arbitrary and exceedingly high. But they were consistent with the idea of encompassing the whole of the gentry's existing indebtedness, and they also reflected Paul's stubborn conviction that there was wealth in the country that was being wasted. One of the basic assumptions on which the Bank was built was that the gentry was in debt because it was wasteful, extravagant, and devoted to the life of luxury. This assumption, however, failed to take into account low agricultural productivity and the nobility's generally depressed income level. The bulk of the landholding gentry was in debt because it was poor, and if a handful of highly visible families set standards of oriental opulence, thousands of others were actually impoverished.[27]

Here we can begin to see some of the broader implications of the Bank for the gentry, and why it was greeted not as a benefit gratefully received, but as a threat and an insupportable burden. The landowners were to be forced to face the accumulated debts that they had been unable or unwilling to discharge, and they were to pay them out of current receipts. If they failed to do so, they lost entirely the income from their lands, and that this would happen seemed almost inevitable. Since the plan was essentially coercive, the high valuations took on a sinister connotation, amounting almost to a license to confiscate. The average rental income for the last decade of the eighteenth century was in the neighborhood of 5 or 6 rubles per soul. Depending on where the lands were located, the Bank plan proposed that the landowner would dedicate 40 to 60 percent of his rental income simply to pay the interest on the amount he had borrowed. The principal reductions would be an additional burden. Thus even a relatively well-to-do landholder on a Class I territory with five hundred serfs to mortgage would be hard put to meet his obligations. He could discharge up to 37,500 rubles in old debts, but to do so would cost him 2,250 rubles in interest alone, while his rental income, though probably higher than the 6 ruble interest, would not be likely to run above 4,000 rubles. And by the time his principal reductions began in the loan's sixth year, he would be giving nearly 75 percent of his anticipated income from the land to the government. His only hope would be a substantial outside income, but this was available only to a few members of the gentry. Put in these terms, the Bank of Assistance for the Nobility appeared to be a catastrophe.[28]

If the Auxiliary Bank plan as described in the decree of December 1797 could have been fully implemented and enforced, it would have brought the gentry's domestic economy directly under the state's control, and it more than likely would have resulted in the state's administering a substantial part of the gentry's lands, while alienating the landholders from their source of income. Land valuations were set so high, the gentry's debts were so extensive, and the Bank's competence was so broad, that it is difficult to see any other result. This, however, would have contradicted the idea of preserving the gentry as a class, and while Paul believed that the nobility needed to be disciplined, even coerced, and while he insisted on its subordination, he was also committed to its preservation as a part of the monarchical system. When the plan was published, and the dangers inherent in it were perceived, there was such a violent public outcry from all affected interests, nongentry as well as gentry, that Paul, though angered, had to take another look at his proposals.[29] The result was a number of revisions that were finally announced nearly seven months after the Bank opened its doors. The revisions reduced the cost of contracting a loan, permitted borrowers to use Bank scrip to pay interest, attempted to make the scrip more acceptable, and set the date on which a loan was made as the date from which the borrower paid interest, rather than the arbitrary date of 1 March, when the Bank had opened.[30] These revisions responded to the criticism that the credit that the Bank offered cost too much, and they did ease matters for borrowers. They did not, however, change the basic conception of the Bank, and though the public's protests subsided, the Bank remained a coercive means to force the gentry to pay its debts and regularize its life, while making the gentry debt itself a source of income for the crown.

Though potentially destructive, the Bank's actual functioning, so far as we can determine it, was far looser than it was intended to be. Both the original decree and the *Règlamente* that appeared in February stressed tightly controlled adminitrative procedures, and the latter went into the most minute detail, leaving nothing to chance. There were, however, substantial loopholes that made the plan tolerable for the landowners. These same loopholes, of course, militated against the plan's effectiveness in dealing with the gentry's debts.

Initially it was reported that the Auxiliary Bank would be the sole source of credit for the gentry in the future, as well as holding all past debts.[31] This proved to be no more than rumor, since neither the December decree nor its successors touched on the point. Even so, there was a great scramble either to sell properties or to borrow enough to pay off pressing obligations before the Bank opened in March 1798.[32] And since the original Bank proposal refused to accept Bank scrip for discharge of interest on its loans, it was clear that nobles could not have recourse to the Auxiliary Bank for additional loans to discharge their accumulated interest charges. Other government credit sources remained available for loans, however, and the 1798 revisions in the Bank plan permitted the use of scrip for interest payments.[33] Indeed, this provision had been weakened earlier when, in answer to complaints from private creditors that the scrip they were receiving was worthless, an official exchange and discount office was established.[34] The plan's original provision, of course, was to allow the scrip to be used primarily, if not exclusively, for the settlement of old debts. This provision was badly bent if not destroyed by the introduction of relatively free conversion very early in the plan's life. In addition, though the Bank administration was held to be responsible for providing honest and efficient service, the substantive decisions concerning validating properties for security, sequestering defaulters' lands, or granting creditors' petitions for forced loans were vested in the Noble Assemblies. This provision guaranteed at the very least a lenient approach on questions of enforcement, and turned the bulk of the regulatory decree into an exercise in legal formalism.[35]

The practical effect of these various weak points in the Bank's implementation was to open the door to a further pyramiding of gentry indebtedness. Between March 1798 and October 1799, great landholders and small pledged 708,050 serfs of all classifications, receiving nearly forty-six million rubles in scrip. There was, however, no demonstrable lessening of the gentry's indebtedness. Indeed, the contrary occurred, since the massive sums issued through the Auxiliary Bank simply became a platform on which a further structure of indebtedness was built. Every lending agency saw a significant increase in the amounts it had outstanding through this period, while the budget books of individual families showed a sharp upward swing in the amounts owing. Paul himself saw that the plan was not working, and when he announced the revisions in the Bank's operations in the fall of 1798, he included a sharp warning to those who were abusing their credit privileges. No further attempts were made, however, to plug the leaks, and the Bank was closed abruptly in the fall of 1799, six months before its term expired.[36]

The Bank failed as a measure to aid the gentry to escape its burden of debt largely because it concentrated on a moral issue and ignored economic realities. There was no way, given the state of the domainal economy, that the gentry could have fulfilled Paul's expectations, and the incredible gap between valuations and repayment schedules on the one side, and income from the land on the other, made the point dramatically. The effort to bridge that gap, to ease somewhat the tension between the plan's expectations and costs and the gentry's ability to pay, only weakened barely adequate barriers against abuse, while the failure to control credit from other institutions combined with faulty disciplinary provisions and long-standing traditions of favoritism and corruption made the plan, as conceived, essentially inoperable. In its results, the Auxiliary Bank proved to be no more successful than its predecessors. It not only failed to halt the rise of gentry debts but contributed to their increase, and there is no evidence, either in the last year of Paul's life or under his successor, that any serious effort to reform the Bank was contemplated.

Ironically, the interests of private creditors weakened Paul's plans to discipline the gentry, and on the whole the Bank had a disruptive effect on the economy. This effect was in part attributable to an attitude toward business and the business community that was not favorable to competition or a success ethic. Paul paraded thrift, moderation, and hard work as personal values that he approved and hoped to inculcate, but he married these ideas to subordination, self-control, and recognition of place. Paul believed firmly that obligations had to be met, and he considered debts moral obligations.[37] Consequently, in his preamble to the Bank decree, he stressed the necessity for helping creditors recover what was owing to them, and he noted the burden that creditors bore when debts went unpaid. This view of obligation, however, was a limiting one. Although creditors might have legitimate claims, they were flatly told not to press those claims, nor to disturb any further those who owed them. Once they had been promised payment, they should be quiet. Article 37 of the *ukaz* makes the point specifically:

> After having thus established on firm foundations the means for freeing Noble families from their onerous and ruinous debts, and having assured creditors the exact payment of the Capital [owing them], WE order that the latter, finding themselves delivered from all uncertainty in this regard, will not torment their debtors by pressing and premature demands; but that they remain calm and full of confidence until the Bank begins its operations and satisfies without delay their claims according to the means that WE have just established.

Persistent indebtedness led to excessive dunning, and the perpetually unpaid creditor begging his lordly client for even a little on account was a familiar Russian theme.[38] Read in that context, Article 37 makes considerable sense. But the significance of the attitudes expressed here goes further. The tone of the decree where private creditors are concerned ranges from condescension through contempt to open warning, and there certainly was no hint that a bourgeoisie contained the future of the state. On the contrary, there was a clearly stated recognition that although private business, small or great, was necessary and was entitled to a fair return for its services, it was entitled to nothing more, and the government determined what was "fair." Paul railed against usurers, but his target was broader than moneylenders who charged excessive interest. The enemies he saw were those thrusting, arrogant, ambitious men who agitated for their own interests, who always demanded more, and who pushed themselves ahead at society's expense. A "usurer" was the antithesis of a public-spirited merchant, a person who preyed on the misfortunes of others while placing personal gain above the common welfare. Thus, for example, any creditor who refused to accept the Bank's certificates in discharge of his debts was declared to be a "grasping usurer," his claims were to be forfeited, and what was owed him was to be paid into the Bank. His crime, and what made him a "usurer," was to refuse what had been declared to be a fair settlement of his accounts.[39] In Article 39 there is a further and particularly interesting reflection of the spirit Paul was seeking to promote:

> Firmly persuaded that WE have in OUR previously described establishment provided equally for the advantage of debtors and creditors, and sheltered from all danger the situation of the one and the other, the former in liberating them from onerous debts, the latter in returning to them the Capital that they have loaned, WE assert in consequence that there may not be any change [in the arrangements] that might work to the detriment of the Bank; and any request presented to this effect, be it by creditors or by debtors, cannot for this reason be admitted. *Anyone who will dare to present such a request will be treated as a man of turbulent and unquiet character.* (Emphasis added.)

In place of ambition and drive, the *ukaz* consistently stresses tranquillity, even passivity, and though Paul openly deplored the evil effects that followed the gentry's refusal to pay its debts, it was apparent that he had no sympathy for pushy capitalists. The decree contains no hint of the success motif, profit is totally ignored, and economic progress is hardly mentioned. The society envisioned is peaceful, prosperous, and unchanging, while the first responsibility of the people inhabiting it is to recognize the obligations of their respective stations and the binding nature of their mutual engagements.

Given this approach, it is small wonder that the Bank was a commercial disaster. In a paternalistic sense, Paul understood that the nongentry, nonbondage groups in Russian society were important and that their interests needed to be protected, but his understanding was limited, and there is no sign that either he or his advisors grasped the functional significance of artisans, small shopkeepers, or middle merchants for the operation of the economy. Voud probably understood all this, but he was less interested in a workable plan for the economy as a whole than he was in a plan that gave maximum benefit to his company. And in the same way, the plan's economic advantage to the crown was considered more important than its effect on private business.

The plan's crucial weakness so far as private creditors were concerned was the scrip or Bank certificates with which debts were to be discharged. When a noble applied for a loan contract, he described and certified the properties he had to pledge. The Bank then issued a certificate that carried the property description on its face. This certificate was to be valid for twenty-five years, or until it was retired by repayment of the principal, and it paid 5 percent interest to its bearer. As principal payments were made, the certificate was to be endorsed to show the liberation of pledged property, and the 5 percent interest was computed each year on a reduced principal. Certificates were issued in round-number denominations—500, 1,000, 2,000, 4,000, 6,000, 8,000, and 10,000 rubles. A 200-ruble denomination was added in the fall of 1798. No effort was spared to convince people that the certificate was worth what it was said to be, and that it was backed by real property. On the other hand, creditors had no choice about accepting the certificates in discharge of debts.[40]

Although the *ukaz* spoke of facilitating the circulation of certificates, the scrip was clumsy to use, and it was not in fact a circulating currency, but rather a negotiable instrument that, in defined circumstances, was also a medium of exchange. Article 28 stated that the Bank billets were to be used by the persons to whom they were issued to pay their debts. This was well and good so far as government-sponsored loans were concerned, but it was no help to an individual creditor. Article 28 was to be read prescriptively. The Bank certificate could only be used to discharge formal debts; it was not fully negotiable, and most certainly was not money. Thus a nobleman who owed his tailor could pay his bill in Bank scrip. The tailor, however, who had to accept the scrip, could not buy bread or kvass, nor could he pay help with it. His only hope was to sell the certificate or exchange it for a circulating currency. This, to put it mildly, was an unfortunate situation. The only person interested in buying such paper would be someone with money to invest who would hold the scrip to collect the 5 percent interest. But this return was too low to tempt anyone, and there was a shortage of investment funds generally. The result was that there was no market for the certificates. They were discounted at between 20 and 25 percent on emission, and the value declined from that point. In sum, private creditors were forced to accept paper worth only a fraction of what was owing to them. The state, however, had no such problem. It could take certificates in payment, hold them for interest, or change them for currency. Since only the government could sequester land and administer it in case of default, only the state had anything approaching a lien on the noble's property. The private creditor had a piece of paper of dubious market value.[41]

This situation was foreseen when the Bank was announced, and it helps to account for the extraordinary unrest that the Bank occasioned in commercial circles. The government was forced to see how serious this problem could be and hastily provided for exchange of the scrip after the Bank had been open for two days. This, however, raised chaos of another sort. Apparently the use of scrip was an attempt to outflank the problem of unsupported paper money. Given the volume of loans the Bank generated, to make those loans in assignats would have deluged the country with rapidly depreciating paper currency. Paul had committed himself to reduce substantially the number of assignats in circulation, and shortly after coming to the throne he publicly burned five million rubles in assignats while promising the retirement of six million more. The Bank certificates created such a storm of discontent, however, that the government agreed to exchange the certificates for assignats without any limits on the amounts exchanged. The result was another huge emission of paper money. More than half of the original amount of Bank certificates issued were exchanged immediately for assignats, and by the time the Bank was reorganized in 1802, less than three million of the nearly fifty million rubles issued were still in circulation as unredeemed scrip. Paul's "hard money" policy collapsed, the number of assignats soared while their value fell fourteen silver kopecks from 79 1/3 to 65 1/3. Times, as Viazzoli pointed out, were bad all over Europe, and Russia's economic problems reflected European conditions; on the other hand, the Auxiliary Bank, in his opinion, was a factor of major importance in substantially weakening the empire's financial position.42

Centralized banking, defined credit procedures, a concern for the strength of a nation's currency, and an effort to build confidence in contracts were all part of the Bank proposal, and may be interpreted as contributions to the growth of a capitalist economy. In this case, however, the interpretation does not follow from either existing conditions or the plan's stated intentions. The Auxiliary Bank focused on the gentry, while its greatest benefit was to the crown. Mercantile interests were benefited incidentally, and the most positive thing the Bank seemed to propose for them was to quiet their complaints and ease their anxieties. For the crown, however, the Bank provided new sources of revenue, not the least of which was the very indebtedness of the nobility itself. It was this aspect of the plan which was most ingenious technically, but which also must be understood to grasp the full intent of the proposal and its significance as a reflection of Paul's political outlook.

In the first place, the Auxiliary Bank was contrived to be entirely self-supporting. Even its administrative costs were to be carried by its noble patrons, and all these costs were paid in advance. This was the purpose of the broker's fee or loan premium. As we have seen, when a loan was approved 8 percent of the amount borrowed was deducted from it, and the borrower then received the net amount. Two percent of this premium was to be paid in assignats or other circulating currency; the remaining 6 percent could be paid in Bank scrip.[43] Although this premium was reduced to 6 percent in the fall of 1798, it yielded almost one million rubles in cash plus at least two million rubles more in scrip. The latter, even if discounted 50 percent, represented another million rubles windfall. And, of course, there was the net gain from interest accumulation on all scrip that the Bank held. The premium with its side benefits paid the Bank's administrative costs. We have no idea what those costs were, but we do know that Paul felt the premium could be reduced and applied to the payment of the first year's interest on the contract.[44] However it might be budgeted, the Bank yielded an absolute minimum of two million rubles on the initial loans, and this without including the fees charged, and profits taken, by its exchange and discounting branches. Moreover, it does not include the seven or eight million rubles in interest due at the end of the first nine months. In the first year of operation, the Bank may have been worth as much as fifteen million rubles to the state, and it certainly promised at least ten million rubles, while in future years there was the whole of the principal plus the accumulating interest to anticipate. This gives us some appreciation of why Paul's ministers, personal greed apart, were so enthusiastic about the Bank; it represented a very major increase in receipts for the treasury, and at least the first round more or less collected itself.[45]

The premium on contracts, special fees, and profits on exchange and discount were really the smallest part of the benefit that was expected, since both interest and principal could be accounted as clear profit. This brings us back to the open-ended capitalization provided in the original decree and the point that the Auxiliary Bank envisioned nothing less than transforming the nobles' debts into a continuing source of crown income, a sort of disguised tax. The method used is interesting. Previous land banks had issued their loans in assignats, a circulating currency that, theoretically at any rate, was based on copper reserves, though Catherine abandoned even that pretense in the later years of her reign. Earlier land bank loans were made either from existing state funds or from new issues of paper money. Paul's Bank, however, was organized to function without touching existing or anticipated treasury receipts; there was, in fact, no capital involved at all, and there was no money loaned. "Borrowers" were required to pay interest and a part of the cost of a "loan" in circulating currency, but the "loans" themselves, as we have seen, were made in a pseudo-currency based on the nobles' properties.

In effect, the Bank gave the nobility a means for converting a stipulated value for its properties into negotiable instruments with which the nobles could then pay their debts. For this privilege, the noble paid the government an initial premium plus interest payments and, eventually, "principal" reductions. The noble paid the Bank as if the Bank had actually advanced him money under an agreement secured by his properties, but in practical terms the noble simply paid over to the crown the stipulated value of his pledged lands plus interest. It was as if he was buying property he already occupied, but with no change in his rights over that property. The crown, with literally no investment or risk of any sort, received the nobles' payments. Though less onerous than a flat percentage tax on assessed valuation of property, the Bank plan had a similar effect, and it meant that the state could count both principal and interest as clear revenue.[46]

In the last analysis, the only consistent beneficiary of the Auxiliary Bank was the crown. Private creditors found that they would collect only a fraction of what they were owed since the Bank scrip depreciated in value on issue, and to realize even that value, they had to exchange it. And until the government set up an exchange bank, the Bank scrip was literally valueless. Exchange, however, meant greatly increasing the quantity of assignats in circulation, and that resulted in a further decline of paper money value with a consequent push to inflation. This affected the whole society adversely, and of course reduced the purchasing power of the state's new revenues.

On the other side of the coin, if nobles did discharge some debts, they added others, and as we have seen, the Auxiliary Bank made it necessary to borrow more than it was possible to repay. There were no provisions to control overextension; investigations of borrowers were limited to determining whether the properties presented for mortgage actually existed and whether they were already encumbered.[47] Beyond that, it was assumed that if the lands were there, the owner could pay. Given the way the Bank functioned, it was to the crown's advantage to loan as much as possible, for that meant the largest volume of cash premiums as well as income from principal and interest payments. And if the borrower defaulted, the crown had the power to administer his lands, absorbing all their income until the debt was paid. The crown won on every count. In the unlikely event that the borrower regularized his life, saved his money, and paid all his debts, the state had income and a moral victory. If the borrower failed, the state still had its income. Since land could not be alienated, the property base for the landed gentry remained; but since debt was considered to be a moral obligation, it would be wrong to allow defaulters to enjoy their properties. On the contrary, they were to be punished for their improvidence. Finally, the plan enabled the crown to recover monies previously loaned to the nobility and to establish a program whereby the nobility paid regularly into the state's coffers. Its burden of debt thus became a source of state income.

Paul closed the Bank to further loans in October 1799, with the bland assertion that it had served its purpose. Perhaps it had. At any rate, it receded rapidly from the public view, and there is no indication that he paid much attention to it during the last year and a half of his reign. Under his successor, the Auxiliary Bank was merged with the Land Bank, and though payments continued to come in over the next two decades, the former Bank of Assistance, now the Twenty-five Year Expedition, had only a minor role to play in Russian finance.[48] From every point of view except that of crown revenues, the Bank had been a grotesque failure, while even its value as a revenue producer was marginal, particularly in view of the mischief it caused. Its provisions demanded that the gentry assume an impossible burden of payments, and ultimately the plan contributed to an increased level of gentry debt. Creditors suffered, money values were further eroded, and since it raised a wave of protest from merchants and nobles alike, the Bank even failed to promote that tranquillity of spirit that Paul envisioned as one of its first benefits. Taking the proposal at face value, the Auxiliary Bank was a disaster that actually worsened the conditions it was intended to remedy.

The Bank's failures, however, were by no means its most important features, especially for the historian. In a very poignant way, the Auxiliary

Bank plan epitomized Paul's brief reign and dramatized his tragedy as a ruler. Superficially, the Bank contained praiseworthy ideas and responded to existing problems; yet it suffered from a confusion of goals and an inappropriateness of method that vitiated whatever useful features it might have had. The Auxiliary Bank was presented as a product of the beneficence of an all-powerful, all-seeing tsar who stood at the apex of the social hierarchy and whose responsibility was to serve the whole society. The plan was formulated to help different parts of society recognize their mutual responsibilities while contributing to the welfare of the whole. No group, including the nobility, could claim a predominant interest at the expense of the whole; only the crown had a general social provenance, and the interests of all groups were always subordinate to the crown, which alone acted for the whole society. The composition was, however, hierarchical. It was obvious that the gentry held a special place, and though this class was to be disciplined and subordinated, it was also the plan's focal point, and by extension, the most important segment in society. Symbolically, peasants appeared in the plan only as a measure of land value, and though the claims of private creditors were to be honored, the most the plan promised merchants and artisans was a settlement of their outstanding accounts. Unreliable though the gentry might be, it was the class on which the autocracy had built its position, and it was the class from which Paul expected the most. The Auxiliary Bank was a measure designed to realize those expectations.[49]

Although the Bank as Paul and his advisers proposed it was a technically innovative, even radical measure, its purpose was to buttress the traditional social order while making it more effective. This meant perpetuating and reinforcing an agricultural economy based on serfdom, while squeezing that economy to maintain the court and the army to pay, in effect, for government and security. Unlike the great French monarchs Henry IV and Louis XIV, whom he affected to admire, Paul made no effort to build a political alliance with the nonprivileged classes or the towns. He accepted the proposition that the landed nobility was the tsar's main support, and while he played out all sorts of chivalric fantasies that dramatized the loyalty, commitment, and personal morality that he expected of the aristocracy, he was fully prepared to use the powers he possessed to whip the recalcitrant into line. The Auxiliary Bank was a prime example of the way legislation could be used to discipline, to direct, or even to exploit.

Although Paul I contributed to the rationalization and centralization of the Russian political system, he was neither a social innovator nor a modernizer, and his primary significance lay in his effort to realize and preserve traditional social and political values. Paul was profoundly opposed to the modern spirit, whether manifested in a skeptical and irreverent intellectualism or in the strident demands of new and unrecognized social groups for a place in the political sunlight. Paul always looked backward to find the forms his policies might fulfill, and he postulated a sort of composite golden age that provided him with criteria to guide his judgments. Those judgments, however, were as eccentric as his view of policies was surreal, and the two together reinforced a fundamental political incompetence that persistently turned his best efforts into caricatures of his purposes. It is only when we look at his successors, particularly Nicholas I, and the character of Russian official conservatism, that we realize to what degree Paul embodied attitudes and values fundamental to the post-Revolutionary generation, and that his adventures in absolutism marked a significant reorientation of the autocracy toward preserving the existing social order in place of forcing the pace and direction of social development. Catherine, of course, reacted very strongly to the French Revolution, but she died before that reaction could in any sense become programmatic. Paul, however, started from the proposition that his first responsibility was to maintain order and monarchical legitimacy, thus becoming one of the first of Europe's modern monarchs to build a program on the principle of preserving the past.

NOTES

1 The diplomatic reports of the Austrian and English missions in St. Petersburg present a detailed picture of Paul's first days as emperor and underline his fear of revolution. See especially Cobenzl to Thugut, Haus-, Hof-, und Staatsarchiv, Vienna (hereafter HHSA), Russland II Berichte, Carton 84, No. 72, 25 Nov. 1796; *ibid.,* apostilles 8 and 17; *ibid.,* No. 75, 7 Dec. 1796. Cf. Whitworth to Grenville, Public Record Office, London (hereafter PRO), FO 65/35, No. 57, 18 Nov. 1796; and No. 62, 5 Dec. 1796. For a full analysis of these materials, and a commentary on Paul's political thinking based on them, see Roderick E. McGrew, "A Political Portrait of Paul I from the Austrian and English Diplomatic Archives," *Jahrbücher für Geschichte Osteuropas,* XVIII (n.s.), 4 (Dec. 1970), 503-529. See also S. B. Okun', *Ocherk istorii SSSR: konets XVIII-pervaia chetvert' XIX veka* (Leningrad, 1956), pp. 26-27, 32-45, 49-68. The best study of Paul's reforms is M. V. Klochkov, *Ocherki pravitel'stvennoi deiatel'nosti vremeni Pavla I* (Petrograd, 1916).

2 Paul was not alone in this conviction. Charles Whitworth, the British minister in St. Petersburg, obtained a detailed survey of the Russian government's resources for 1792, on the basis of which he argued that there was sufficient wealth to support the needs of Catherine's government. All that was required was thrift and regularity in administration. He also pointed out that these were precisely the qualitites Russian government lacked. See PRO, FO 65/28, No. 43, Whitworth to Grenville, 10 Aug. 1794 and enclosure. The English reports are particularly valuable on fiscal questions, including Russia's foreign debt, on commercial policies, and on tariff questions. See R. E. McGrew, "A Note on Some European Foreign Office Archives and Russian Domestic History, 1790-1812," *Slavic Review,* XXIII (Sept. 1964), 535-536. The whole thrust of Heinrich F. Storch's monumental work, *Historisch-statistische Gemälde des russischen Reiches,* 6 vols. (Riga and Leipzig, 1797-1802), was to demonstrate the vast wealth available in Russia to show how its exploitation could be improved. Storch, an early theorist of economic development, shifted his stance from one stressing improvement and fulfillment to one of growth and social change in a series of essays written in the first decade of the nineteenth century, and most especially in his *Cours d'économie politique au exposition des principes qui déterminent la prospérité des nations,* 6 vols. (St. Petersburg, 1815).

3 The fiscal situation Paul inherited was critical. Six months before Catherine's death, von Tauenzien, the Prussian representative in St. Petersburg, wrote that the treasury was empty, the pay of soldiers and civil officials alike in arrears, and that money was flowing out of the country to pay off foreign debts. This condition existed despite increased revenues from the newly acquired Polish lands. When Catherine died, the same correspondent noted that the reign of the "immortal" empress, bedecked with the phantoms of glory and greatness, left behind only an unhappy and impoverished state. See V. Gitermann, *Geschichte Russlands,* II (Hamburg, 1949), 296-297. Gitermann points out that the military costs, expenditures on luxuries for court and favorites, and Potemkin's expensive schemes had added a million souls to the number of the unfree, left unsupported paper money to the amount of 150 million rubles in circulation, and pushed the foreign debt to the level of 50 million rubles. For a detailed discussion, see N. D. Chechulin, *Ocherki po istorii russkikh finansov v tsarstvovanie Ekateriny II* (St. Petersburg, 1906). A recent technical study of the fiscal problem treating the middle years of the eighteenth

century, including the first part of Catherine's reign, is S. M. Troitskii, *Finansovaia politika russkogo absoliutizma v XVIII veke* (Moscow, 1966). For the administrative aspect of Paul's fiscal program, see Klochkov, *Ocherki, passim,* and especially pp. 127-129, 224-270. Fiscal administration was the responsibility of the procurator general's office. A small direct tax on the nobility was introduced to finance functions carried on by the provincial Nobles' Assemblies. See *Polnoe sobranie zakonov Rossiiskoi imperii,* Series I, 30 vols. (St. Petersburg, 1830), XXIV, No. 18278. Count Dietrichstein summarized the fiscal reforms and estimated that increased taxes, new levies, higher fees, and improved administration would yield additional income up to 36,640,000 rubles. Dietrichstein did not include anticipated income from the Auxiliary Bank for the Nobility. His estimate, of which he was skeptical, was based on projections furnished by the government and represented a 33 percent increase over previous income. HHSA, Russ. II Ber. 87, Dietrichstein to Thugut, No. 6, apostille 8, 29 Jan. 1798.

4 *Polnoe sobranie zakonov,* I, XXIV, No. 18274. See also *Manifeste de la banque d'hypothèque établie pour la noblesse* (St. Petersburg, 1798). The administrative regulations for the Bank appeared in February 1798. See *Polnoe sobranie zakonov,* I, XXV, No. 18383. See also *Règlemente de la banque impériale d'hypothèque établie pour la noblesse* (St. Petersburg, 1798). The *Manifeste* and *Règlemente* were circulated and were the form on which contemporaries based their judgments. The copies which I used were filed with Whitworth's correspondence in the Public Record Office. There is no substantive (or substantial) difference between the materials published in 1798 and those reproduced four decades later in *Polnoe sobranie zakonov*.

5 The most detailed analysis of the Bank is S. Ia. Borovoi, "Vspomogatel'nyi bank," *Istoricheskie zapiski*, 44 (1953), 206-230. See especially n. 2, p. 206, for a list of Borovoi's work on banking and credit problems, for a summary of gentry credit problems and government responses, see Jerome Blum, *Lord and Peasant in Russia from the Ninth to the Nineteenth Century* (Princeton, 1961), pp. 379-385. See also M. Confino, *Domaines et seigneurs en Russie vers la fin du XVIIIe siècle* (Paris, 1963), for a very full and perceptive analysis of the domainal economy, especially pp. 136-183. Borovoi argues that the Bank worked against mercantile and commercial interests while subsidizing the landed nobility. Where Borovoi sees this last as the whole of the Bank's function, however, I argue that the intention of the Bank was to discipline the nobility, to strengthen the crown, and to enlarge state revenues. Borovoi presents the Bank as one more cynical grab by the great nobility, represented by Prince Kurakin, at the expense of a complacent and compliant crown. This view, in my opinion, is simplistic, misleading, and only reflects one aspect of the evidence.

6 See Confino, *Domaines et seigneurs.* The same author's *Systèmes agraires et progrès agricole: l'assolement triennal en Russie aux XVIIIe-XIXe siècles* (Paris and The Hague, 1969) presents a brilliant analysis of the reasons for resistance to innovation and the lack of developmental thrust in the agricultural economy. Change, however, did take place, as Confino's own data show, and his work should be compared with I. D. Koval'chenko, *Russkoe krepostnoe krest'ianstvo v pervoi polovine XIX v.* (Moscow, 1967), which develops the thesis of change moving into crisis in the 1830s and 1840s.

7 Borovoi, "Vspomogatel'nyi bank," pp. 207-210; Blum, *Lord and Peasant,* pp. 379-385. See also Confino, *Domaines et seigneurs,* especially pp. 136-183.

8 See Borovoi and Blum; also PRO, FO 65/28, Whitworth to Grenville, No. 43, 10 Aug. 1794.

9 Borovoi, "Vspomogatel'nyi bank," p. 211. Borovoi sees Kurakin as the initiator of the Bank, a position that fits with the view that the Bank was designed to benefit the great serfholders. While Kurakin apparently did draft the proposals, there is no positive evidence to establish him as the originator of the Bank.

10 The contemporary evidence is overwhelming that Voud played this role. See Viazzoli memo, HHSA, Russ. II Ber. 87 (filed with) No. 6, 29 Jan. 1798: "it is Voute [*sic*] who has furnished the plan for the afore-mentioned Bank"; Dietrichstein to Thugut, apostille 1 (cipher), 1 Feb. 1798, which remarks on Voud's role in considering revisions of the original statute; and Carton 88, No. 11, 27 Feb. 1798, for further confirmation. Writing some years after the event, Baron H. F. Storch, the political economist and imperial tutor, clearly identified Voud as the originator of the plan, though not by name. See *Cours d'économie politique,* IV, 35. See also Count S. R. Vorontsov to Count A. R. Vorontsov, 4/15 Mar. 1799, *Arkhiv kniazia Vorontsova,* X (Moscow, 1876), 41-42, in which Count S. R. Vorontsov speaks of protesting to Hope and Company about Voud. See Karl Ludwig Blum, *Ein russischer Staatsmann: des Grafen Jakob*

Johann Sievers Denkwürdigkeiten zur Geschichte Russlands, 4 vols. (Leipzig and Heidelberg, 1857-1858). Sievers worked closely with Mariia Fedorovna on problems of the domestic economy, including canal building. Paul was too busy to be involved. See, for example, *ibid.,* IV, 413-419, for a survey of canals reported to the empress and her reply of 26 Apr. 1798, p. 421. Sievers was very much involved in promoting economic growth and capitalist principles; his career deserves closer study.

11 HHSA,Russ. II Ber. 87, Dietrichstein to Thugut, No. 6, apostille 1 (cipher) 29 Jan. 1798; Carton 88, No. 7, 1 Feb. 1798. See also Count S. R. Vorontsov to Count A. R. Vorontsov, Dec. 1802, No. 58, *Arkhiv kniazia Vorontsova,* VIII, 185; *ibid.,* No. 41, 18 Apr. 1799, pp. 206-207.

12 Stockholm Riksarkivet, Diplomatica Muscovitica, vol. 459, Stedingk to king, 19/30 Mar. 1798 (apostille). Stedingk also reported that Voud extracted one million rubles from Hope and Company as his price for establishing this arrangement. Dietrichstein reported that Voud was buying up huge quantities of nobles' loans at discount which he planned to collect when the Bank went into operation. Voud, of course, would have had no problem in exchanging scrip for assignats. The Hope and Company archives, which have not been available, would be invaluable for studying this particular period. Borovoi, "Vspomogatel'nyi bank," makes no mention of any of these factors, none of which fit the schemata of his analysis, and further confirmation or elucidation will have to wait for Soviet archival finds or the Hope Company archives. The ideal, of course, would be to have both.

13 Viazzoli memo, HHSA, Russ. II Ber. 87 (filed with) No. 6, 29 Jan. 1798. Cf. Count [P. V.] Zavadovskii [to the Vorontsovs], No. 122, 23 Dec. 1797, *Arkhiv kniazia Vorontsova,* XII, 190.

14 *Polnoe sobranie zakonov,* I, XXIV, No. 18274, p. 823; *Manifeste* (Preamble). The translation has been made from the Russian text compared with the French; the use of capitals follows the French text.

15 Article 39.

16 Article 1; Borovoi, "Vspomogatel'nyi bank," p. 212.

17 Articles 2, 7, 20.

18 Article 37. In the *Règlamente,* article 37, this power shifted to the governor of the province. This provision, of course, was only effective against debtors who had land and serfs; other measures, including debtors' prison, dealt with the landless, but this was not discussed in the Auxiliary Bank proposal.

19 See article 11.

20 *Polnoe sobranie zakonov,* I, XXIV, No. 18274, article 11, p. 825 and appendix G, p. 831, cover the repayment schedule and include a tabular presentation from which the examples given in the text were taken.

21 See articles 30 and 31. The idea that even a defaulter would retain possession (though not use) of the hereditary lands reflected the tsar's determination to stabilize the gentry's social position.

22 See article 28.

23 See Preamble and article 29.

24 Articles 5-16 deal with Bank certificates. Validating certificates are exemplified in annexes D, E, and Z. *Polnoe sobranie zakonov,* I, XXIV, 831-833. *Règlamente* provides supplementary detail on handling notes.

25 Article 31. Cf. *Règlamente* for procedures.

26 The classes and *gubernii* are given in appendix B as follows: Class I: Riazan'; Iaroslavl'; Kostroma; Tula; Kaluga; Vladimir; Simbirsk; Orel; Kursk; Tambov; Voronezh; Viatka; Nizhegorod; Kazan'; Saratov. Class II: Moscow; Tver'; Smolensk; Astrakhan'. Class III: Pskov; Vologda; St. Petersburg; Tobolsk; Orenburg; Minsk; Slobodsko-Ukraine; Novorossiia; Belorussia; Kiev; Podol'ia; Malorossiia; Litovsk; Volynia; Voisko Donskago. Class IV: Perm'; Arkhangel'sk; Irkutsk; Novgorod. For a tabular picture of the number of peasants pledged from each *guberniia,* see Borovoi, "Vspomogatel'nyi bank," p. 221.

27 See especially Confino, *Domaines et seigneurs* and *Systèmes agraires* for this point. Blum, *Lord and Peasant,* gives a more traditional view; see especially pp. 384-385.

28 Average *obrok* is obviously a very inexact concept, but it does provide a guideline. Borovoi, "Vspomogatel'nyi bank," p. 215, cites Semevskii's data as providing the six-ruble figure for yearly *obrok* in the period 1790-1800. Semevskii himself suggested five rubles as the yearly quit-rent at the end of Catherine's reign, but he also noted that *obrok* was rising. V. I. Semevskii, *Krest'ianskii vopros v tsarstvovanie Imperatritsy Ekateriny II,* (St. Petersburg, 1903), 52-53;

detailed data are given in appendix 9, pp. 593-595. See Blum, *Lord and Peasant,* pp. 367-385, for a description of the economic status of the gentry. Only a very few of the richest nobles had a large enough income to pay off their debts under Paul's plan. Once the loans were made, only failure to enforce the rules would save the borrowers. We have no idea whether and how Paul would have done this since he died before the plan's long-range implications could come into play. Previous land banks or gentry loan plans simply had not attempted to collect what was owed them. Paul obviously had no intention of letting the loans go unpaid, but implementing his plan was another matter. Contemporaries, however, felt the threat. Dietrichstein reported that some shrewd spirits were selling properties to pay debts rather than suffer the consequences of a forced Bank loan; others went to usurers to get the needed money. HHSA, Russ. II Ber. 87, No. 6, apostille 1, 29 Jan. 1798. Earlier he referred to the plan as literally encompassing the economic ruin of the gentry. *Ibid.,* No. 1, 22 Dec./2 Jan. 1797/1798.

29 On public reactions to Paul's fiscal proposals, see HHSA, Russ. II Ber. 84, Cobenzl to Thugut, No. 72, apostille 15, 25 Nov. 1796; Carton 87, Dietrichstein to Thugut, No. 1 (cipher) 22 Dec./2 Jan. 1797/1798 and annex; No. 3, 29 Dec./9 Jan. 1797/1798; and especially No. 5, apostille 1 (cipher), 29 Jan. 1798. See also Consul General (for economic affairs) Viazzoli's special memorandum, 29 Jan. 1798, filed with Dietrichstein to Thugut, No. 6. Cf. PRO, FO 65/38, Whitworth to Grenville, No. 64 ("Most Secret and Confidential"), 14 Dec. 1797; FO 65/39, Whitworth to Grenville, No. 68, 9 Jan. 1798. See also HHSA, Russ. II Ber. 88, Dietrichstein to Thugut (cipher), No. 7, 1 Feb. 1798; No. 10, 23 Feb. 1798; No. 11, 27 Feb. 1798; No. 12, 2 Mar. 1798, for reports on revision plans. No. 61, 14 Nov. 1798, reports the reforms and includes a copy of the Manifesto of 25 Oct. 1798, which revised the plan.

30 *Polnoe sobranie zakonov,* I, XXV, No. 18718, 25 Oct. 1798, p. 424.

31 See HHSA, Russ. II Ber. 87, annex to No. 1, 22 Dec./2 Jan. 1797/1798.

32 *Ibid.,* No. 1 (cipher), Dietrichstein to Thugut, 22 Dec./2 Jan. 1797/1798.

33 Decree of 25 Oct. 1798, *Polnoe sobranie zakonov,* I, XXV, No. 18718, articles 1,2.

34 This point is discussed in detail below.

35 Borovoi, "Vspomogatel'nyi bank," describes the plan's failures and abuses, particularly those of the gentry. The *Règlamente (Polnoe sobranie zakonov,* I, XXV, No. 18383) is an essay in bureaucratic formalism with attention given to a host of particular details. These are interlarded with exhortations to administrators and gentry alike.

36 Borovoi, "Vspomogatel'nyi bank," pp. 217-227; cf. Blum, *Lord and Peasant.*

37 In this, as in other matters, Paul was inclined to go too far, especially when his sympathies were engaged. So, for example, he accepted the principle that Russia was responsible for obligations contracted by Poland. Once he accepted the principle he allowed no compromises, taking on not only those debts Poland owed to recognized banking houses, but accepting as well Russia's responsibility to fulfill the subsidies and return the income on land promised to the Polish *langue* of the Knights of Malta. Here Paul not only accepted the obligation, he actually tripled the amount the knights were to receive. See M. J. Rouët de Journel, S.J., *Nonciatures de Russie d'après des documents authentiques, I, Nonciature de Litta, 1797-1799: Studi e Testi,* 167 (Vatican City, 1943). See especially the introduction to the documents. When the émigré community became troublesome, and Louis XVIII's court too expensive, Paul tried to cut loose, but again the sense of obligation intervened, though continued expenditures on the émigrés were draining the treasury. See, for example, Stockholm Riksarkivet, Dipl. Musc. vol. 459, Stedingk to king, apostille 23 July/3 Aug. 1798, in which Stedingk reports Paul's dilemmas with Louis XVIII and the question of a regular pension. Paul placed primary stress on the moral issue; what was owed had to be paid, regardless of the sacrifices it might entail. This attitude was quite different from Catherine's, and it reflected that respect for contracts and agreements the lack of which Alexander Gerschenkron considers a major reason for Russia's failure to develop economically. On the other hand, it was integral to Paul's entire personal philosophy, reflecting his fundamental commitment to duty as the moral mainspring for man in society, and it was in no sense given any special economic significance.

38 See Blum, *Lord and Peasant*, p. 384.

39 See article 28.

40 *Polnoe sobranie zakonov,* I, XXIV, 831-833, articles 5-16; annexes D, E, and Z. See also *Règlemente* for administrative detail.

41 The position is explained clearly and with precision in H. F. Storch, *Cours d'économie politique,* VI, 35-41. Cf. Dietrichstein and Viazzoli.

42 See Borovoi, "Vspomogatel'nyi bank," pp. 224 ff.; E. Amburger, *Geschichte der Behördenorganisation Russlands von Peter dem Grossen bis 1917* (Leiden, 1966), p. 212. See also Storch, Viazzoli, and Dietrichstein. For publicity on reduction of assignats, see HHSA, Russ. II Ber. 84, No. 78, Cobenzl to Thugut, 18 Dec. 1796; No. 72, apostilles 11 and 15, 25 Nov. 1796.

43 Article 11. See above.

44 *Polnoe sobranie zakonov,* I, XXV, No. 18718. 25 Oct. 1798.

45 See Borovoi, "Vspomogatel'nyi bank," pp. 218 ff., for a discussion of who received loans, the amounts involved, and the repayments.

46 Contemporaries understood only part of all this, and even the critical assessments cited above missed the finer points of the plan. Baron Storch identified the Bank scrip as promissory notes and explained the limits on its value (see above), and the conviction was general that debtors and creditors alike would suffer. The main fears voiced, however, were that the scrip would fall in value from the moment of issue while the repayment schedules would absorb available cash income. Beyond this, the point was regularly made that only the state would benefit from the plan, while society would have to bear the burden. The forced loan idea was considered especially onerous. There were charges that the bank was not at all what it appeared to be, but no one specifically identified it as a taxing instrument, though Dietrichstein recognized the differences between this plan and the preceding ones, and notes especially the shift from circulating currency to scrip. See above, n. 29, especially HHSA, Russ. II Ber. 87, Dietrichstein to Thugut, No. 6, apostille 1, 29 Jan. 1798 and Viazzoli memo.

47 The *Règlamente* dealt with methods and procedures of valuation and validation.

48 See Borovoi, "Vspomogatel'nyi bank," pp. 223-227.

49 Paul viewed the nobility as an essential element of society, but what he hoped to promote was a dedicated, loyal, service-oriented class that would be an ornament of the monarchy and its main support. He was also convinced, however, that the nobility had developed a dangerous independence of outlook and action. It was this that he intended to curb. In conversation with Stedingk he pointed out that the main difference between southern and northern Europe was that in the south the people were rebellious and the nobility loyal; in the north, especially in Russia and Sweden, the nobles threatened the monarchies' stability, while the common people were loyal. This comment came when Paul was urging Stedingk to use a Russian army to quiet alleged popular disturbances in Swedish Finland. Stockholm Riksarkivet, Diplomatica Muscovitica, vol. 464, Stedingk to king, 30 Mar./11 Apr. 1800. Paul's fear of the great nobility stood in marked contrast to his sympathy, calmness, and courage when dealing with ordinary people, and when the peasants revolted, Paul, as he told Count Cobenzl, believed it was because they had been inspired to do so by educated influential courtiers determined to wrong him. See HHSA, Russ. II Ber. 84, No. 10, Cobenzl to Thugut, 17 Feb. 1797. See also McGrew, "Political Portrait," pp. 511-515. This does not mean, however, that Paul intended to destroy the nobility, or that his reign did for Russia what the Revolution did for France. This exaggerated view appears in V. Zubow, *Zar Paul I: Mensch und Schicksal* (Stuttgart, 1963); see especially pp. 40-41. Kliuchevskii was closer to the point when he emphasized that Paul saw the law as written for everybody, not simply to underwrite the privileges of a particular class, and that he intended to bring the nobles under the law. V. O. Kliuchevskii, *Kurs russkoi istorii,* in *Sochineniia v vos'mi tomakh,* V (Moscow, 1959), 236-237. Cf. notes to Lecture LXXXII, *ibid.,* pp. 437-441; and *ibid.,* p. 190. Klochkov, *Ocherki,* follows a similar line of reasoning, identifying Paul with enlightened absolutism and the development of rationalization, centralization, and administrative efficiency. What is missing in these interpretations is an appreciation of the importance Paul attached to the nobility, and the spirit he hoped to inculcate among its members.

8

THE POLITICS OF ASSASSINATION

James J. Kenney, Jr.

"Politics is the science of how who gets what, when and why."
—Sidney Hillman

"Modern politics is, at bottom, a struggle not of men but of forces."
—Henry Adams

For over one hundred years it was officially maintained in Russia that the Emperor Paul died in his bed, suddenly but naturally, during the night of 11-12 March 1801. The manner of his death was not, however, a secret to those who made it their business to know about such things. Many more or less accurate accounts of Paul's murder circulated in Russia long into the reign of his son and successor, Alexander, and foreign diplomats naturally collected and reported these stories to their home governments.[1] Moreover, some of those involved directly in the successful assassination plot either dictated or put into writing their versions of what had happened on that fateful night. Thus, authoritative descriptions of the murder spread, and actually appeared in print in western Europe, as early as 1819.[2]

The fact of Paul's murder, then, and the manner in which it was committed have never been much of a mystery, if we overlook some minor contradictions and inconsistencies in the versions that have come down to us. All of them agree that the assassination plot, effectively a coup d'état in the name of Grand Duke Alexander, was engineered by Count P. A. Pahlen, military governor of St. Petersburg and, since February 1801, head of the College of Foreign Affairs and director of the Post. Pahlen acted with the knowledge and approval of the grand duke, and with the assistance of Prince Platon Zubov and his brothers, Counts Nikolai and Valerian. The Zubovs, powerful figures at the court of the late Empress Catherine, were banished from the capital during most of Paul's reign but were recalled in December 1800 to receive the rank of senator along with comfortable sinecures at court. The commandants of the aristocratic guards regiments were initiated into the conspiracy against the tsar, as were many officers of these regiments and several regimental adjutants.[3] A key figure on the night of the murder was General L. L. Bennigsen, a Hanoverian in the Russian service, who was initiated into the conspiracy by Pahlen on the eve of the assassination. The conspirators chose to act on a night when regimental units favorable to the grand duke were on duty at the Michael Palace, the tsar's new residence. After fortifying themselves with drink, the officers positioned themselves around the palace, while a party including Bennigsen and two of the Zubovs proceeded to force their way into the emperor's bedchamber. Several accounts identify Nikolai Zubov, who had the reputation of a bully and a coward, as the man who first struck the hapless emperor. Paul was then beaten and strangled to death by the very men who were sworn to defend him.

After the murder, Grand Duke Alexander was summoned from his chambers on the floor below. Flanked by Pahlen and Prince Zubov, he accepted oaths of allegiance from the units of the guard there present. The sullen if not hostile attitude of the enlisted men in the regiments is noted by several accounts. The new emperor then retired to the Winter Palace, taking with him the other members of the imperial family, including his somewhat hysterical mother, Mariia Fedorovna. Bennigsen was left in command of the Michael Palace. Within a few hours, the oath of allegiance to the new emperor had been successfully administered to all the important military and civil functionaries in the capital. There was no resistance once it was understood that Paul was truly dead, and Paul himself was the only casualty of the coup d'état.[4]

Traditionally, the causes of Paul's assassination have been found in both his domestic and foreign policies. Most memoirists and historians have stressed the despotic character of his reign, the capriciousness and folly of his administration, the brutality of his treatment of his officers, and the danger that was assumed to threaten the members of the imperial family from this unpredictable, suspicious man.[5] Prince Adam Czartoryski wrote of a "reign of terror" and stated that virtually the entire politically conscious population of Russia was "more or less" convinced that Paul was mad. He claimed to have seen "universal aversion" to Paul as far back as the autumn of 1799. Only hesitation on the part of Grand Duke Alexander prevented Russian statesmen from acting earlier to secure the removal, but not necessarily the murder, of Tsar Paul. Czartoryski described the efforts of Vice-Chancellor N. P. Panin (banished in December 1800) and Count Pahlen, "the two best heads in Paul's Council," to persuade the grand duke to sanction a coup in his name. Alexander withheld his consent for more than six months until, convinced that immediate danger threatened his brother and himself, he allowed the coup to proceed. But Czartoryski also felt it necessary to explain why it was that the Russian nobles, who had endured so many other despots, resolved to act against Paul. "A sovereign can do many wrongs without exposing himself to death," he explained. "But when the sovereign authority weighs at every moment on each individual . . . and continually disturbs the peace of families, passions are excited which are more formidable. . . . This was the real motive of Paul's assassination."[6]

The manner in which foreign policy was conducted aroused suspicions that Paul was incapable of governing rationally and that Russia's peace and well-being depended on his removal.[7] The international situation was unsettled, and war threatened Russia as a result of Paul's abrupt reversal of foreign policy in 1800. The previous year, Paul had been an ardent supporter of the coalition of anti-French powers. Allied with Great Britain, Austria, and the Ottoman Empire, Russian forces had helped to drive the French out of Italy, liberating the Adriatic and threatening for a time to carry the war into France itself. Then a series of military setbacks, coupled with quarrels with his allies over the administration of occupied territories and the fate of the fortress island of Malta, led Paul to consider a different policy. Concluding that he had been the dupe of the Austrians and the English, Paul expelled the ambassadors of these powers from his capital in May 1800. Eventually, he revived the idea of a league of Baltic powers to challenge Britain's supremacy on the seas. In the autumn, an embargo was laid on trade with Britain; British ships were seized in Russian waters, and their crews were incarcerated. In November, Paul accepted as the basis of his new policy a memorandum submitted by Count F. V. Rostopchin, acting head of the College of Foreign Affairs. Rostopchin urged Paul to seek a rapprochement with the French as a counterweight to the British and to consider the possibility of partitioning the territories of the Ottoman Empire.[8] But even without waiting for this new negotiation to bear fruit, Paul ordered a Cossack army under General V. P. Orlov to march against the British in India.[9] In March 1801, a British fleet entered the Baltic and subjected Copenhagen to a fearful bombardment. Only the news that Paul was dead and that his successor wished to prevent hostilities saved St. Petersburg from a similar fate.[10] It is no wonder, then, that many contemporaries, including the French first consul, Napoleon Bonaparte, believed that the British government and pro-British factions in St. Petersburg were behind the assassination of the tsar.[11]

Thus the traditional explanations present the view that Paul's administration was irregular, an aberration in the course of Russian history that resulted logically, if not inevitably, in regicide.[12] The assassination is regarded as an antidote to the emperor's madness, a method of restoring Catherinian normalcy. But is this view justified? The results of recent reappraisals of the reign of Paul suggest not only that Paul's basic policies were rational but also that they set the style and foreshadowed developments in the nineteenth century. Must we not then reconsider the politics of Paul's assassination?[13] If the assassination was not the instrument for setting right a reign that had gone awry, what was it? We must try to answer this question by looking, not, as previously, at Emperor Paul, but rather at those who conspired against him.

First, let us establish who the conspirators were. Using the memoirs of the participants themselves and of men like Czartoryski and Fonvizin who collected information directly from the participants, it is possible to list the names of sixty-eight Russians who took part in the conspiracy against Tsar Paul. (This is, of course, but a fraction of the total number, according to Sablukov and others.[14]) Standard Russian reference works contain quite a lot of information about these people, thus permitting us to answer basic questions concerning age, rank, and branch of service and sometimes to infer the existence of personal motivations and connections among the conspirators known to us. This information is shown in Table 1.[15]

TABLE 1

The Conspirators Against Paul

Name	*Age*	*Rank & Regiment*	*Connection with Zubovs*	*Other Connections*	*Personal Grievance*	*Punished by Alexander*
A. V. Argamakov	(20s)	lieut., Preobrazh.	-	brother	-	-
P. V. Argamakov	(20s)	lieut., Preobrazh.	-	brother	-	-
A. M. Belosel'skii	49	Senator	-	favorite of Paul	?	-
L. L. Bennigsen	56	general, infantry	service	Pahlen	-	temporarily
(N. I.) Bibikov	(30s)	colonel, Izmail.	-	-	-	-
D. N. Bolgovskii	(30s)	captain, Izmail.	-	Speranskii, later	-	possibly
N. M. Borozdin	24	general-maior, Kavaler.	by marriage	-	-	no
Chertkov	(30s)	guards ?	-	-	-	-
P. A. Chicherin	23	lieut., Horse	-	-	yes	-
L. I. Depreradovich	35	general, commandant of Semenov.	-	-	-	no
P. P. Dolgorukov	24	general-maior, ADC of Izmail.	-	Alexander	-	no
Efimovich	(20s)	lieut., Semenov.	-	-	-	-
(V. I.) Filat'ev	(20s)	kornet, Horse	-	-	-	no
P. V. Golenishchev-Kutuzov	29	general-maior, commandant of Hussars	-	-	-	no
B. A. Golitsyn	35	general-lieut., Horse	-	-	forcibly retired in 1800	-
V. F. Gorbatov	(20s)	lieut., Kavaler.	-	-	-	-
E. S. Gordanov	24	ADC of Kavaler.	-	Alexander	-	yes

TABLE 1 (*cont'd.*)

Name	*Age*	*Rank & Regiment*	*Connection with Zubovs*	*Other Connections*	*Personal Grievance*	*Punished by Alexander*
I. S. Gorgoli	31	major, guards ?	-	-	-	no
I. F. Iankovich-de-Mirievo	(30s)	colonel, commandant of Horse	-	son of one of Catherine's favorites	-	no
V. M. Iashvil'	37	colonel, Horse	-	-	yes	yes
P. N. Ivashev	(30s)	-	-	former ADC to Suvorov; father of Decembrist	possibly	-
Ivashkin	(20s)	sublieut., Semenov.	-	-	-	-
Karpovskii	-	-	-	-	-	-
A. Z. Khitrovo	25	Horse	-	Alexander; brother	forcibly retired in 1799	no
N. Z. Khitrovo	(20s)	Horse	-	Alexander; brother; later, Speranskii	-	possibly
P. A. Kikin	26	Semenov.	-	Alexander	-	no
A. F. Klokachev	32	commander, imperial fleet	-	-	-	no
D. S. Kositskii	-	-	uncle	-	-	-
A. P. Kutuzov	24	lieut., Izmail.	-	-	forced into active service	no
Leont'ev	(20s)	lieut., Preobrazh.	-	-	-	-
V. A. Mansurov	35	colonel, Izmail.	-	-	-	-
S. N. Marin	25	lieut., Preobrazh.	-	-	-	-
A. N. Mordvinov	19	lieut., Izmail.	-	brother	father retired in 1796	-
D. N. Mordvinov	16	lieut., Izmail.	-	brother	"	-

TABLE 1 (*cont'd.*)

Name	*Age*	*Rank & Regiment*	*Connection with Zubovs*	*Other Connections*	*Personal Grievance*	*Punished by Alexander*
I. N. Mordvinov	18	lieut., Izmail.	-	brother	"	-
N. M. Murav'ev	44	Senator	-	former tutor to Alexander; father of Decembrists	-	no
Orlov	-	-	-	-	-	-
P. A. Pahlen	56	general, military governor	service connection	Bennigsen	yes	yes
N. P. Panin	31	former vice-chancellor	-	Alexander	-	yes
Pisarev	(20s)	lieut., Semenov.	-	-	-	-
K. M. Poltoratskii	19	lieut., Semenov.	-	father a favorite of Catherine; Alexander	-	no
O. M. Ribas	51	admiral	service connection	-	yes	died, 1800
G. V. Rozen	19	shtabs kapitan, Preobrazh.	-	-	-	no
Savel'ev	(20s)	lieut., Semenov.	-	Panin's cousin?	-	-
V. N. Shensin	17	lieut., Izmail.	-	-	-	no
Ia. F. Skariatin	(20s)	shtabs kapitan,	-	-	-	probably
A. I. Talyzin	(30s)	captain, Izmail.	-	-	-	no
P. A. Talyzin	34	general, commandant of Preobrazh.	-	-	yes	died, 1801
(I. M.) Tatarinov	(20s)	lieut., Kavaler.	-	Alexander	yes	no
N. V. Titov	(20s)	Kavaler.	-	-	-	-
P. A. Tolstoi	32	general-lieut., Semenov.	-	Alexander	-	no

TABLE 1 (*cont'd.*)

Name	*Age*	*Rank & Regiment*	*Connection with Zubovs*	*Other Connections*	*Personal Grievance*	*Punished by Alexander*
D. P. Troshchinskii	47	Senator	-	Vorontsovs	-	no
P. A. Tuchkov	25	-	-	-	-	-
Ushakov	-	commandant of "Senate" battalion	-	-	-	-
N. V. Ushakov	(20s)	lieut., Kavaler.	-	Alexander	-	possibly
F. P. Uvarov	28	general, commandant of Kavaler.	yes	favorite of Paul	yes	-
Vederevskii	(30s)	commandant of Keksgol'm regiment	-	-	-	-
Viazemskii	(30s)	commander of 4th battalion, Preobrazh.	-	-	-	-
Viazemskii	-	captain, Izmail	-	-	-	-
Viazemskii	-	Semenov.	-	-	-	-
I. I. Vilde	-	-	-	-	-	-
P. M. Volkonskii	25	ADC of Semenov.	-	Alexander	-	no
N. A. Zagriazhskii	55	Court Master	-	friend of Mariia Fed.	possibly	no
Zapol'skii	(30s)	colonel, Preobrazh.	-	-	-	-
O. A. Zherebtsova	25	-	sister	Whitworth	yes	no
N. A. Zubov	38	Senator	yes	brother	yes	yes
P. A. Zubov	34	Senator	yes	brother	yes	yes
V. A. Zubov	30	Senator	yes	brother	yes	no

As Table 1 indicates, significant information is available for about 75 percent of the names on the list, leaving us with only seventeen men about whom little or nothing is known. We can determine the rank and position of fifty-eight of the conspirators (85 percent of those known to us) as of the time of the assassination. The ages of thirty-eight (56 percent) of the persons on the list have been definitely determined, while approximate ages for another twenty-four individuals (35 percent) can be reasonably inferred from other data (e.g. rank, or ages of siblings).

The conspirators ranged in age from sixteen to fifty-six. Over 40 percent of those whose ages can be determined were under thirty years of age, including six officers and subofficers who were still in their teens. Some of these men were hardly more than children when the Empress Catherine died; many of them began their active service after 1797, when Paul decreed that all sons of noblemen who had passed the age of majority (sixteen) must begin active service. Although they could not have been motivated by actual memories of better days under Catherine, it is possible that they were influenced by the contrast between the harsh reality of service under Paul and an idealized version of life under Catherine. It should also be noted that the men in this age group were roughly the contemporaries of Grand Duke Alexander and may have been motivated by the hope of better opportunities under a new, young tsar than they could expect under Paul, who came to the throne already surrounded by middle-aged *Gatchintsy*.

At the same time, the data confirm that the largest single bloc of conspirators consisted of men between the ages of thirty and forty. The men in this age group were the contemporaries of the Zubov brothers, and like them, they had been in the service during the final years of the reign of Catherine. Such men might well have been influenced, at least in part, by reminiscences of her "golden" rule. Conspicuous by their absence are men between the ages of forty and fifty (there are only three). This age corresponds, of course, to the age of the Emperor Paul and many of his favorites. Lastly, there were four conspirators, among them Pahlen and Bennigsen, who were over fifty years of age. These men were old enough to remember not only the reign of Catherine, but also the coup d'état that put her on the throne.

A breakdown of the conspirators by occupation is also interesting. It is no surprise to learn that over two thirds of the persons listed were members of the aristocratic guards regiments. The disposition of the military in the capital, especially of the guards, had proved to be absolutely crucial at every change of reigns since the death of Peter the Great. The distribution of the conspirators among these regiments was remarkably even: the list shows eight in the Preobrazhenskii, ten in the Semenovskii, twelve in the Izmailovskii, seven in the Horse Guards, and seven in the newly formed Cavalier Guards. The commandant of the Leib Kompaniia of Hussars is also on the list. In addition to these guardsmen, there were five conspirators in other branches of the military: two in honor regiments that were not officially part of the guard, two in the navy, and one (Bennigsen) in the regular army. It is most significant that eleven civilians (16 percent of the total) are known to have participated in the conspiracy. This number includes six senators (three of them Zubovs). Also included here are the men who were the acknowledged initiators of the plot,

Panin and Pahlen,[16] as well as key bureaucrats such as D. P. Troshchinskii. The participation of a sizable group of nonmilitary men is one of the factors that distinguishes the coup of 1801 from its eighteenth-century predecessors and suggests a resemblance between this conspiracy and the later one of the Decembrists.

The remaining columns on the table represent an attempt to indicate the answers to questions of personal connections, influences, and private motives among the conspirators. It is difficult to generalize about such highly individualistic data. Without doing too much violence to the facts, one can say that there was a close relationship between Grand Duke Alexander and twelve of the conspirators on the list. There are also two striking examples of what must be termed the blackest ingratitude: Belosel'skii and Uvarov were close personal favorites of the Emperor Paul who betrayed his friendship. At least one of the conspirators (Zagriazhskii) was a close friend of the Empress Mariia Fedorovna and may have been motivated by a desire to protect her interests (it was rumored that Paul intended to put her away in favor of his new mistress, Gagarina). On the other hand, Zagriazhskii may have become involved because of the disfavor into which his wife, *née* Nataliia Razumovskaia, had fallen, along with her young friend, Viktor Kochubei. At least ten of the conspirators were linked to the Zubov family, either by blood or through their careers in the army. There are indications that sixteen of the conspirators held personal grievances against Tsar Paul, either because he had insulted them publicly (e.g., Iashvil') or because he had interrupted their careers with banishment or demotion (the Zubovs, Golitsyn, Khitrovo). It is interesting, though perhaps irrelevant, that two of the conspirators against Paul sired future Decembrists (Ivashev and Murav'ev). Two others were later linked with the reformer Michael Speranskii and shared his disgrace (Bolgovskii and Khitrovo). Finally, it should be noted that the Emperor Alexander was remarkably lenient to those who conspired against their lawful sovereign. Only seven of the conspirators can definitely be said to have suffered some form of punishment or discouragement in their later careers, although there may have been others. However, the later careers of most of the conspirators show absolutely no sign of persecution or punishment.

The table contains some of the oldest and most distinguished names in Russian history. There are Rurikovichi and Gediminovichi such as Dolgorukov and Golitsyn; and those with post-Petrine titles, such as Count Tolstoi and Baron Rozen. There is also a Georgian prince, Iashvil'. Many ancient but untitled Muscovite families are represented: Khitrovo, Murav'ev, Kutuzov. A number of eighteenth-century parvenus appear: for example, Ribas, Poltoratskii, and Iankovich-de-Mirievo. Finally, there are the Germans, Pahlen and Bennigsen. In short, the list is a fairly complete microcosm of the eighteenth-century Russian aristocracy, which is exactly what we would expect to find in the guards regiments, the Senate, and high government offices. Socially, the conspirators formed a homogeneous group drawn from the highest layer of Russian society. There is no reason to posit any significant divergence of motives based on social origin.

What we do not know, of course, is the nature of the relationship between these aristocratic conspirators and the majority of soldiers and servitors who composed the bulk of Russian officialdom. By analogy with other coups in Russian history, especially with that of 1730, we would suspect that there was no important link between the conspirators and the lesser gentry. Presumably, the aristocrats acted on the basis of their own knowledge and experience, and there is no reason to think that their views were representative of the *dvorianstvo* as a whole. The memoir literature contains some information to support this hypothesis. Sablukov, who was himself rather cool toward the conspirators, told of an enlisted man in the Horse Guards who shrugged his shoulders at the announcement of the change of sovereigns, with the remark, "Kto ni pop, tot i bat'ka." Czartoryski expressly excluded the "lower ranks" when speaking of the widespread sympathy for the conspirators.[17]

To date, only a few attempts have been made to investigate political attitudes among the lesser gentry during the reign of Paul. Utilizing material from the archives of Paul's Secret Chancery, T. G. Snytko examined a group of "Jacobins" among army officers in the Smolensk district whose complaints about Paul's military reforms came to the attention of the central authorities in 1799.[18] Led by A. M. Kakhovskii the group, numbering about a dozen, discussed the possibility of armed rebellion and tried unsuccessfully to win the support of Field Marshal A. P. Suvorov (who was known to be an opponent of Paul's "Prussian" reforms in the army). To the chagrin of the emperor's zealous prosecutors, all attempts to establish a connection between this group of dissidents and the Zubov brothers, who were then living on their estates in western Russia, failed. The leaders of the group were imprisoned but were eventually freed upon the accession of Alexander.[19]

Another Soviet historian, O. S. Gvinchidze, investigated the case of the Gruzinov brothers, guardsmen who were demoted and sent to serve in a Don Cossack regiment in 1800. Since they continued to stir up trouble, they were eventually tried by a military court and executed for advocating rebellion against the tsar.[20] Gvinchidze uses the records of the court and the "confessions" of the prisoners in an attempt to show that the political consciousness of the men was well developed and included a number of "republican" concepts, such as the idea of popular sovereignty.

Both Snytko and Gvinchidze make a distinction in principle between the conspiracy of 1801 and earlier palace revolutions, noting that the conspiracy against Paul was not the result of personal motivations, but of an organization that "expressed the feelings of broader strata of the *dvorianstvo* and urban population."[21] Both historians profess to see divisions among the conspirators between "republicans," like N. I. Bibikov, who is reported to have "demanded" the extermination of the entire imperial family; "constitutionalists," including Panin, Pahlen, and Zubov; and "absolutists," who were animated by mere personal hatred of Tsar Paul and wished to replace him with another autocrat.[22] As Snytko notes, distinctions of this type look forward to the Decembrist revolt a generation later.[23] However, we must observe that these categorizations rest on very little solid evidence. Even if we accept the reporting of Bibikov's words as accurate, his remarks may be ascribed to the extravagance of drink. There is no other indication of republicanism among the conspirators. The constitutionalism of Panin is problematical. He left no drafts or projects of any sort of constitution; it is noteworthy that he also played no role whatsoever in the reformist movement at the beginning of the reign of Alexander. Likewise, in the statements attributed to Pahlen there is no mention of constitutionalism. We will consider the case of Zubov presently. Much more work needs to be done on the political consciousness of the Russian *dvorianstvo* before we can challenge Count Stroganov's harsh assessment of this class as "the most ignorant, dull-witted, and insignificant" in Russia.[24]

As to the conspirators on our list, we repeat that there is no solid evidence of any division in principle among them. Most of them remain mere names to us, useful thus far only to the extent that they allow us to compile a few shaky statistics. Certainly there must have been among them men of intelligence who could articulate their views and explain their reasons for participating in the conspiracy. N. A. Sablukov, an officer in the Horse Guards whose memoirs constitute one of our most important sources, was a man similar in many respects to the men who made up the conspiracy. Sablukov in fact knew most of the conspirators and surmised much concerning the plot, which he refused to join out of a strong sense of commitment to his oath of allegiance.[25] Perhaps we will yet see the appearance from some forgotten archive of the memoirs of one of those guardsmen who decided to break his oath to Tsar Paul. Meanwhile, it is premature to speak of grouping these aristocrats into "republicans," "constitutionalists," and "absolutists."

We are on much firmer ground when we speak of the hatred of the aristocracy as a whole for the Emperor Paul. The memoir literature is full of the complaints of members of this class against Paul's violations of the Charter of the Nobility, his interference in their private lives, and restrictions imposed on their right to travel abroad and to import goods from western Europe.[26] Many aristocrats fled from St. Petersburg to the comparative safety of Moscow, or else sought refuge in the capitals and *Kurorten* of Europe. Count Dietrichstein, an Austrian observer, noted Paul's "mania for issuing orders and prohibitions." The Russians, he explained, either had to "get used to everything, even blows of the *baton,*" or else "leave as soon as they can."[27]

It was indeed Paul's intent to destroy what he viewed as the harmful and counterproductive pretensions of the aristocracy. Whereas his predecessor Catherine had held that the Russian nobles could be Europeanized by a slow process combining education with government inducements, Paul believed only force could compel the nobles to accept the concepts of honor and duty. He condemned equally the swinish recalcitrance of the provincial nobility and the selfish indulgence of the aristocracy. All must shoulder the burden of responsibility to the state. He also believed in the efficacy of administrative reform. Therefore, he ignored the Charter of the Nobility and willingly violated any of its provisions that stood in the way of his reforms or hampered his efforts to inculcate what he believed to be the real sense of *noblesse oblige* among his nobles.[28]

As an enlightened ruler, Paul wished to promote the well-being of all classes of society, including the peasantry. Although far from embracing the concept of egalitarianism, Paul recognized the debt owed to these producing members of society, and he clearly intended for his justice to filter down through all classes. In particular, he wished to prevent the peasants from being exploited grotesquely or abused by their lords. His famous law limiting *barshchina* to three days a week, although unenforceable in practice, served notice on the nobles that the state reserved the right to intervene in the landlord-peasant relationship in the interest of social harmony and justice.[29]

The Russian aristocrats, however, missed the point of Paul's social policy. The blows of the *baton* were more apparent to them than the emperor's concern for social justice. The erratic and uneven enforcement of Paul's policies no doubt obscured many of their positive qualities.[30] Baron S. A. Korf, writing shortly before the First World War, was persuaded that this was the primary problem of Paul's reign, for which, however, he blamed the emperor personally. "No one knew for sure what tomorrow was preparing for him; Russia as a whole knew not what awaited her tomorrow. Precisely this, more than anything else, led to Paul's downfall in the end."[31]

Nowhere was the aristocrats' concern more evident than in the area of foreign policy. If Paul's domestic policies were regarded as confused and potentially damaging, his foreign policy came to be considered by many aristocrats as utterly ruinous for Russia. Thus, as Fonvizin noted, the conspiracy against Paul was for many a "truly patriotic affair" (*istinno-patrioticheskoe delo).*[32]

Paul's foreign policy was not always viewed in such a bad light, and the reasons for the change tell us something about the origins of the conspiracy against him. At the commencement of his reign, Paul followed both the inclination of his conscience and the practical advice of experienced statesmen like A. A. Bezborodko, adopting a policy of temporary withdrawal from Transcaucasia and neutrality in Europe. Although this course disappointed the Zubovs and other advocates of Russian expansion, as well as proponents of counterrevolution like Count S. R. Vorontsov, the Anglophile minister to London, the policy had the support of many who understood the precarious state of Russian finances and the need for military reform.[33] But even while observing neutrality in the affairs of Europe, Paul refused at first to deal with the representatives of the regicide government of France, thus giving hope to Vorontsov and like-minded aristocrats that he would eventually take an active role in the counterrevolutionary cause.[34] His decision in 1798 to enter the Second Coalition against France seemed to justify their expectations.

From the point of view of Vorontsov, Panin and other Francophobes, the real trouble began with the death of Prince Bezborodko in the spring of 1799. This misfortune deprived Russia of "the only Minister who could permit himself the slightest contradiction vis-à-vis the Emperor."[35] Count Rostopchin, who succeeded Bezborodko as head of the College of Foreign Affairs, was bitterly criticized for cooling Paul's ardor for the anti-French coalition and for encouraging him to break with England and Austria and seek an accomodation with France.[36] Count Panin could scarcely find words to express his disgust for Rostopchin, whom he called a "très mauvais fils," who sought high office only for the sake of enriching himself. He considered Emperor Paul and Rostopchin together "capable of anything, the one because of fits of passion (*emportement*), the other because of renunciation of all principle."[37] Thus, the incompetent tsar was linked with an evil and unscrupulous adviser. Count Vorontsov curtly informed his friend Lord Grenville, the

British foreign secretary, "Back home, everything is decided by passion and violence."[38]

Vorontsov was disturbed not merely by the change in Russian foreign policy, which he considered wrong, but also by the abrupt manner in which this change was announced. The Emperor Paul simply did not bother to prepare the world for his about-face in foreign policy in the spring of 1800. As late as February, Panin and Vorontsov, to say nothing of the courts of London and Vienna, still hoped to open an new campaign against the French with Russian assistance. Suddenly came word that the emperor had requested the recall of the English and Austrian ambassadors. Sir Charles Whitworth, the English minister, warned his government that "the Emperor is literally not in his senses."[39] Vorontsov confessed to Grenville that he was "weary of serving a court which behaves in such a strange manner. I cannot publicly find fault with it, but I will never have the baseness to defend it." He later remarked that he was in despair over the "more than bizarre manner" in which Paul treated foreign affairs and that he was "ashamed and humiliated by our diplomacy."[40] This attitude was shared by many of the conspirators.

Thus it was no accident that Count Panin, whose duties as vice-chancellor brought him into daily contact with the representatives of foreign powers, was the first Russian statesman to approach Grand Duke Alexander with a proposal to remove Paul from power.[41] Paul's misconduct of foreign policy was simply one folly too many. In a letter to Vorontsov, Panin "protested solemnly" against Russia's withdrawal from the coalition. He dissociated himself from the policy of rupture with the courts of London and Vienna, and "from all acts relative to the Order of Malta," which he believed to be "extremely damaging" to Russian interests.[42] Like Vorontsov, Panin felt that the question of further Russian expansion must recede before the question of the Revolution, which Russia was duty-bound to destroy, "that in so doing we might raise ourselves to the highest degree of glory and power."[43] Panin did not regard himself as betraying his oath to the Emperor Paul; his higher obligation was to Russia, which he saw threatened by the activities of an insane tsar. Vorontsov stated this view plainly in a famous letter to N. N. Novosil'tsov, a friend and confidant of Grand Duke Alexander. He compared Russia to a ship whose captain had gone mad and whose only hope lay in the prompt, responsible action of the ship's second-in-command, "a nice, intelligent young man in whom the crew has confidence."[44] Elsewhere, Vorontsov expressed the view that Paul's policies might well "plunge Russia into popular revolt, producing millions of Stenka Razins and Pugachevs."[45] To these conservative aristocrats, a policy of accommodation with France was not merely a blunder, but a direct threat to their social order. From their point of view, the very attempt to reach such an accomodation was criminal—whether or not it succeeded.

Vorontsov was only peripherally connected with the conspiracy against Paul, but Panin approached Grand Duke Alexander with a plan to declare Paul incompetent and to establish a regency. It is quite possible that Panin acted with the knowledge and encouragment of his friend, Lord Whitworth.[46] In any event, Alexander hesitated to approve this plan. It was necessary for Alexander to be persuaded that his own life was threatened by Paul, as well as the lives of his brother and mother, before he would give his consent and, even then, only on condition that his father's life be spared.[47] But by this time, the emperor had brought Russia to the brink of war with England, and the Francophobe Panin had been banished from the capital. The conspiracy against Paul was now directed by Count P. A. Pahlen, newly appointed to the College of Foreign Affairs and the grand duke's associate as military governor of St. Petersburg.

According to the account of the conspiracy that he later gave Count Langeron, Pahlen's primary concern was to preserve the peace, "to save Russia, perhaps also Europe, from a bloody and inevitable Time of Troubles."[48] However, in his version of the story of the assassination, this latter-day Cincinnatus exaggerated his part and presented his actions as being more deliberate and systematic than they probably were. Without even mentioning Panin, Pahlen said that he took it upon himself to persuade Grand Duke Alexander of the necessity of a coup d'état. He took steps to secure the return of the Zubovs and the participation of Bennigsen. Finally, he used his power as military governor, director of the Post, and acting head of the College of Foreign Affairs to make Paul's orders and *ukazy* appear even more arbitrary and eccentric than they were.[49] Indeed, it would be difficult to imagine how the conspiracy could have succeeded without the assistance of the man who controlled the key departments of the secret police, the postal service, and the garrison of the city of St. Petersburg. But at the same time, it is preposterous to attribute to Pahlen power as great as he claimed to have. The conspiracy was not initiated by him, nor was he responsible for the support that it enjoyed. Pahlen, a Baltic German, could play an important role only insofar as he was sustained by ties among the Russian aristocracy. The days of Empress Anna and her Germans had long since been repudiated by the native Russian reaction under Empress Elizabeth.

Pahlen had long been a friend and supporter of the Zubov family. Originally a member of Potemkin's entourage, Pahlen had found a new protector in Platon Zubov, whose ascendancy over the aging empress knew practically no bounds in the last years of her reign. Pahlen was associated with the vigorous annexationist policy that the Zubovs proposed at the expense of Poland. He became the first Russian governor general of the province of Courland in 1795.[50] He even acknowledged his gratitude toward Prince Zubov when, as governor general, he gave a magnificent reception to the fallen potentate in Mitau, through which Zubov was passing on his way to his estates. Because of this uncalled-for display of partisanship, Pahlen was dismissed from his post by Paul in the spring of 1797.

As often happened during Paul's reign, the chastised victim was received back into the service.[51] Within a year, Pahlen rose from commandant of the Horse Guards (Zubov's old regiment) to general of cavalry. In 1799, he became military governor of St. Petersburg. There is some indication that Pahlen participated in the first discussions of deposing Paul, beginning as early as the autumn of 1799. He shared Panin's alarm at the precipitous break with England, though not necessarily for the same reasons.[52] There is no reason to doubt that Pahlen used his influence to help arrange for the return of the Zubovs from banishment, as he claimed.[53] As a non-Russian, whose ties to the Russian aristocracy were largely professional, Pahlen could not really hope to lead the conspiracy himself. He needed the Zubovs to recruit enough supporters to attempt a coup d'état.

The Zubov brothers were then the key members of the conspiracy against Paul. They possessed the name, rank, and social and political connections among the guards and the civilian aristocracy that Pahlen lacked. They were associated popularly with the Empress Catherine, the policy of expansion of the Russian Empire, the guards regiments (especially the Horse and Cavalier Guards), and the idea of noble privilege. One encounters them or their relations at every stage of the conspiracy, from the first days when the conspirators met at the home of Ol'ga Zherebtsova to consider the possibility of a regency, to the night of the murder, and afterwards. According to Sablukov, the Zubov brothers organized the social gatherings at which officers of the guard were initiated into the conspiracy and at which the plan of action was discussed.[54] Two of the brothers, Nikolai and Platon, were among those present at the scene of the murder, while Count Valerian accompanied Pahlen and his regiment to the Michael Palace. Both Platon and Valerian Zubov were appointed to Emperor Alexander's new State Council and played a prominent role in the politics of the new reign.[55]

The activities of the Zubovs and other aristocrats during the first months of the reign of Alexander were a logical continuation of their participation in the conspiracy against Paul. One of their chief concerns was foreign policy. The Zubovs were energetic opponents of intervention in Europe; instead, they vigorously supported a policy of Russian expansion in the Caucasus.[56] They abhorred the policy of war with Britain because they had a use for Orlov's Cossacks closer to home. Count Valerian, who had previously commanded the army in the Caucasus, hoped to resume that command, and busied himself with projects relating to the annexation of Georgia and Russian commercial penetration of the Caspian region and Persia. Although his projects were accepted in principle by Alexander and his "Unofficial Committee," they felt that Zubov was not the appropriate man to be entrusted with the task of conquering and adminstering Transcaucasia.[57] Georgia was indeed annexed, but Zubov was denied the opportunity to serve in the army. He remained a respected but powerless member of the State Council until his death in 1804.

Meanwhile, Prince Platon Zubov was one of several senators and members of the State Council who took an active part in the consideration of legal and administrative reform at the beginning of Alexander's reign. Many aristocrats were optimistic that the time had come to place Russia's autocratic system of government on a sound legal footing. The new tsar had agreed, although reluctantly, to confirm the Charter of the Nobility that had been so flagrantly violated by his father. But Alexander was extremely suspicous of the aristocracy, whom he regarded as the selfish and short-sighted enemies of reason and progress.[58] By playing off one group of aristocrats against another, he and his Unofficial Committee succeeded during the first year and a half of his reign in emasculating every proposed reform that would have placed limits on his autocratic powers. The aristocrats, in turn, considered a variety of safeguards to protect themselves from the recurrence of an Emperor Paul, centering on the administrative and legislative power of the Governing

Senate, the idea of "fundamental laws," and the role of the Senate as "guardian" of the laws.

Senate reform and the related notion of a "Charter to the Russian People," a kind of Magna Carta, stood at the heart of the aristocratic reaction during the first year of Alexander's reign. Several projects for senatorial reform have come down to us, along with notes of discussions of these projects by the Unofficial Committee and the State Council.[59] The most important projects were submitted by members of the Vorontsov circle: the brothers Counts Alexander and Semen and Count P. A. Zavadovskii. They all stressed the ancient and honorable character of the institution, the authority it had enjoyed under its founder, Peter the Great, and the necessity of selecting senators of the highest moral and intellectual caliber. They were careful to put forth the theory that power emanates from the sovereign, but only via lawful institutions such as the Senate and the State Council. It was clearly their intention that the Senate should serve as a bulwark against despotism, an idea that the young tsar found offensive, and to which he reacted with hostility. In particular, their projects all reserved to the Senate the "right of remonstrance" *(pravo predstavleniia),* according to which the Senate would have the right and even the obligation to protest any legislation that stood in contradiction to existing laws (such as the Charter of the Nobility) or that might, in their view, prove harmful to the interests of the state.[60]

Of the conspirators, only P. A. Zubov submitted a proposal for Senate reform. Unfortunately, it has not survived, the notes made by the Unofficial Committee being the only indication of its character. Zubov apparently did not speak of the need to curb despotism and so avoided the mistake of antagonizing the young tsar. His project called for a clear division of power between executive and judicial branches of government, presumably by vesting the latter powers entirely in the Senate. It is not clear what legislative powers, if any, the Senate would receive. At first, Tsar Alexander showed some warmth for this project, which he considered to be more than just another example of aristocratic pretension. However, in the end his friends succeeded in dissuading him from permitting any division of powers that would imply a diminution of his own power.[61]

The most striking feature of all these projects is their political conservatism, bordering on naïveté. The aristocrats could not accept the notion of popular sovereignty and went out of their way to avoid any taint of revolutionary doctrine. Even so staid a concept as Montesquieu's balance of power was suspect and incompletely developed in the Russian context. They were left with the idea of a *Rechtstaat,* a state in which power emanating from the crown would be directed along legal channels and the Senate, as guardian of the laws, would protect the interests of their class and those of the society at large. In order to work, their scheme required that the tsar be surrounded by the proper ministers. As Count Semen Vorontsov put it, what was needed were men who would not be afraid to say, even to the brother of the tsar, "Monseigneur, what you propose is contrary to the good, and I will not stand for it."[62] One of the most grievous sins of the Emperor Paul had been precisely that he had surrounded himself with creatures who were not influenced by the collective wisdom of the aristocracy.

Although they could all agree in principle on the need for "good men" to govern Russia, the aristocrats failed to reach agreement among themselves as to who these good men were. Neither Panin nor Vorontsov lifted a finger to protest the dismissal of Count Pahlen, whom the emperor dismissed at the first opportunity. They too felt that there was something not quite right about this German schemer, who was, moreover, a supporter of their rivals, the Zubovs. Moreover, Panin and the Vorontsovs were soon locked in a bitter feud, ostensibly over issues of foreign policy, but really over the question of who was going to be the tsar's chief adviser on foreign policy. Both parties did their best to ruin the other in the sight of the emperor and the court. Unable to overcome the tsar's suspicion because of the role he had played in initiating the conspiracy against Paul, Panin fell victim to an intrigue led by the Vorontsovs. He was dismissed from the post of vice-chancellor in October 1801.[63] In precisely the same way, the aristocrats undermined each other's senatorial reform projects. Alexander's strategy of *divide et impera* worked only too well. Novosil'tsov in the Unofficial Committee administered the coup de grâce to A. R. Vorontsov's proposed Charter to the Russian People, with its dangerous and inconvenient implications of limits on the power of the autocrat.[64] For all intents and purposes, this ended the aristocratic reaction against the autocracy that had cost Emperor Paul his life. Alexander was crowned in Moscow with all the ancient powers and prerogatives of the tsars intact.

The conspiracy against Paul was essentially an aristocratic revolt against the policy of centralization by an "enlightened" despot. The issue was not really whether or not the tsar was mad; the fact is that Paul's domestic and foreign policies were interpreted by the aristocrats as being hostile to their interests, and hence, in their view, contrary to the interests of their country. The tsar's madness was merely a convenient pretext to justify deposing him in the hope that his successor would be more compatible with their way of thinking. As far as we know, no other segments of the population were involved in the assassination. Indeed, the attempts at reform under Alexander struck no responsive chord in the population at large, not even among the *dvorianstvo*. The conspiracy was organized by aristocrats like Panin, who believed that Paul was betraying the just cause of conservative Europe. It matured through the participation of aristocrats like the Zubovs, identified by their fellows with the historic policies of Catherine the Great, i.e., the recognition of noble privilege and foreign expansion. It was carried out by the armed representatives of the aristocracy, the officers of the guards regiments. There is as yet no evidence of important political divergences among the conspirators and no evidence that their views were shared by the lesser gentry.

Although it succeeded in bringing about a change of rulers and helped to avert an unnecessary and potentially disastrous war with Great Britain, the conspiracy must be judged a failure in its larger aim of winning real political freedom and power for the Russian aristocracy. The aristocracy was too small in proportion to the bulk of Russian servitors who felt they still had something to gain from supporting the autocracy. The aristocrats were too suspicious of each other and not sufficiently aware of a common purpose to succeed in the difficult task of wresting political power from the tsar. One by one, they succumbed to the power of the autocrat. Their failure set an unfortunate precedent for future political reforms in Russia and left less room for compromise in the great political struggles of the next century.

NOTES

1 For example, the reports of Viazzoli to Count Trautmansdorf, Haus-, Hof-, und Staatsarchiv, Vienna (hereafter HHSA), Russland II Berichte, Carton 95, 22 Mar. 1801; Locatelli to Trautmansdorf, *ibid.*, No. 16, 27 Mar. 1801; Prince Schwarzenberg to Trautmansdorf, *ibid.*, No. 2, apostille 1, 9 July 1801; and the report of St. Helens to Lord Hawkesbury, Public Record Office, London (hereafter PRO), FO 65/48, 31 May 1801.

2 For a full discussion of these sources, see Leo Loewensen, "The Death of Paul I (1801) and the Memoirs of Count Bennigsen," *Slavonic and East European Review,* XXIX (1950), 212-232. Bennigsen left at least three distinct versions of the assassination. Bennigsen and Zubov told their stories to Major Ernst Wedell in 1812; Pahlen and Zubov had earlier recounted the story to Count Langeron in 1804. Both these versions are conveniently printed in the anonymous volume entitled *Tsareubiistvo 11 marta 1801 g.: zapiski uchastnikov i sovremennikov,* 2nd ed. (St. Petersburg, 1908). This volume also includes the memoirs of N. A. Sablukov, A. N. Veliaminov-Zernov, and August Kotzebue, with excerpts from the memoirs of Adam Czartoryski, Princess Lieven, Baron Heyking, and M. A. Fonvizin. Some of these materials were published earlier by Theodor Schiemann, *Zur Geschichte der Regierung Paul I und Nikolaus,* 2nd ed. (Berlin, 1906).

3 In addition to the Preobrazhenskii, Semenovskii, and Izmailovskii guards regiments, there were in Paul's day the Horse Guards, the Cavalier Guards (formed in 1800 out of the Horse Guards), the Leib Kompaniia of Hussars and Jägers, and a number of honor regiments that were not officially considered part of the guards.

4 This summary closely follows the accounts of the conspiracy and assassination related by Czartoryski, *Memoirs of Prince Adam Czartoryski and his Correspondence with Alexander I,* I (London, 1888), 222-255; Kazimierz Waliszewski, *Paul the First of Russia* (London, 1913), pp. 410-472; and Valentin Zubow, *Zar Paul I* (Stuttgart, 1963), pp. 159-227.

5 See the accounts given by Wedell, *Tsareubiistvo,* p. 162; Langeron, *Tsareubiistvo,* p. 178; Bennigsen, in his letter to Fock, *Historische vierteljahrschrift* (1901), p. 60; and Princess Lieven in Schiemann, *Zur Geschichte,* pp. 35-40.

6 Czartoryski, *Memoirs,* I, 228-233.

7 Standard treatments of Paul's foreign policy are Dmitrii Miliutin, *Istoriia voiny 1799 goda v tsarstvovanie imperatora Pavla I,* 5 vols. (St. Petersburg, 1852-1853) and Waliszewski, *Paul the First,* pp. 291-378. An excellent reassessment of this policy is done by Hugh Ragsdale, "Was Paul Bonaparte's Fool?: The Evidence of the Danish and Swedish Archives," *Canadian-American Slavic Studies,* VII, (Spring 1973), 52-67 (a revised version is published in this volume). Although Russian historians have, on the whole, tended to play down the significance of foreign affairs in the conspiracy against Paul, the anonymous preface to a posthumous article by S. B. Okun', "Dvortsovyi perevorot 1801 goda v dorevoliutsionnoi literature," *Voprosy istorii,* 1973, No. 11, p. 34, states that the conspiracy was the result of a combination of aristocratic interests and the activity of English agents and pro-English Russians.

8 Rostopchin's memorandum is printed in *Russkii arkhiv,* 1878, pp. 103-110.

9 On this episode, see Norman E. Saul, *Russia and the Mediterranean, 1797-1807* (Chicago, 1970), pp. 149-150. Princess Lieven makes the interesting comment that one of the conspirators, on bursting into Paul's room, cried "Où sont les Cosaques?" See her account in Schiemann, *Zur Geschichte,* p. 43.

10 That the Russians were extremely worried about the presence of an English fleet off their shores can be seen in the official instructions sent Count Vorontsov in London, published in *Arkhiv kniazia Vorontsova,* X (St. Petersburg, 1876), dated 6 Apr. and 2 May 1801. Lord Hawkesbury's instructions to St. Helens, PRO, FO 65/48, 30 Apr. 1801 were firm: the Russians must agree to make restitution to all Englishmen who had suffered from the seizure of their property, and they must either cancel the new Convention of Armed Neutrality which Paul had signed in December or sign an agreement stipulating that they recognized the right of a belligerent to seize enemy goods carried on neutral ships. Otherwise, St. Helens was to declare his mission terminated. Admiral Pavel Chichagov, who handled the preliminary negotiations with the English Admiral Parker, told Emperor Alexander that he considered the capital "indefensible under current conditions." (See his letter to Count Vorontsov, 12 May 1801, *Arkhiv kniazia Vorontsova,* XIX, 39-41.)

11 *Le Moniteur,* quoted in M. A. Thiers, *History of the Consulate and the Empire under Napoleon I,* II (London, 1845), 246; see also Napoleon's remarks cited in Waliszewski, *Paul the First,* p. 371.

12 For a good review of this bias in the historical literature, see Okun', "Dvortsovyi perevorot."

13 In addition to the article by Ragsdale, see also J. L. H. Keep, "Paul I and the Militarization of Government," *Canadian-American Slavic Studies,* VII (Spring 1973), 1-14; and R. E. McGrew, "The Politics of Absolutism: Paul I and the Bank of Assistance for the Nobility," *ibid.,* pp. 15-38 (both reprinted in this volume).

14 Sablukov, in *Tsareubiistvo,* p. 87, claims that there were about 180 men involved. Fonvizin, who entered the guards in 1803, collected names of 37 conspirators from his fellow officers; *ibid.,* pp. 201-202.

15 My table is based on a slightly amended version of the list of conspirators given by Zubow, *Zar Paul,* pp. 314-315. Biographical data were compiled from the *Russkii biograficheskii slovar',* 25 vols. (St. Petersburg, 1896-1918); the Brokgauz-Efron *Entsiklopedicheskii slovar',* 43 vols. (St. Petersburg, 1890-1907); and the standard genealogical reference works by P. V. Dolgorukov, *Rossiiskaia rodoslovnaia kniga,* 4 vols. (St. Petersburg, 1854-1857), N. Ikonnikov, *La noblesse de Russie: éléments pour servir à la reconstitution des registres généalogiques de la noblesse russe,* 51 vols., 2nd ed. (Paris, 1957-1966), and V. V. Rummel' and V. V. Golubtsov, *Rodoslovnyi sbornik russkikh dvorianskikh familii,* 2 vols. (St. Petersburg, 1886-1887). This compilation involved numerous difficulties. First, the memoirists who furnished the names were of different degrees of reliability. Often, they gave only a last name. They did not always indicate an officer's rank or regiment. Typical of the problems encountered is the case of the name "Prince Viazemskii." Fonvizin mentions a *general-maior* by that name, commander of the 4th battalion of the Preobrazhenskii Guards. Bennigsen mentions an officer by that name in the Semenovskii Regiment. Kotzebue says that a Prince Viazemskii, colonel in the Izmailovskii Regiment, was one of those present at the scene of the murder. Unable to resolve these discrepancies, I have listed three persons by that name on my table.

Another difficulty involved determining correct first name and patronymic or initials. In the case of Bibikov, for example, a Soviet historian gives N. I. as the proper initials (T. G. Snytko, "Novye materialy po istorii obshchestvennogo dvizheniia kontsa XVIII veka," *Voprosy istorii,* 1952, No. 9, p. 121). However, none of the genealogical sources I consulted list such a person. Ikonnikov, *La noblesse de Russie,* tome "B1," pp. 15-21, offers only two possibilities, V. I. and B. I. Bibikov, brothers in the Horse Guards during the reign of Paul. Where I have been unable to determine the correct initials with certitude, I have indicated them in parentheses. I have also indicated approximate ages in parentheses.

16 Pahlen, of course, was the military governor of St. Petersburg. His authority extended over several military forces in the city, but his duties also included many that we would regard as primarily civilian today. The distinction between military and civilian in tsarist Russia was always somewhat arbitrary. I prefer to list Pahlen among the civilians because his affinities were more with high government officials than with the military men in the War College.

17 Sablukov, *Tsareubiistvo,* p. 85; Czartoryski, *Memoirs,* I, 243.

18 Snytko, "Novye materialy," pp. 111-122.

19 *Ibid.,* p. 121.

20 O. S. Gvinchidze, *Brat'ia Gruzinovy* (Tbilisi, 1965).

21 Snytko, "Novye materialy," p. 121.

22 *Ibid.*; also Gvinchidze, *Brat'ia Gruzinovy,* pp. 47-49.

23 Snytko, "Novye materialy," p. 122.

24 Grand Duke Nikolai Mikhailovich, *Le Comte Paul Stroganov,* II (Paris, 1905), 61-62.

25 Sablukov resorted to a bit of "*iezuitstvo*" to rationalize his decision to keep quiet about his suspicions. See *Tsareubiistvo,* pp. 70-71.

26 See M.V. Klochkov, *Ocherki pravitel'stvennoi deiatel'nosti vremeni Pavla I* (Petrograd, 1916), pp. 1-46, for a discussion of the memoir literature and its bias.

27 Dietrichstein to Thugut, HHSA, Russ. II Ber. 87, No. 14, apostille, 2, 23 Mar. 1798; also No. 18, 18 Apr. 1798.

28 See Baron S. F. Korf, "Pavel i dvorianstvo," *Golos minuvshego,* No. 7 (1913), pp. 5-18; cf. Klochkov, *Ocherki,* pp. 501 ff.

29 For a discussion of Paul's policy with regard to the peasants, see Klochkov, *Ocherki,* p. 583 ff.

30 Among those who noted Paul's positive characteristics were Sablukov, *Tsareubiistvo,* pp. 14-17, and Princess Lieven, *Zur Geschichte,* pp. 37-38.

31 Korf, "Pavel i dvorianstvo," p. 6.

32 Fonvizin, *Tsareubiistvo,* p. 205.

33 See Klochkov, *Ocherki,* pp. 284-293. The reports of the English agent William Eton, PRO, FO 65/35, to Hammond, 21 Dec. 1796, and to Grenville, 21 Dec. 1796, are an interesting confirmation, from a party who had reason to argue the reverse, that Russia's financial affairs were in a parlous state and that Paul's military reforms were sorely needed.

34 See the letter of Count Semen Vorontsov to Lord Grenville, dated 9 Jan. 1797, in the Dropmore MSS recently acquired by the British Museum. When I examined these papers, they had not yet been assigned Additional Manuscript numbers. However, each letter is readily identifiable by its date. (A report on the collection of which these letters were once a part was published by the Historical Manuscript Commission—*Report on the Manuscripts of J. B. Fortescue preserved at Dropmore,* [London, 1892-1927.] 10 vols. Also Whitworth to Grenville, PRO, FO 65/35, No. 59, 22 Nov. 1796.

35 Cobenzl to Thugut, HHSA, Russ. II Ber. 91, No. 25, apostille 9, 7 Apr. 1799. Compare Czartoryski's statement about Bezborodko, *Memoirs,* I, 194.

36 Whitworth to Grenville, PRO, FO 65/44, No. 94, 10 Oct. 1799, and FO 65/45, No. 102, 13 Nov. 1799. See also the letters of Panin to Vorontsov, 4 Oct. 1799, *Arkhiv kniazia Vorontsova,* XI, 93, and 3 Nov. 1799, *ibid.,* XI, 96-97.

37 Panin to Vorontsov, 20 Apr. 1800, *Arkhiv kniazia Vorontsova,* XI, 110-114.

38 Vorontsov to Grenville, Dropmore MSS, 19 Nov. 1799.

39 Whitworth to Grenville, PRO, FO 65/46, No. 17, 18 Mar. 1800.

40 Vorontsov to Grenville, Dropmore MSS, 27 Apr. and 27 June 1800.

41 Czartoryski, *Memoirs,* I, 228-231.

42 Panin to Vorontsov, 20 Apr. 1800, *Arkhiv kniazia Vorontsova,* XI, 110-114.

43 *Ibid.*

44 Vorontsov to Novosil'tsov, 5 Feb. 1801, *ibid.,* XI, 380-381.

45 Vorontsov to Panin, 16 Apr. 1801, in Alexander Brückner, ed., *Materialy dlia zhizneopisaniia Grafa N. P. Panina,* VI (St. Petersburg, 1892), 423-425.

46 For more discussion of this point, see my article "Lord Whitworth and the Conspiracy against Tsar Paul: the New Evidence of the Kent Archive," *Slavic Review,* XXXVI (June 1977), 205-219.

47 Czartoryski, *Memoirs,* I, 231.

48 Pahlen (as reported by Langeron), *Tsareubiistvo,* p. 178.

49 *Ibid.,* pp. 178-182. Pahlen's version is accepted by the playwright Dmitrii Merezhkovskii in his play, *Smert' Pavla Pervago.* See Okun', "Dvortsovyi perevorot," p. 48.

50 These and other details of Pahlen's career are taken from *Russkii biograficheskii slovar',* XIII, 138-139.

51 Among those who experienced similar reversals in their careers, we can mention Suvorov, Rostopchin, Bennigsen, and, of course, the Zubovs. The same applies to several of the conspirators on my table.

52 See the letter of Pahlen to Lord Whitworth dated 26 May 1800, printed in my "Lord Whitworth and the Conspiracy," pp. 205-219. In his desire to avert war with Great Britain, Pahlen may have been motivated by desires similar to those of the Zubovs, i. e., he may have desired mere neutrality, not alliance with England against France.

53 Pahlen (as reported by Langeron), *Tsareubiistvo,* p. 182. The report of Locatelli to Trautmansdorf, HHSA, Russ. II Ber. 95, No. 19, apostille 9, 7 May 1801, says that Kutaisov, Paul's favorite, was bribed through the agency of his mistress, Mme. Chevalier, to bring about the return of the Zubovs. See also Shumigorskii, *Imperator Pavel I, zhizn' i tsarstvovanie* (St. Petersburg, 1907), pp. 195-196.

54 Sablukov, *Tsareubiistvo,* p. 69.

55 *Arkhiv Gosudarstvennago soveta,* III (St. Petersburg, 1878), 5. Locatelli to Trautmansdorf, HHSA, Russ. II Ber. 95, No. 16, 27 Mar. 1801, identifies the Zubovs as the most powerful men in the new government.

56 See the long monograph on Zubov by "P. P.," "Kniaz' Platon Zubov," *Russkaia starina,* XVII (1876), especially pp. 691-693. Foreign diplomats frequently referred to the Zubovs as proponents of neutrality in the wars of Europe and of Russian expansion in Transcaucasia. For example, see Cobenzl to Thugut, HHSA, Russ. II Ber. 82, Nos. 66 and 67, 16 and 24 Nov. 1795; and Whitworth to Grenville, PRO, FO 65/33, No. 7, 20 Jan. 1796.

57 See the memoir by V. A. Zubov on trade with Asia, *Russkii arkhiv,* 1873, pp. 879-894. On the annexation of Georgia, see *Vneshniaia politika Rossii XIX i nachala XX veka,* I (Moscow, 1960), 24-26; and the protocol of the session of the Unofficial Committee for 13 Aug. 1801, in *Le Comte Paul Stroganov,* II, 48-52.

58 N. K. Schilder, *Imperator Aleksandr I, ego zhizn' i tsarstvovanie,* II (St. Petersburg, 1897), pp. 28-30. See also *Stroganov,* II, 37-38. Alexander shared his father's suspicion and dislike for the Russian aristocrats as a class.

59 The suggestions of several aristocrats regarding Senate reform are published in *Arkhīv Gosudarstvennago soveta,* III, 15-19. Derzhavin's "Mnenie" appears in *Chteniia imperatorskago obshchestva istorii i drevnosti rossiiskikh,* 1858, No. 3, part 5, pp. 122-127; Zavadovskii's "Mnenie" in *Chteniia,* 1864, No. 1, part 5, pp. 100-107; and Count A. R. Vorontsov's in *ibid.,* pp. 108-111. An anonymous "Zapiska o senate," dated 19 May 1801, was also found among the Vorontsov papers and published in *Arkhiv kniazia Vorontsova,* XII, 456-462. The letters of Count Semën to Panin, 16 Apr. 1801, *Materialy,* VI, 423-425; and to Novosil'tsov, 18 May 1801, *Arkhiv kniazia Vorontsova,* XI, 389-391, are also germane to the issue of Senate reform. The reform projects were discussed several times by the tsar and his Unofficial Committee; for example, on 24 June 1801 (*Stroganov,* II, 31-32), on 1 July 1801 (*ibid.,* pp . 33-34), on 5 Aug. 1801 (*ibid.,* pp. 44-46), and on 11 Sept. 1801 (*ibid.,* pp. 55-56).

60 Count Semën Vorontsov told Stroganov that the Senate must be "above suspicion, like Caesar's wife" (cited in *Stroganov,* II, 165). See also Count Alexander Vorontsov's and Zavadovskii's "Mneniia," cited above, and the anonymous "Zapiska." The tsar's reaction is reported in *Stroganov,* II, 46.

61 *Stroganov,* II, 55-56 (11 Sept. 1801). For widely varying estimates of the importance of the proposed Senate reforms, compare E. N. Berendts, "Proekty reformy Senata v tsarstvovaniia Imperatorov Aleksandra I i Nikolaia I," in S. F. Platonov et al., *Istoriia Pravitel'stvuiushchego senata za 200 let, 1711-1911,* III (St. Petersburg, 1911), 1-69; A. V. Predtechenskii, *Ocherki obshchestvenno-politicheskoi istorii Rossii v pervoi chetverti XIX veka* (Moscow, 1957); and Allen McConnell, "Tsar Alexander I's Hundred Days," *Slavic Review,* XXVIII (Sept. 1969), 373-393.

McConnell perhaps exaggerates the power of Pahlen, Panin, and Zubov, whom he calls at one point "the only real power" behind reform in Russia at that time. The period during which Alexander felt himself to be under pressure from these people was, in my opinion, more like fifty than one hundred days. Pahlen and Zubov were perceived as a *physical* threat on the night of 11 March, but this threat ceased to exist once Alexander had removed himself to the Winter Palace. For the next several weeks, Alexander was uncertain to what extent these people posed a *political* threat to him, precisely because he was not sure to what extent they represented the aristocracy as a whole. By late April, when he and Stroganov came up with the idea of the Unofficial Committee, Alexander had had time to take stock of the situation; his fear of Pahlen and Zubov was greatly diminished. By the end of May, when he had gathered around him his Committee, Alexander had already worked out the strategy of divide and conquer against the aristocracy. He knew then that he could dismiss Pahlen with impunity, and he did. He treated Prince Zubov with more respect, because he did not want to antagonize the aristocracy needlessly. I know of no evidence anywhere that Alexander ever feared Panin. Panin was simply a useful, temporary minister for foreign affairs. He was dismissed not because he had ceased to be feared, but because he had ceased to be useful.

62 Reported by Count Stroganov, *Stroganov,* II, 159-166. See also Vorontsov's letter to Panin, 16 Apr. 1801, *Materialy Panina,* VI, 423-425.

63 For a full account of this intrigue, see *Materialy Panina,* VI, 622-635 and 645-650.

64 Vorontsov's "Zapiska o milostivom manifeste na koronatsii Imperatora Aleksandra I s materialami dlia sego manifesta," appendix to *Russkii arkhiv,* 1908, pp. 4-19. This includes Novosil'tsov's detailed criticisms. See also the discussions of the Unofficial Committee, 15 July, 23 July, and 13 Aug. 1801, *Stroganov,* II, 36-51. Because at least three versions of the Charter survived into the twentieth century, there was some confusion over its authorship. For a time, Soviet scholars maintained that Alexander Radishchev was somehow involved in its composition (e.g., V. P. Semennikov, *Radishchev, ocherki i issledovaniia* [Moscow, 1923]). This view has been persuasively attacked by a German scholar, Georg Sacke, *Graf A. Voroncov und der Gnadenbrief für das russische Volk* (Emsdetten, 1937). A complete summary of the controversy can be found in Predtechenskii, *Ocherki obshchestvenno-politicheskoi istorii Rossii,* pp. 191-199. An English translation of one of the later versions of the Charter is printed in Marc Raeff, *Plans for Political Reform in Imperial Russia, 1730-1905* (Englewood Cliffs, N. J., 1966), pp. 84-94.

IV
SOURCES AND HISTORIOGRAPHY

9

THE FURTHER STUDY OF PAUL*
(Werner Phillip in Verehrung zugeeignet)

Christian D. Schmidt

This essay is organized in five parts: Introduction; Historiography; Published Documents; Archival Materials; and Memoirs. It makes no pretense of being exhaustive. It suggests where further materials may be found when that is appropriate. As memoirs of Paul and his time are both the most controversial materials treated here and the most difficult, at least in many cases, to locate and to evaluate, they receive more attention than the other items.

I. *Introduction*

"Historical scholarship has not been well served by having the 'crowned Hamlet' in St. Petersburg handed down as merely a poor caricature of Frederick the Great or Joseph II; for even in the caricature lies a figure of importance." Thus did Dietrich Geyer[1] some years ago testify to the reawakening interest of Western as well as Soviet historical scholarship in the person, and above all in the brief reign, of Paul I of Russia. The traditional view is that this intermezzo between the age of the Enlightenment and the beginning of the new century was largely unimportant or even annoying, that the figure of Paul was a largely negative phenomenon sandwiched between the incomparably more illustrious and attractive profiles of Catherine II and Alexander I. Whether we dispute this view or not, we must admit, unless we are willing to ignore important insights into modern Russian history, that a serious examination of these judgments and prejudices is necessary. It is not merely a question of an all too moralistic rectification by historical scholarship of the presumed injustice done Paul. Nor has there been anything like a revolution in the sources that demands an imperative reconsideration of the subject. Rather, we must recognize that a short transition period, such as the brief four-and-one-half-year reign of Paul I, can serve as a hinge of both continuity and change in Russian history from 1762 to 1855. This is especially true if

*Translated by David and Karin Griffiths.

Russian history is not treated in isolation, but within the context of European history as a whole.

The purpose of this essay is to facilitate further study of the subject. It seemed reasonable not to confine this survey to specialized scholarly studies but to expand it to include contemporary memoir literature. The memoirs certainly did not originate as scholarly contributions to modern history or, initially, as primary sources. Frequently written down as eyewitness accounts of contemporary history, only much later have they come to be regarded as sources of a sort. It has therefore not always been easy to distinguish them from older works of history, and the distinction will appear at times a bit arbitrary. Furthermore, considerations of space make it impossible to include everything on the subject. In spite of that, here and there a long-forgotten curiosity from the profusion of literature on Paul and his times has been cited. In the memoir literature, which is mostly Russian, care has been taken to select those works that focus on the figure of the ruler, including his life prior to 1796, or his reign, regardless of the general or specific approach. The overly general has been omitted here. The general histories of Russia, whatever their scope, have not been considered. Likewise, it would not have made sense to list shorter works not directly related to the theme unless they were of a genuinely essential character. Those remaining are monographs dealing with Paul's person, his reign, or particular problems of his policy, i.e., works that might be considered biographies or contributions that have biographical significance. For this reason, Soviet literature is barely represented here: biographies of autocrats do not belong to Soviet tradition, and specialized Soviet works that encompass Paul I and his times as their major concern have remained rather sporadic until recent times.

Despite all endeavors to make a historiographic as well as a bibliographic contribution, there can be no question of an extensive, critical discussion of the opinions represented in the works. Such an enterprise would require a book in itself. Moreover, we already have such critical reviews of literature, the most important of which is M. V. Klochkov, *Ocherki pravitel'stvennoi deiatel'nosti vremeni Pavla I* (St. Petersburg, 1916), pp. 1-92. The more prominent works on Paul are reviewed in the introduction to this book. Enough informaton will be reported about each of the works discussed here to allow a preliminary familiarity with it and a comfortable classification of the viewpoint of the author.

II. *Historiography*

Most of the basic works in the literature on Paul are biographies, but there are a few other essential kinds of contributions among them: E. S. Shumigorskii, *Imperator Pavel Pervyi; zhizn' i tsarstvovanie* (St. Petersburg, 1907; see also his article on Paul in *Russkii biograficheskii slovar'*, XIII); N. K. Schilder, *Imperator Pavel I: istoriko-biograficheskii ocherk* (St. Petersburg, 1901) and *Imperator Aleksandr Pervyi: ego zhizn' i tsarstvovanie*, I, 2nd ed. (St. Petersburg, 1900); D. F. Kobeko, *Tsesarevich Pavel Petrovich, 1754-1796* (St. Petersburg, 1882; Fr. tr., *La jeunesse d'un tsar* [Paris, 1896]); Pierre Morane, *Paul I de Russie avant l'avènement, 1754-1796* (Paris,

1907); Kazimierz Waliszewski, *Le fils de la Grande Catherine, Paul I, empereur de Russie: sa vie, son règne et sa mort, 1754-1801,* 2nd ed. (Paris, 1912; Eng. tr., *Paul the First of Russia* [London, 1913]; also Russian and Polish translations); V. F. Chizh, "Imperator Pavel I: psikhologicheskii analiz," *Voprosy filosofii i psikhologii,* 1907, *passim*; D. A. Miliutin, *Istoriia voiny Rossii s Frantsiei . . . v 1799 g.,* 5 vols. (St. Petersburg, 1852-1853; 2nd ed., 1854-1855, 3 vols.; Ger. tr. by Christian Schmitt, *Geschichte des Krieges Russlands mit Frankreich unter der Regierung Kaiser Pauls I.* [Munich, 1856-1858. 5 vols.]); M. V. Klochkov, *Ocherki pravitel'stvennoi deiatel'nosti vremeni Pavla I* (St. Petersburg, 1916); Valentin Graf Zubow, *Zar Paul I: Mensch und Schicksal* (Stuttgart, 1963); A. M. Stanislavskaia, *Russko-angliiskie otnosheniia i problemy Sredizemnomor'ia, 1798-1807* (Moscow, 1962); David L. Ransel, *The Politics of Catherinian Russia: The Panin Party* (New Haven, 1975); and Norman E. Saul, *Russia and the Mediterranean, 1797-1807* (Chicago, 1970).

Most of these works are reviewed in the introduction. With the exception of Stanislavskaia, they are either pre-Revolutionary Russian or Western. Soviet literature on Paul, as noted, is limited. We have the general work of Semen Bentsianovich Okun', *Ocherk istorii SSSR: konets XVIII-pervaia chetvert' XIX veka* (Leningrad, 1956). In chronological and conceptual terms, the work represents a continuation of the last (ninth) volume of the large and similarly named series *Ocherki istorii SSSR* (Moscow, 1953-1956). See also Anatolii Vasil'evich Predtechenskii, *Ocherki obshchestvenno-politicheskoi istorii Rossii v pervoi chetverti XIX veka* (Moscow-Leningrad, 1957) and V. I. Samoilov, *Vnutrenniaia i vneshniaia politika Pavla I* (Khlebnikovo, 1946). Stanislavskaia has recently published *Rossiia i Gretsiia v kontse XVIII-nachale XIX vv.* (Moscow, 1976). None of these works is much concerned with the person of Paul.

Of the other biographical studies, Shumigorskii's *Imperatritsa Mariia Fedorovna* (St. Petersburg, 1892) and *Ekaterina Ivanovna Nelidova (1758-1839): ocherki iz istorii Pavla I* (2nd ed. St. Petersburg, 1902) are essential. The work on Mariia Fedorovna was planned in several volumes, but only the first volume appeared. See also Johann-Heinrich Schnitzler, *La jeunesse de l'Impératrice Maria Feodorovna jusqu'à son mariage* (Colmar, 1864) and Shumigorskii, "1800 god," *Russkaia starina,* Jan.-Mar. 1913, pp. 37-54, 263-279, Apr.-June 1913, pp. 223-236.

There are two studies of Paul that are useful for students, though they make no pretense of being works of research: Martha Edith Almedingen, *So Dark a Stream: A Study of Emperor Paul I of Russia, 1754-1801* (London, 1959) and Constantine de Grunwald, *L'assassinat de Paul I; tsar de Russie* (Paris, 1960).

A. N. Korsakov did a study of Paul's accession based primarily on memoir literature, "Votsarenie Imperatora Pavla," *Istoricheskii vestnik,* XVII (1896), 495-535, 921-966.

On internal administration, there are several works that bear comparison with the study of Klochkov: Sergei Aleksandrovich Korf, *Dvorianstvo i ego soslovnoe upravlenie za stoletie 1762-1855 godov* (St. Petersburg, 1906); A. E. Nol'de, "Pravitel'stvuiushchii senat v tsarstvovanie Pavla I," *Istoriia*

Pravitel'stvuiushchego senata za dvesti let, II (St. Petersburg, 1911), 695-779; and P. Zhukovich, "Zapadnaia Rossiia v tsarstvovanie Imperatora Pavla," *Zhurnal Ministerstva narodnago prosveshcheniia,* June 1916, pp. 183-226, Aug. 1916, pp. 207-263, Oct. 1916, pp. 175-186. In addition, there is a valuable study of Paul's political program in terms both of his plans and his reign: Claus Scharf, "Staatsauffassung und Regierungsprogramm eines aufgeklärten Selbstherrschers; die Instruktion des Grossfürsten Paul von 1788," in Ernst Schulin, ed., *Gedenkschrift Martin Göhring* (Wiesbaden, 1968), pp. 91-106.

For Paul's early contacts with the French republic, see the valuable study of Georges Grosjean, *La France et la Russie pendant le Directoire* (Paris, 1896). The important subject of the influence of the émigrés in St. Petersburg is admirably covered in Ernest Daudet's well-known work, *L'histoire de l'émigration,* 3 vols. (Paris, 1904-1907). An extremely influential work on Russian aspirations toward the straits and relations with the Turks is that of the Russian archivist Sergei Goriainov, *Bosfor i Dardanelly—issledovanie voprosa o prolivakh po diplomaticheskoi perepiske khraniashcheisia v gosudarstvennom i s-peterburgskom glavnom arkhivakh* (St. Petersburg, 1907). Perhaps even more important is the revealing critique of it, Jacob Hurewitz, "Russia and the Turkish Straits: A Revaluation of the Origins of the Problem," *World Politics,* XIV (1961-1962), 605-632. See also the somewhat superficial account of Boris Mouravieff, *L'alliance russo-turque au milieu des guerres napoléoniennes* (Neuchâtel, 1954). On Paul's relations with Bonaparte, see Sergei S. Tatishchev, "Paul I et Bonaparte," *La nouvelle revue,* XLVII (1887), 631-665, XLVIII (1887), 41-58, XLIX (1887), 233-260, 754-785; Hugh Ragsdale, "Russian Influence at Lunéville," *French Historical Studies,* V (1968), 274-284; and Ragsdale, "A Continental System in 1801: Paul I and Bonaparte," *Journal of Modern History,* XLII (1970), 70-89. There are two very useful studies of Paul's relations with the Italian states: Carlo di Somma, *Une mission diplomatique du Marquis de Gallo à Saint-Pétersbourg en 1799* (Naples, 1910) and Giuseppi Greppi, *Révélations diplomatiques sur les relations de la Sardaigne avec l'Autriche et la Russie pendant la première et la deuxième coalition* (Paris, 1859).

On military history, in addition to Miliutin, a good modern account of the war of 1799 is in Alexander Bankier Rodger, *The War of the Second Coalition: A Strategic Commentary, 1798-1801* (Oxford, 1964). For a particular aspect of both military and social history, see S. A. Panchulidzev, *Istoriia Kavalergardov, 1724-1899,* 2 vols. (St. Petersburg, 1899-1901). See also the documentary collections on Ushakov, Suvorov, and Kutuzov, and the memoirs of Chichagov (cited below). A valuable study of the Russian navy in the Mediterranean is Evgenii V. Tarle, "Admiral Ushakov na Sredizemnom mor'e, 1798-1800," in his *Tri ekspeditsii russkogo flota* (Moscow, 1956). The important works of Saul and Stanislavskaia have already been mentioned.

Paul's assassination was a taboo subject in Russia until after the revolution of 1905, though the facts of the matter were known abroad in both memoirs and works of history. The Kobeko biography does not extend into Paul's reign. Schilder's biography does not relate this death. The first biography to do so in Russia was that of Shumigorskii (1907). The memorial volume by Aleksandr Geno, *Pavel I: sobranie anekdotov, otzyvov, kharakteristik, ukazov i prochikh* (St. Petersburg, 1901) conveys official ignorance of the cause of death without batting an eye. In the meantime, Alexander Brückner, writing under the pseudonym "R. R.," published a conscientious but now outmoded study of Paul's death, its causes, and surrounding circumstances, a problem which at that time increasingly demanded explanation: *Kaiser Pauls Ende* (Stuttgart, 1897). The essay by Albert Sorel, "La mort de Paul I," *Revue bleue,* XVII (1902), 1-7 was superseded by Theodor Schiemann's pioneering study, *Die Ermordung Pauls I. und die Thronbesteigung Nikolaus I.* (Berlin, 1902). These foreign works were eventually reflected in the basic Russian publication of the materials on Paul's death, *Tsareubiistvo 11 marta 1801 g.: zapiski uchastnikov i sovremennikov* (St. Petersburg, 1907; 2nd ed., 1908). At the same time, Brückner's study was published in Russian, *Smert' Pavla I* (St. Petersburg, 1907). Curiously, and evidently uniquely, Panchulidzev, *Istoriia Kavalergardov* (1901), calls Paul's death a murder in spite of the censorship. See also *Vremia Pavla i ego smert': zapiski sovremennikov sobytiia 11-go marta 1801 goda* (Moscow, 1908).

Paul's reign, like others in eighteenth-century Russia, was the subject of a good deal of writing in the genre of contemporary history. In February 1801, Heinrich Reimers presented Paul a handwritten book of homage entitled *St. Petersburg During the First Four Years of the Glorious Reign of His Imperial Majesty Paul the First.* Paul's death the next month and the political climate of the new reign rendered the book obsolete. Two years later, however, a revised text with a revised title was published to commemorate in a jubilee edition the centennial of the capital: *Petersburg am Ende seines ersten Jahrhunderts.* Excerpts appeared in Russian in *Russkaia starina,* July-Sept. 1883, pp. 443-474.

At almost the same time, that is, a few weeks before the assassination, an anonymous and peculiar biography of Paul appeared in a German magazine: "Paul der Erste, Kaiser von Russland, von einem unbefangenen Beobachter," *Monatsschrift für Deutsche zur Veredelung der Kenntnisse, zur Bildung des Geschmacks und zur Unterhaltung* (Leipzig), Feb. 1801.

Another almost contemporary and anonymous biography of Paul is *Leben Pauls des Ersten, Kaisers und Selbstherrschers aller Reussen, nebst einer authentischen Geschichte der Feldzüge der Russen in Italien in der Helvetischen und Batavischen Republic gegen die Franzosen und vieler bisher unbekannt gebliebener Anekdoten und Züge aus dem Leben dieses merkwürdigen Monarchen, freimütig beschrieben von einem russischen Offizier* (Frankfurt/Main, 1804). The author turned out to be the Saxon-Meiningen chamberlain Georg Freiherr von Tannenberg (1740?-1805), a somewhat mysterious figure who entered Russian service as a young man, rose quickly to the rank of major of a cavalry regiment, and accompanied Suvorov on all his campaigns for a period of eighteen years. He is probably also the author of the life of Catherine II that appeared in Leipzig in 1797, of a Suvorov biography that appeared in Nuremberg in the same year, and of several other books on Russia. His book on Paul was published by Kotzebue's translator Kriazhev in Moscow in 1805. See the information on Tannenberg in Hamberger-Meusel's *Das Gelehrte Teutschland.*

The secretary of the Saxon embassy wrote an account of the Russian court under Catherine and Paul that is concerned almost entirely with the system of favorites: Georg-Adolf-Wilhelm von Helbig, *Russische Günstlinge* (Tübingen, 1809). A Russian translation by V. A. Bil'basov was published in *Russkaia starina,* July 1886, pp. 1-20, Oct. 1886, pp. 1-24, Jan.-Mar. 1887, pp. 299-328, 533-552, Apr. 1887, pp. 35-46, Oct.-Dec. 1887, pp. 1-30, 425-444. There is also a Swedish translation, *Rysska Gunstlingar* (Stockholm, 1821).

III. *Published Documents*

On the internal administration, vols. 24-26 of the *Polnoe sobranie zakonov Rossiiskoi imperii,* First Series (St. Petersburg, 1830) are indispensable. This collection also contains the text of treaties. Another important source is *Senatskii arkhiv,* I (St. Petersburg, 1879). *Arkhiv Gosudarstvennago soveta: sovet v tsarstvovanie Imperatora Pavla* (St. Petersburg, 1888) is not what we ordinarily think of as the State Council, which was not founded until 1810, but its distant predecessor, the Sovet pri vysochaishem dvore, which was replaced in 1801 by the Nepremennyi sovet.

Documents of a more personal nature dealing with Paul's life abound. Mikhail Ivanovich Semevskii published what was in effect Paul's political testament, full of insights into his objectives, "Materialy k russkoi istorii XVIII veka," *Vestnik Evropy,* Mar. 1867, No. 2, pp. 297-330. See here the work of Claus Scharf (cited above) based on these documents. Of lesser significance at first glance but of considerable importance for a description and comprehension of the ruler's everyday affairs are the orders and instructions of Paul published by B. M. Fedotov, "Imperator Pavel I: reskripty i zapiski Gosudaria Imperatora Pavla I k grafu Arakcheevu, 1794-1799 gg.," and "Ukazy, rasporiazheniia i rezoliutsii Imperatora Pavla 1796-1799 gg.," *Russkaia starina,* Apr. 1873, pp. 476-516, and "Ukazy, rasporiazheniia i rezoliutsii Imperatora Pavla 1799-1800 gg.," *ibid.,* May 1873, pp. 622-634. (Compare Léonce Pingaud, "L'empereur Paul I de Russie d'après des documents nouveaux," *Le Correspondant,* 269, No. 5 (1912), 926-946.)

These citations are used here to illustrate the nature of many documentary publications on Paul that appeared in nineteenth-century periodicals. To list all of them here would be quite a ponderous business. Rather, we shall list the periodicals that abound in such material:

Sbornik (Imperatorskago) Russkago istoricheskago obshchestva (St. Petersburg, 1867-1916).

Chteniia v Obshchestve istorii i drevnostei rossiiskikh pri Moskovskom universitete (Moscow, 1845-1916).

Russkii arkhiv (Moscow, 1863-1917).

Russkaia starina (St. Petersburg, 1870-1918).

Drevniaia i novaia Rossiia (St. Petersburg, 1875-1881).

Istoricheskii vestnik (St. Petersburg, 1880-1917).

There are a variety of indexes for such journals, for example: Vasilii A. Popov, *Sistematicheskii ukazatel' statei pomeshchennykh . . . s 1836 po 1884 g.* (St. Petersburg, 1885) and Sergei R. Mintslov, *Obzor zapisok, dnevnikov, vospominanii, pisem' i puteshestvii otnosiashikhsia k istorii Rossii,* 5 vols. in 1 (St. Petersburg, 1911). For others, including cumulative indexes for individual journals, see Karol Maichel, ed., *Guide to Russian Reference Books,* II: *Historical Sciences* (Stanford, 1964), pp. 45-49. See also the extensive work of Vladimir I. Mezhov and B. P. and P. P. Lambin, eds., *Russkaia istoricheskaia bibliografiia* (St. Petersburg, 1861 ff.).

Petr Bartenev, ed., *Os'mnadtsatyi vek,* 4 vols. (St. Petersburg, 1869) is rich in materials on Paul. There are a variety of very valuable publications from private archives: Petr Bartenev, ed., *Arkhiv kniazia Vorontsova,* 40 vols. (Moscow, 1870-1895); M. I. Semevskii and V. N. Smol'ianinov, eds., *Arkhiv kniazia Kurakina,* 10 vols. (St. Petersburg, 1890-1902); and Alexander Brückner, ed., *Materialy dlia zhizneopisaniia grafa N. P. Panina,* 7 vols. (St. Petersburg, 1888-1892). Though they are really histories, in fact A. A. Vasil'chikov, *Semeistvo Razumovskikh,* 5 vols. (St. Petersburg, 1880-1894) and Nikolai I. Grigorovich, *Kantsler kniaz' Aleksandr Andreevich Bezborodko v sviazi s sobytiiami ego vremeni,* II (Moscow, 1881; vol. 29 of *SIRIO*) have abundant documentary materials. The Vorontsov papers are especially rich for foreign affairs matters. N. P. Panin was the nephew of Paul's tutor, and he was a moving force in the conspiracy of March 1801.

For military history, there are three exceptionally important publications: R. N. Mordvinov, ed., *Admiral Ushakov: sbornik dokumentov,* 3 vols. (Moscow, 1951-1956); G. P. Meshcheriakov, ed., *A. V. Suvorov: sbornik dokumentov,* 4 vols. (Moscow, 1949-1953); and L. G. Beskrovnyi, ed., *M. I. Kutuzov: sbornik dokumentov,* 5 vols. (Moscow, 1950-1956). See also Hermann Hüffer, ed., *Quellen zur Geschichte der Kriege von 1799 und 1800,* 2 vols. (Leipzig, 1900-1901).

On foreign affairs, A. S. Trachevskii, ed., *Diplomaticheskiia snosheniia Rossii s Frantsiei v epokhu Napoleona I,* I (St. Petersburg, 1890; vol. 70 of *SIRIO*) is basic. It contains documents from both French and Russian archives. Fedor F. Martens, ed., *Sobranie traktatov i konventsii zakliuchennykh Rossieiu s inostrannymi derzhavami,* 15 vols. (St. Petersburg, 1874-1909) contains much diplomatic history in the editorial commentary on the treaties. *Vneshniaia politika Rossii XIX i nachala XX veka: dokumenty rossiiskogo Ministerstva inostrannykh del,* Series I, I (Moscow, 1960) has some documents pertinent to Paul's reign.

There are several valuable publications on the foreign affairs of the era from Western archives. The English diplomatic correspondence with St. Petersburg and legation records in the Russian capital are in Walter Fitzpatrick, ed., *The Dropmore Papers: The Manuscripts of J. B. Fortescue Preserved at Dropmore,* 7 vols. (London, 1892-1910). The corresponding Austrian materials are in Alfred von Vivenot, ed., *Vertrauliche Briefe des Freiherrn von Thugut,* 2 vols. (Vienna, 1872). There is much useful information on Russia in Paul Bailleu, ed., *Preussen und Frankreich von 1795 bis 1807,* 2 vols. (Leipzig, 1881-1887). On the armed neutrality, see F. T. Piggott and G. W. T. Omond, eds., *Documentary History of the Armed Neutralities* (London, 1919) and James Brown Scott, ed., *The Armed Neutralities of 1780 and 1800: A Collection of Official Documents . . .* (New York, 1918). On Maltese issues, see McGrew, "Malta," below.

Two contemporary Russian newspapers ought not to be forgotten: *Sankt-peterburgskie vedomosti* and *Moskovskie vedomosti.* If a file of it could be located anywhere, the *Hamburgische Zeitung (Gazette de Hambourg)* for the period would be invaluable. The Library of Congress has very good holdings of *Sankt-peterburgskie vedomosti* for the reign of Paul. One other source is indispensable for recording the activities of the court: *Kamer-fur'erskii tseremonial'nyi zhurnal*. Initiated by Peter I, it was a kind of logbook of court life. It recorded all the comings and goings of the ruler and the entire imperial family and receptions and banquets, along with the order of precedence, number, and names of invited guests. It was published a hundred years after the events it records.

IV. *Archival Materials*

The contents of Soviet archives and manuscript repositories constitute an increasingly important collection of sources on modern Russian history for the Western scholar. Though problems of access continue, this situation is improving, and it is becoming more imperative for us to give these sources our attention.

The most general and comprehensive guide to Soviet archives is *Gosudarstvennye arkhivy SSSR: kratkii spravochnik* (Moscow, 1956). As it deals with more than one hundred fifty such institutions, most of them provincial or local, the attention given to each is very brief. It does not deal with libraries at all and hence ignores several large manuscript collections. It does not cite more detailed guides or inventories. Moreover, it is out of date in some respects. Several Soviet archives have been reorganized in important ways since its publication, and one archive mentioned in the *Kratkii spravochnik* has been closed down, its contents divided among others.

A more up-to-date and satisfactory guide for our purpose is P. K. Grimsted, *Archives and Manuscript Repositories in the USSR: Moscow and Leningrad* (Princeton, 1972). This volume details the fate of major relocations of materials since the publication of *Kratkii spravochnik*. It centers on the more important national institutions in the two traditional capitals, includes manuscript collections in libraries, and cites at length more detailed guides and inventories. Most of the information that follows here is from Grimsted, though some is from *Kratkii spravochnik*.

There are two other important volumes that deal with a wide variety of archival and manuscript collections. *Lichnye arkhivnye fondy v gosudarstvennykh khranilishchakh SSSR: ukazatel'*, 2 vols. (Moscow, 1962-1963) is one of the most valuable of Soviet finding aids and should be used along with the guides that apply to particular institutions. *Rukopisnye fondy leningradskikh khranilishch: kratkii spravochnik po fondam bibliotek, muzeev, nauchno-issledovatel'skikh i drugikh uchrezhdenii* (Leningrad, 1970), a ninety-two-page pamphlet, is a very general and somewhat scant guide to the subject. It is also rather rare, having been produced in just two hundred mimeographed copies (Harvard Libraries have one). But it is the only organized commentary on some of the significant research collections in the city.

One of the more important archives for the study of Paul is the Tsentral'nyi gosudarstvennyi arkhiv drevnikh aktov (TsGADA). TsGADA contains, among other things, records of the Pravitel'stvuiushchii senat and of the eighteenth-century colleges of the central government and much information on landholding, peasant affairs, and manufacturing. The standard guide to the archive is *Tsentral'nyi gosudarstvennyi arkhiv drevnikh aktov: putevoditel'*, 2 vols. (Moscow, 1946-1947), but a later reorganization of the archive has made the guide somewhat obsolete. For pertinent updating, see Grimsted, *Archives,* p. 160.

The bulk of the old Senate materials (in addition to those in TsGADA) as well as the materials of the Holy Synod and a wide variety of other records, including material on foreign trade, internal economic development, administrative history, state banks, and the papers of many prominent Russian families, are in the Tsentral'nyi gosudarstvennyi istoricheskii arkhiv SSSR (TsGIA). The basic guide is *Tsentral'nyi gosudarstvennyi istoricheskii arkhiv SSSR v Leningrade: putevoditel'* (Leningrad, 1956). See also *Opis' dokumentov i del, khraniashchikhsia v Senatskom arkhive,* 9 vols. (St. Petersburg, 1909-1917). On economic development, manufacturing, and trade, see Grimsted, *Archives,* pp. 178-179.

The Arkhiv Leningradskogo otdeleniia Instituta istorii SSSR AN SSSR (LOII) contains collections of papers on southern and western European countries and the major part of the well-known Vorontsov archive. It is this part of the Vorontsov papers that forms the basis for the published collection (cited above). The standard guide to LOII is *Putevoditel' po arkhivu Leningradskogo otdeleniia Instituta istorii* (Moscow-Leningrad, 1958).

The foreign affairs documents for the reign of Paul have been transferred from TsGADA to the Arkhiv vneshnei politiki Rossii (AVPR). The best guide is still that part of the TsGADA *Putevoditel'* that described them when they were a part of that collection. But see also other guides and descriptions in Grimsted, *Archives,* pp. 253-255.

The military materials of the period of Paul are housed in the Tsentral'nyi gosudarstvennyi voenno-istoricheskii arkhiv SSSR (TsGVIA). Materials on related subject matter, e.g., peasant uprisings, may also be found there. The standard guide is *Putevoditel' po Tsentral'nomu gosudarstvennomu voenno-istoricheskomu arkhivu* (Moscow, 1941). It is quite dated but still useful. An important treatment of the whole subject of sources of Russian military history, including this archive and others, is Liubomir Grigor'evich Beskrovnyi, *Ocherki po istochnikovedeniiu voennoi istorii Rossii* (Moscow, 1957). An important inventory of the papers of an exceptionally significant figure in the reign of Paul is *Suvorov, Aleksandr Vasil'evich (1730-1800): opis' dokumentalnykh materialov arkhivnogo fonda no. 43* (Moscow, 1952).

Naval materials are in the Tsentral'nyi gosudarstvennyi arkhiv voenno-morskogo flota SSSR (TsGAVMF). The published inventories are quite extensive: see Grimsted, *Archives,* pp. 140-141. The archive is officially closed to foreign scholars, but materials from it are sometimes made available in the reading room of TsGIA.

The manuscript division of the Gosudarstvennaia biblioteka SSSR imeni V. I. Lenina (GBL) contains quite a variety of personal and family collections. There are two indexes to the repository: *Kratkii ukazatel' arkhivnykh fondov otdela rukopisei* (Moscow, 1948), dated but useful; and *Ukazatel' vospominanii, dnevnikov i putevykh zapisok XVIII-XIX vv. (iz fondov otdela rukopisei)* (Moscow, 1957). See also *Lichnye arkhivnye fondy.*

The manuscript collection of the Gosudarstvennaia biblioteka imeni M. E. Saltykova-Shchedrina (GPB) is much larger than that of the Lenin Library (GBL) in Moscow, but unfortunately there is no comprehensive guide to the collection. See *Lichnye arkhivnye fondy: Rukopisnye fondy leningradskikh khranilishch*; the many specialized guides in Grimsted, *Archives,* pp. 310 ff.; and, especially, *Opis' bumag N. K. Shil'dera postupivshikh v 1903 godu v Imperatorskuiu Publichnuiu biblioteku* (St. Petersburg, 1910).

Finally, the Gosudarstvennyi istoricheskii muzei (GIM) has extensive collections of private archives, especially for the late eighteenth and the nineteenth centuries. The appropriate guides are *Putevoditel' po fondam lichnogo proiskhozhdeniia Otdela pis'mennykh istochnikov Gosudarstvennogo istoricheskogo muzeia* (Moscow, 1967) and *Pis'mennye istochniki v sobranii Gosudarstvennogo istoricheskogo muzeia,* I (Moscow, 1958). See also *Lichnye arkhivnye fondy.*

Problems of access to Soviet archival institutions as well as further problems of use of their inventories after access is granted considerably enhance the value of other European archives for the study of both Russian foreign policy and Russian internal history. See in this regard Daniel H. Thomas and Lynn M. Case, eds., *Guide to the Diplomatic Archives of Western Europe* (Philadelphia, 1959). More specialized is Basile Spiridonakis, ed., *Mémoires et documents du Ministère des Affaires étrangères de France sur la Russie* (Quebec, 1962). For more explicit references to the type of material available on Paul in the Public Record Office, the Ministère des Affaires étrangères, and the Haus-, Hof-, und Staatsarchiv, see R. E. McGrew, "A Note on Some European Foreign Office Archives and Russian Domestic History, 1790-1812," *Slavic Review,* XXVIII (1964), 531-536. For an excellent example of the use to be made of such materials—an example that does not appear, judging by the article just cited, to exhaust the possibilities of research in these archives—see R. E. McGrew, "A Political Portrait of Paul I from the Austrian and English Diplomatic Archives," *Jahrbücher für Geschichte Osteuropas,* XVIII (1970), 503-529.

V. *Memoirs*

In attempting to survey the contemporary memoir literature, it is well to keep in mind that Paul's personality, his governmental measures, and the period 1796-1801 in general were unusually controversial in contemporary judgments. The memoirs themselves are therefore rarely impartial. Hence the viewpoint of the author, above all as it pertains to his professional or social status, will be emphasized here. These materials are treated in alphabetical order.

First to be mentioned, therefore, are the so-called memoirs of Armand-François Comte d'Allonville, *Mémoires tirés des papiers d'un homme d'état sur les causes qui ont déterminés la politique secrète des cabinets dans les guerres de la Révolution,* 13 vols. (Paris, 1828-1837). To put it more precisely we are dealing here with an anonymous work. It actually reports in memoir style on the background of European history from 1792 to 1815. In the eighth volume, which sketches the development of European international affairs from Marengo to Austerlitz, the primary concerns are the peace treaties of Lunéville and Amiens and the confrontation between Pitt and Bonaparte. Following p. 85 we find material on the March events in St. Petersburg in 1801 and speculations on their possible repercussions.

Aleksandr Aleksandrovich Bashilov (1777-1847) left "Zapiski o vremenakh Ekateriny II i Pavla I," *Zaria,* Dec. 1871, pp. 192-223.[2] Bashilov may be considered one of those favored by the regime. Entering the corps of pages in 1792, he was soon introduced to the aging empress and quickly rose to become her personal page. Strangely enough, he became at the same time the favorite chamber page of the tsarevich. Promoted to the rank of lieutenant in the Preobrazhenskii Guards in 1798, he was immediately given seemingly adventurous assignments and was soon dispatched on a secret mission to Vienna. During Suvorov's campaign, he delivered to the general his new title of "Kniaz' italiiskii" and to the king of Sardinia an offer of credit of three hundred thousand rubles. Commissioned to transport from Malta to Russia the presumed relics of John the Baptist, the patron saint of the Maltese Order, he arrived with them at Gatchina in October 1799. Paul rewarded him for this effort by the bestowal of the diamond cross of the order. Under Alexander, his career continued to flourish. His extensive memoirs, of which only a fraction have been published, were written shortly before his death.

An interesting source on Paul as tsarevich, and one to which little attention has been paid, is the series of reports of the imperial couple's trip to France as "Comte et Comtesse du Nord," recorded in the so-called "Mémoires de Bachaumont" (Louis Petit de, 1690-1771). In fact, after the death of the famous journalist his friends continued the "Mémoires" (the actual title was "Mémoires secrets de la République des lettres"), and Paul's visit to Versailles in 1782 was treated as the event of the year. Paul's French secretary Lafermière made excerpts at the time, but it was to be a century before they appeared in Russian translation: "Tsesarevich Pavel Petrovich vo Frantsii v 1782 godu; iz zapisok Bashomont'a," *Russkaia starina,* Oct.-Dec. 1882, pp. 321-334.

When we come to the writings as well as the indirect testimony of Count Bennigsen (Levin-August-Theophil, 1745-1826), a body of materials dealing primarily with the conspiracy against Paul, and his assassination, we are treating a topic that has remained controversial down to the present day even though the ink has flowed in streams on the subject. It cannot be dealt with in detail, but an introduction to the bibliographical state of affairs is in order here. The subject itself entails a whole series of memoirs.

On the fatal evening, Bennigsen was in the inner circle of the conspirators. He subsequently offered revelations concerning Paul's assassination and his own role in it on several occasions. For example, he talked about it with his friend Count Andrault de Langeron (1763-1831). De Langeron, descended from the ancient French nobility, emigrated in 1790 and entered Russian military service. He was promoted to the rank of general in 1799, and he later participated in the campaigns against Napoleon. In March 1801 he was stationed in Brest-Litovsk as commander of an infantry regiment and therefore had no direct hand in the conspiracy. His knowledge of it comes from the accounts of Bennigsen and others. He left extensive writings on military and political topics, most of which have remained unpublished in the archives of the French Ministry of Foreign Affairs in Paris. The Vicomte de Grouchy published brief excerpts on the events of March 1801: Aleksandr Fedorovich Andrault de Lanzheron (name russified), "De la mort de Paul I," *La revue britannique,* Oct. 1895, pp. 58-79. They doubtless reflect the stories that Bennigsen told him. Parts of his writings dealing with the Russian army of the time were published by N. K. Schilder, "Russkaia armiia v god smerti Ekateriny," *Russkaia starina,* Mar. 1895, pp. 147-166, May 1895, pp. 185-202. Finally, the excerpts dealing with the assassination appeared in *Tsareubiistvo* and in *Vremia Pavla I.*

Further conversational observations of Bennigsen have been handed down by his nephew and aide-de-camp, Major (later Major General) Ernst von Wedell. Von Wedell left a manuscript entitled "Aufschlüsse über die Ermordung des Kaisers Paul I. nach den Depositionen des Generals Freiherrn von Bennigsen und des Fürsten Plato Subow zu Wilna im Jahre 1812." Along with a manuscript by another colleague and confidant on the staff of Bennigsen, Prince Eugene of Württemberg (1788-1858), von Wedell's writings were transmitted by the son of the German military historian and diplomat, Theodor von Bernhardi, to Theodor Schiemann, who included them in his collection of documents, *Zur Geschichte der Regierung Pauls I. und Nikolaus I.* (Berlin, 1906), pp. 72-82 and 83-89. Much the same material had appeared in two previous editions in Berlin in 1902 and 1906 under the title *Die Ermordung Pauls I. und die Thronbesteigung Nikolaus I.* Von Bernhardi himself had already, though anonymously, made use of these and other pertinent documents in two essays on Paul's death: "Die Ermordung von Kaiser Paul," *Preussische Jahrbücher,* I (1858), 420-428 and "Die Ermordung des Kaisers Paul I. von Russland am 23. März 1801," *Historische Zeitschrift,* III (1860), 133-168. See Zubow, *Zar Paul I,* pp. 260-261, and especially Leo Loewenson, "The death of Paul I (1801) and the Memoirs of Count Bennigsen," *Slavonic and East European Review,* XXIX (1950-1951), 212-232. Shortly after von Bernhardi's essays, the detailed memoirs of the Prince of Württemberg appeared: *Aus dem Leben des Kaiserlich-Russischen General der Infanterie Prinz Eugen von Württemberg ...,* 4 vols. (Berlin and Frankfurt/Main, 1861-1862). The parts pertinent to Paul's reign are in vol. I, 74-160. Excerpts appeared in *Russkii arkhiv,* 1878, pp. 43-75, 330-359.

It is not only Bennigsen's discussions with third parties that have been handed down, but his own "Mémoires de mon temps" as well. These memoirs, because of their provocative content, became after his death the subject of negotiations between his family and the Russian government. An agreement was at length reached. Maria-Leonarda von Bennigsen, his widow, was to leave the sole copy of her husband's memoirs in the hands of the Russian diplomatic representative at the court of Hanover—in exchange for twelve thousand rubles. The agreement was broken, however, by both sides. The Russian government paid only four thousand rubles, while Bennigsen's family retained copies of the "interesting parts" of the papers, a fact that was at first kept a strict secret. One of these copies remained in the possession of the Hanoverian branch of the family until it too was left to Theodor Schiemann

kazaka donskago, atamana Adriana Karpovicha Denisova, 1763-1841," *Russkaia starina,* May-Aug. 1874, pp. 1-45, Sept.-Dec. 1874, pp. 379-409, 601-641, Jan.-Apr. 1875, pp. 27-49, 237-271, 467-479. Denisov also participated in the Italian campaign (during which he was raised to the rank of commander of the Maltese Order) as well as in Paul's controversial Indian campaign. Denisov was standing at the Irgiz when news of Paul's death reached him.

The famous Russian poet and statesman Gavrila Romanovich Derzhavin (1743-1816) wrote his memoirs in 1811-1813: "Zapiski," in *Sobranie sochinenii Derzhavina,* VI (St. Petersburg, 1869). They convey a sharply etched picture of the conclusion of Catherine's era and the reign of Paul and extend through Derzhavin's resumption of service as Minister of Justice under Alexander (1802-1803).

We also have something approaching memoirs from the two Dmitrievs, Ivan Ivanovich (1760-1837) and his lesser-known nephew, Mikhail Aleksandrovich (1796-1866). Despite the differences in personality and significance, they—like many representatives of the Russian intelligentsia of the time—have one thing in common: a life in the civil service and another as man of letters. Ivan Ivanovich left a well-known work that extends from approximately 1760 to 1820: *Vzgliad na moiu zhizn': zapiski deistvitel'nago tainago sovetnika Ivana Ivanovicha Dmitrieva,* ed. by M. A. Dmitriev (Moscow, 1866). In addition to interesting descriptions of Russian life in the capital and the provinces, it contains important sections devoted to the personality of Paul and to his activities as a statesman. I. I. Dmitriev was chief procurator of the Senate under Paul. The nephew was not fated to follow the path of his famous uncle: as civil servant, he rose over the course of a not-always-smooth career to the rank of actual privy councillor, though not in Paul's time. Shortly before his death, he published his uncle's memoirs. His own reminiscences appeared posthumously: *Melochi iz zapasa moei pamiati* (Moscow, 1869). In comparison to the former, they are anecdotal gems that portray many a celebrity of political and cultural life of the generation preceding his own though he had not known them personally. His memoirs are not, however, as significant as his uncle's.

We meet another representative of the statesman and man of letters in the person of Prince Ivan Mikhailovich Dolgorukii (also occasionally called Dolgorukov, 1764-1823). He was the author of now-forgotten lyric verses and also held office in the provincial administration. He left witty autobiographical notes in the form of an album or biographical inventory: "Kapishche moego serdtsa ili slovar' vsekh tekh lits s koimi ia byl v raznykh otnosheniiakh v techenii moei zhizni," *Russkii arkhiv,* Jan.-May 1890, Nos. 1-5, Supplement.[7] Under Paul, he served as vice-governor of Penza until 1797, when a romantic escapade forced him to resign from service temporarily.

Egor Antonovich Engelgardt's (1775-1862) *Zapiski* (Moscow, 1867) provide an account of the Vice-Chancery in Paul's reign. Engelhardt served directly under Kurakin but survived the fall of the latter in 1799 to be named secretary of the Maltese Order. In 1811, Alexander appointed him director of the famous lycée at Tsarskoe Selo.

In the accounts and notes of Aleksei Petrovich Ermolov (1777-1861)—*Zapiski,* 2 vols. (Moscow, 1865-1868) and "Rasskazy," *Chteniia OIDR,* Oct.-Dec. 1863, Part V (Smes'), pp. 214-232—we possess contemporary documents from the hand of one of the most celebrated Russian generals of the Napoleonic wars. He participated in the Persian campaign of 1796. He was arrested in 1798 as a "free-thinker," reduced to the ranks, and banished to Kostroma. Not until Paul's death was he rehabilitated and reinstated to his former rank. Subsequently, he was to cover himself with glory at Borodino, Bautzen, and Leipzig.

The "Zapiski," *Russkaia starina,* Mar.-Apr. 1884, pp. 31-66, May-June 1884, pp. 281-302, of M. A. Fonvizin (1788-1854), the nephew of the famous Russian writer D. I. Fonvizin, center upon the immediate circumstances of the tsar's assassination. Fonvizin was in 1801 a candidate for a commission in the Engineering School established in the Michael Palace after Paul's death. He often stood guard duty there, and he had sufficient occasion to become familiar with the place. He recounts his own interrogations of eyewitnesses, his perusal of foreign dispatches, and his personal views on the event, which was then still shrouded in mystery.

A colonel in the artillery and an administrator of Potemkin's vast possessions in St. Petersburg, Mikhail Antonovich Garnovskii (1764-1810) recorded observations in "Zapiski," *Russkaia starina,* Jan.-Apr. 1876, pp. 9-38, 237-265, 471-499, 687-720, May-Aug. 1876, pp. 1-32, 207-238, 399-440.

The French abbé Jean-François Georgel (1731-1813) left an extensive account of life and affairs in St. Petersburg in 1799-1802. It has special reference to the Maltese Order. See both his *Voyage à St.-Pétersbourg en 1799-1800 fait avec l'ambassade de l'Ordre de St.-Jean de Jérusalem allant offrir à l'Empereur Paul la Grande-Maîtrise de l'Ordre* (Paris, 1818) and *Mémoires pour servir à l'histoire des événements de la fin du XVIII siècle,* VI (Paris, 1820).

The future chief procurator of the Holy Synod (1805), minister of education (1816), minister of spiritual affairs (1817), and president of the Russian Bible Society, Prince Aleksandr Nikolaevich Golitsyn (1773-1844), left a short but interesting account of his youth, "Rasskazy pro Ekaterinu, Pavla, Aleksandra, Nikolaia i ikh sovremennikov: misticheskie mechty i chteniia," *Russkii arkhiv,* 1886, pp. 305-333. As the offspring of a family close to the court, he was among the childhood friends of the Grand Dukes Aleksandr and Konstantin Pavlovich. *Russkii arkhiv,* 1869, pp. 621-644, also published the contemporary papers, "Rasskazy," of Prince Sergei Mikhailovich Golitsyn (1774-1859), the senator, actual privy councillor, and eventual member of the State Council.

We have various editions of the memoirs of Countess Varvara Nikolaevna Golovina, née Golitsyna (1766-1821), former confidante of Empress Elizabeth. The *Zapiski grafini Goloviny* appeared in St. Petersburg in 1899 and *Souvenirs de la Comtesse Barbe Golovine* in Paris in 1910. As an ardent admirer of the great Catherine, her attitude toward Paul was extremely hostile.

The memoirs of Fedor Golovkin, *La cour et le règne de Paul I: portraits, souvenirs et anecdotes* (Paris,1905), are gossipy, colorful, trivial, and unreliable.

We also have the youthful remembrances of the Russian author and journalist Nikolai Ivanovich Grech, *Zapiski moei zhizni* (St. Petersburg, 1886; reprinted Moscow-Leningrad, 1930). He describes the turbulent days of March 1801 and gives an account of Paul's funeral.

The theater and opera producer Sergei Nikolaevich Glinka (1775-1847, not to be confused with his distant relative the composer) left his *Zapiski* (St. Petersburg, 1895).

The important memoirs of the Courland noble, Baron Karl-Heinrich von Heyking (1751-1809), are well known. A partial German translation of the French original is *Aus den Tagen Kaiser Pauls: Aufzeichnungen eines kurländischen Edelmannes,* 2 vols. (Leipzig, 1886). Excerpts were translated into Russian in *Russkaia starina,* Nov.-Dec. 1887, pp. 365-394, 783-815, as well as in *Tsareubiistvo* and *Vremia Pavla*. A Russian edition appeared in St. Petersburg in 1907. Heyking served with distinction during the Russian assumption of power in Courland after the third partition of Poland, and he was rewarded accordingly. In 1796, he was summoned to St. Petersburg by Paul and appointed to the posts of senator and president of the College of Justice for Livonia, Estonia, and Finland. He fell into disgrace, however, in 1798, for supporting the Mariia Fedorovna party in a court intrigue, and he had to return to Mitau. His mother-in-law had been director of the Smol'nyi Institute under Catherine, which explains why Heyking belonged to the circle of Nelidova and Mariia Fedorovna—he met Nelidova at Smol'nyi. His memoirs reflect clearly their point of view.

The memoirs of Nikolai Stepanovich Il'inskii (1761-1846), "Iz zapisok," *Russkii arkhiv,* 1879, pp. 377-434, represent, on the other hand, the work of a middle-level civil servant who also harbored certain literary ambitions. He began his career in 1771 as a copyist with the College of Commerce, served a long term as a government official in Pskov (1781-1795), and eventually returned to the Senate Chancery in St. Petersburg. In 1801, he became a close aide of the Chief Procurator Obol'ianinov.

In the memoirs of Count Dmitrii Borisovich Mertvago (1760-1824), "Zapiski," *Russkii arkhiv,* 1867 (a special supplement), we possess a rich source for the social history of Russia from the Pugachevshchina to the Arakcheevshchina.

The memoirs of the Izmailovskii officer Evgraf Fedorovich Komarovskii (1769-1843), "Iz zapisok," *Russkii arkhiv,* 1867, pp. 220-248, 521-576, 748-788, 1276-1330, provide valuable source material for the military history of the reign, although from the point of view of a steep "climber." Still a lieutenant in a famous guards regiment in 1792, he became adjutant to Grand Duke Constantine in 1796, colonel in 1798, major general in 1799, in recognition of his services under Suvorov, and, finally, imperial adjutant general in 1801. The continuation of his career under Alexander I was far less dramatic.

The Russian archeologist Pavel Fedorovich Karabanov (1767-1851) left us his historically valuable notes. In his passion for collection, Karabanov abandoned grand historical perspective and gathered enormous quantities of genealogical and biographical information dealing with some of the prominent families in Russian society at the end of the eighteenth century. His notes offer a wealth of detail from daily life and from the contemporary Russian oral tradition. In fact, Karabanov was not so much an archeologist in the modern sense of the term as an "ar heographer" in the Russian sense: that is, primarily a collector of "Slavic antiquities," such as were found in Russia and also in Poland at the end of the eighteenth and the beginning of the nineteenth centuries. His "Istoricheskie rasskazy i anekdoty," appeared complete in *Russ-*

kaia starina, June-Sept. 1871, pp. 583-587, 685-696, Jan.-June 1872, pp. 129-147, 457-468, 670-680, 767-772, July-Dec. 1872, pp. 285-290.

A vast change of scale is involved in turning from these seemingly "microscopic" notes of Karabanov to Grand Duke Karl Friedrich von Baden's (1728-1811) *Politische Korrespondenz 1783-1806,* 5 vols., ed. by B. Erdmannsdörfer and K. Obser (Heidelberg, 1888-1901). The correspondence contains important information on the development of international affairs in Europe in the reigns of Catherine, Paul, and Alexander.

Nikolai Osipovich Kotlubitskii (1749- ?) was an officer in the Gatchina forces. He became a lieutenant general and adjutant general to the tsar early in Paul's reign and was commander of the palace guard at the Michael Palace on the night of the assassination. His memoirs are in his "Rasskazy," *Russkii arkhiv,* 1866, pp. 1301-1331.

August von Kotzebue (1761-1819) evidently felt, at the end of Paul's reign, that he owed his public a sentimental report on Russia's problems as well as a retort to the rather vicious work of Masson (see below). His interesting memoir is *Das merkwürdigste Jahr meines Lebens,* 2 vols. (Berlin, 1801). English and French editions appeared soon afterward, and several new German editions also appeared. Though Kotzebue was, like Masson, a victim of the regime, unlike Masson he was rehabilitated. See also Gerhard Giesemann, *Kotzebue in Russland: Materialien zu einer Wirkungsgeschichte* (Frankfurt/Main, 1971), esp. pp. 169 ff.

The *Mémoires de Frédéric-César Laharpe* (Paris-Geneva, 1864), the tutor of Alexander and Constantine, reveal much of the influential role that the author was able to play at the court and in Catherine's entourage.

Princess Lieven (Daria Khristoforovna, or Dorothea, 1785-1857), one of the most striking personalities of the period, left memoirs that have been published in various places. A French manuscript version was left in the library of the Winter Palace, and other copies were apparently left to such friends as Metternich, Canning, and Guizot. A copy was used by Schiemann and published in Russian translation several years later. See Schiemann, *Zur Geschichte,* pp. 35-52; *Tsareubiistvo,* pp. 171-199 (same excerpt); and the complete English translation, *The Unpublished Diary and Political Sketches* (London, 1925).

"Zapiski nekotorykh obstoiatelstv zhizni i sluzhby Deistvitel'nago tainago sovetnika Ivana Vladimirovicha Lopukhina [1756-1816], sochinnenye im samym," *Russkii arkhiv,* 1884, pp. 1-154, are notes probably designed for an autobiography that was never written. Lopukhin, like his friend Fonvizin, was co-founder and co-owner of a progressive publishing company, the "Tipograficheskaia kompaniia." He was also intimately involved in the Masonic movement in Russia.

Senator Fedor Petrovich Lubianovskii (1777-1869) eventually made his career in the upper levels of the ministerial bureaucracy under Alexander and Nicholas. But his younger years, when he was still serving as an officer in the Preobrazhenskii Guards and as adjutant to several commanding generals (Repnin, Lassi, 1790-1801), occupy an important place in his memoirs: "Vospominaniia," *Russkii arkhiv,* 1872, pp. 98-185, 450-533.

Two well-known memoirs require no more than a mention: *Mémoires politiques et correspondance diplomatique de Joseph de Maistre* [1753-1821] *avec explications et commentaires historiques par Albert Blanc,* 2nd ed. (Paris, 1859) and James Harris, Earl of Malmesbury, *Diaries and Correspondence,* 4 vols., 2nd ed., ed. by James Howard Harris, Earl of Malmesbury (London, 1845).

The famous-infamous work of Charles-François-Philibert Masson (1762-1807), *Mémoires secrets sur la Russie et particulièrement sur la fin du règne de Catherine et le commencement de celui de Paul I, formant un tableau de moeurs de St. Pétersbourg à fin du 18 siècle,* 3 vols. (Paris, 1801-1802), began to appear even prior to Paul's death. Masson was motivated in part by revenge, for he had been expelled from Russia in 1796. A second edition appeared in four volumes in 1804. At the same time, English and German translations appeared. The work turned out to be unexpectedly successful. The last complete French edition came out in 1859. For a long time, it was regarded as an indispensable source. Masson also published a rebuttal to Kotzebue: *Lettre d'un français à un allemand servant de réponse à M. de Kotzebue et de supplément aux "Mémoires," suivie d'un précis historique de la déportation et de l'exil de l'auteur* (Paris-Coblenz, 1802). A German translation appeared the same year.

The daughter of the Master of the Horse who served Catherine and Paul published memoirs of her father, Sergei Ilich Mukhanov (1762-1842). They are marked by the wealth of detail on life at court: Mariia Sergeevna Mukhanova, "Iz zapisok," *Russkii arkhiv,* 1878, pp. 209-216, 299-329.

In the same category as the memoirs of Princess Lieven, Joseph de Maistre, and Malmesbury are those of the future foreign minister Count Karl-Robert Nesselrode (1780-1862), *Des russischen Reichskanzlers Grafen Nesselrode Selbstbiographie* (Berlin, 1866), although his career began only in the year of Paul's death.

That portion of the memoirs of Baroness Henriette-Louis Oberkirch (1754-1803) pertinent to Paul's early life is written from a narrowly personal and apolitical point of view: *Mémoires publiés par le Comte de Montbrisson, son petit-fils* (Paris, 1853). They are full of vivid detail and are ambitious from the literary point of view. A new edition was brought out by Suzanne Burkhart, *Mémoires de la baronne d'Oberkirch sur la cour de Louis XVI et sur la société française avant 1789* (Paris, 1970), vol. XXI of the series *Le temps retrouvé.* The baroness was a childhood friend of Mariia Fedorovna. Her memoirs pertain to the period before 1789.

A. S. Pishchevich (1764- ?) was a cavalry officer in Catherine's second Turkish war and in the Caucasus campaign. He left important information on the military history of the time, although his autobiography remained incomplete, ending in 1798: "Zhizn' Aleksandra Semenovicha Pishchevicha, im samym opisanaia," *Chteniia OIDR,* 1885, I, 1-112, II, 113-273.

The Russian diplomat Petr Ivanovich Poletika (1778-1849) wrote his memoirs toward the end of 1843: "Vospominaniia," *Russkii arkhiv,* 1885, pp. 305-336 (fragments). Though his eventful career later took him to North and South America among other places, he was in 1796 a mere lieutenant "à la suite"; in 1798, however, he entered the service with the College of Foreign Affairs, and from 1799 he worked in the chancery of the College under the immediate supervision of Kochubei.

Written from the perspective of "higher politics" by one of the key figures of eighteenth-century European dynastic history are the memoirs of the last king of Poland, Stanislaw August Poniatowski (1732-1798). They are a source that should not be overlooked for the period of Paul. The memoirs were announced at the Warsaw Diet of 1767 as his apologia before the court of history, and they were found among his extensive papers when he died at the Marble Palace in St. Petersburg, 2 February 1798. Bezborodko personally had the king's effects sealed and stored immediately. But shortly before Poniatowski's death, probably in 1797, copies of parts of these manuscripts had come into the possession of his nephew, Adam Czartoryski, who took them along with him to Parisian exile after 1831. They evidently served as the basis for the French edition of the memoirs: *Mémoires secrets inédits de Stanislas II Auguste, roi de Pologne,* 2 vols. (Paris, 1862). To a large extent, they are identical with the first two volumes of the subsequent St. Petersburg edition. Another French edition of somewhat different form appeared in Paris in 1895 under the title *Souvenirs.* The papers of the king that remained in Russia, on the other hand, belonged to the emperors personally until Nicholas donated them to the newly founded State Archive in 1832. By this time they were probably no longer complete. They remained there until 1907, when they were released by Sergei Goriainov, then director of the State Archive, for publication by the Imperial Academy of Sciences. The first four volumes appeared in the original French in 1914, when publication was stopped: *Mémoires du Roi Stanislas Auguste.*

In the *Zapiski* (St. Petersburg, 1881) of Semen Andreevich Poroshin (1741-1769), we possess a very important document from Paul's tutor in mathematics and history when the heir to the throne was ten to eleven years old.

Aleksandr Ivanovich Ribop'er (Count Rappolstein-Ribaupierre, 1781-1865) was a page at court and a gentleman-in-waiting during Catherine's reign. See his "Zapiski," *Russkii arkhiv,* 1877, pp. 460-506.

Count Fedor Vasil'evich Rostopchin (1763-1826) was one of the more provocative and intriguing figures of the period, and his life is not as fully documented as we would like. On the period down to 1801, much of his correspondence with the Vorontsovs is published in the *Arkhiv kniazia Vorontsova.* He left an interesting account of Paul's accession: *Poslednii den', Imperatritsy Ekateriny II i pervyi den' tsarstvovaniia Imperatora Pavla I* (Moscow, 1864). His famous memorial on the French alliance and the partition of the Ottoman Empire is in *Russkii arkhiv,* 1878, pp. 103-110. See in addition André Rostopchin, ed., *Matériaux en grande partie inédite pour la biographie future de Comte Théodore Rastaptchine* (Brussels, 1864) and Lydie Rostopchin, ed., *Oeuvres inédites de comte Rostoptchine* (Paris, 1894). See also his *Sochineniia* (St.Petersburg, 1869). Perhaps the greater part of Rostopchin's memoirs remained unpublished.

The memoirs of the future director of the St. Petersburg educational district, Dmitrii Pavlovich Runich (1780-1860), are very rich on Paul's reign: "Sto let tomu nazad; iz zapisok D. P. Runicha," *Russkaia starina,* Oct. 1896, pp. 281-319 (fragments). The same is true of the former Smol'nyi pupil G. I. Rzhevskaia-Alymova (1759-1826), who left memoirs relating to her friendship with Ekaterina Nelidova: "Pamiatnye zapiski," *Russkii arkhiv,* 1871, pp. 1-51.

In General N. A. Sablukov's (1776-1848) memoirs we are faced with a document with a complex publishing history, though not so complex as in the case of Bennigsen. The author's father was a senator and vice-president of the College of Manufacturing. The son belonged from 1793 to a Horse Guards regiment whose commander was Grand Duke Constantine himself. In 1801, Sablukov served as squadron leader. He evidently enjoyed the tsar's complete confidence without interruption, something that few were fortunate enough to do. He thus belonged to the immedate entourage of the imperial family, and he is a first-rate eyewitness of the genesis of the crisis of 1801. His memoirs first appeared in English anonymously and incompletely in *Fraser's Magazine for Town and Country,* LXXII (1865), 222-241, 302-327: "Reminiscences of the Court and Time of the Emperor Paul I of Russia up to the Period of His Death: From the Papers of a Deceased Russian General Officer." An incomplete Russian version identifying the author appeared in *Russkii arkhiv,* 1869, cols. 1872-1953. A complete Russian version appeared in Leipzig in 1902: *Zapiski N. A. Sablukova o vremenakh Pavla I i o konchine etago gosudaria.* A complete version also appeared in *Tsareubiistvo,* pp. 9-105 and again in St. Petersburg in 1911.

Iakov Ivanovich de-Sanglen (1776-1864) was a minister of police in the reign of Alexander I. His memoirs, like those of von Wedell and Lanzheron, relate not events in which he participated but reports of conversations with the conspirators who took Paul's life. See "Pavel i ego vremia," *Russkaia starina,* Oct.-Dec. 1882, pp. 442-498, Jan.-Mar. 1883, pp. 1-46, 375-394, 539-578, Apr.-June 1883, pp. 137-150. Also, *Tsareubiistvo.*

The adventures of the Livonian pastor Fedor Nikolaevich Seider are similar to those of Kotzebue and Masson. He was beaten with the knout and banished to Nerchinsk because of a minor infraction of the censorship regulations, but he was also summoned to return, and a small monument was erected to his memory in the park at Gatchina after his death. See his *Todeskampf am Hochgericht oder Geschichte des unglücklichen Dulders F. Seider, ehemaligen Predigers zu Randen in Estland* [sic], *von ihm selbst erzählt, ein Seitenstück zum "Merkwürdigsten Jahr meines Lebens" von Aug. v. Kotzebue* (Hildesheim-Leipzig, 1803; 2nd ed., Berlin, 1803). A partial Russian translation appeared in *Russkaia starina,* Jan.-Apr. 1878, pp. 462-490.

Count Jakob Johann Sievers (1731-1808) had an illustrious career under Catherine II and in 1796 became a senator and member of the Sovet pri vysochaishem dvore. He received the grand cross of Malta from Paul. Only the last volume of his memoirs covers the period of Paul: Karl Ludwig Blum, ed., *Ein russischer Staatsmann: des Grafen Jakob Sievers Denkwürdigkeiten zur Geschichte Russlands,* 4 vols. (Leipzig-Heidelberg, 1857-1858).

The memoirs of Admiral Aleksandr Semenovich Shishkov (1754-1841), *Zapiski, mneniia i perepiska admirala Shishkova* (Berlin, 1870), have more to do with the literary history of the time of Paul than with the military history.

One of the really important diplomatic memoirs of the period is that of the long-standing Swedish ambassador at the court of Catherine and Paul: Count Curt von Stedingk (1746-1837), *Mémoires posthumes du feldmaréchal Comte de Stedingk, rédigés sur des lettres, dépêches et autres pièces authentiques,* 2 vols. (Paris, 1844-1845). See also Countess B. de la Gardie, *Un ambassadeur de Suède à la cour de Catherine II,* 2 vols. (Stockholm, 1919).

Aleksandr Mikhailovich Turgenev (1772-1863) was a distant relative of the novelist of the same name. As a corporal in the Horse Guards, he happened to be standing duty on the day of Catherine's death, and like many other such persons, he later suffered the personal disfavor of Paul. The viewpoint in his memoirs was influenced accordingly: "Zapiski 1772-1801," *Russkaia starina,* July-Sept. 1885, pp. 365-390, Oct.-Dec. 1885, pp. 55-82, 247-282, 473-486.

The famous French court and portrait painter Madame Marie-Anne-Elizabeth (Vigée) Lebrun (1755-1842) was in Russia in 1796-1797, and she devoted several chapters of her memoirs to the experience: *Souvenirs,* 3 vols. (Paris, 1835-1837; 2nd ed., Paris, 1869). Those parts relating to Paul's reign were published in *Drevniaia i novaia Rossiia,* 1876, Nos. 10-12.

In the memoirs of Filipp Filippovich Vigel' (1786-1856), *Zapiski,* 7 vols. (Moscow, 1891-1893; republished Moscow, 1928) we have the work of both a high state official and a man of letters. Vigel' was vice-governor of Bessarabia and chief administrator of Kerch as well as a member of the Arzamas circle. His memoirs contain abundant material on both the court and the literary and theatrical life of Russia during the reigns of Paul and Alexander.

Prince Petr Andreevich Viazemskii (1792-1878) was a child at the time of Paul's reign, but his memoirs, evidently relying heavily on the extensive family archives, nevertheless extend back into the period: *Polnoe sobranie sochinenii,* 12 vols. (St. Petersburg, 1878-1896). It is interesting to note that no fewer than three of the conspirators of 11 March 1801 bore this family name, though they are not identifiable by Christian names.

Prince Petr Mikhailovich Volkonskii (1776-1852) also belonged to the inner circle of the conspirators. As Alexander's adjutant in the latter's role of commander of the Semenovskii Guards, however, he was not present on the night of the assassination. His career flourished in the reign of Alexander. His secretary took down his not very extensive memoires of the period of Paul: "Rasskazy zapisannye s ego slov A. V. Viskovatym v ianvare 1845 g.," *Russkaia starina,* May 1876, pp. 176-190.

This completes the survey of memoirs. Two further observations are in order.

There are three noteworthy fictional interpretations of Paul: Iurii Nikolaevich Tynianov, *Podporuchik Kizhe* (Leningrad, 1930); Dmitrii Sergeevich Merezhkovskii, "Smert' Pavla I," a play, in *Polnoe sobranie sochinenii,* XV, part 2 (Moscow, 1913); and Friedrich von Bodenstedt, *Kaiser Paul: eine Tragödie in fünf Akten* (Stuttgart, 1875).

Finally, for further bibliography, see especially Klochkov, *Ocherki,* pp. 605-613; Ransel, *The Politics of Catherinian Russia,* pp. 291-314; McGrew, "Malta," notes; Ragsdale, "A Continental System in 1801," notes; Saul, *Russia and the Mediterranean,* pp. 229-256; and Stanislavskaia, *Russko-angliiskie otnosheniia,* notes.

NOTES

1 "Staatsaufbau und Sozialverfassung: Probleme des russischen Absolutismus am Ende des 18. Jahrhunderts," *Cahiers du monde russe et soviétique,* VII (1966), 375.

2 No less than seven periodicals have borne the title *Zaria* over the course of time. Here we are dealing with a relatively short-lived "literary-scientific-political" organ with clear pan-Slav tendencies that appeared under the editorship of S. Kashpirev in St. Petersburg from 1869 to 1872.

3 Soon thereafter a translation of this publication—not Bennigsen's French original—appeared in *Bibliothèque historique ou recueil de matériaux pour servir à l'histoire du temps,* XIII (Paris, 1820), 257-269. It was subsequently republished in Alphonse Rabbé, *Histoire d'Alexandre I, empereur de toutes les Russies, et des principaux événements de son règne,* I (Paris, 1826), 297-313; and in the partial translation of this work under another author's name, H. E. Lloyd, *Alexander I, Emperor of Russia, or a Sketch of His Life and of the Most Important Events of His Reign* (London, 1826), pp. 6-29. During his London exile, Alexander Herzen published a Russian translation: Iskander, "Smert' Imperatora Pavla I: otryvok iz dnevnika odnago sovremmenika," *Istoricheskii sbornik Vol'noi russkoi tipografii v Londone,* I (1859), 46-61. A second Russian translation, totally independent of Herzen's, did not appear in Russia until 1914: "Poslednie dni tsarstvovaniia Pavla; otryvok dnevnika odnago zagovorshchika," *Russkii arkhiv,* Sept.-Dec. 1914, pp. 443-459.

4 A partial edition was brought out by Alexander Herzen in London in 1859, *Mémoires de l'impératrice Catherine II écrits par elle-même,* an edition that appeared in German translation the same year. Another German edition is by E. Boehme, *Katharina II. in ihren Memoiren* (Berlin, 1916). The Russian edition is in her *Sochineniia,* 12 vols. (St. Petersburg, 1901-1907).

5 This edition is vol. VII of *Bibliothèque russe et polonaise, Nouvelle série.* A second edition by Charles G. de Lahovary appeared in Paris in 1909 under a new title, *Mémoires de l'amiral Paul Tchitchagof, commandant en chef de l'armée du Danube, gouverneur des principautés de Moldavie et de Valachie en 1812.* The 1858 Berlin edition and the 1862 Leipzig edition are described as "falsified" by Zubow, *Zar Paul I,* p. 248, without any explanation. They were serialized in *Russkaia starina,* 1883-1887, and they finally appeared in Russian translation in a single volume, *Arkhiv admirala Chichagova: zapiski* (St. Petersburg, 1885).

6 This edition is vol. XXI of *Arkhiv kniazia Vorontsova.* English editions appeared in London in 1840 and 1858 and a German edition, in 1857; also, *Mémoires de la princesse Daschkoff, dame d'honneur de Catherine II, écrits par elle-même avec la correspondance de cette impératrice et d'autres lettres,* 4 vols. (Paris, 1858-1862), vols. IX-XII of *Bibliothèque russe et polonaise.* In London, the first Russian translation was brought out by Alexander Herzen in 1859. Numerous excerpts can be found in *Russkaia starina, Russkii arkhiv,* and *Chteniia OIDR.*

7 Previously published incomplete in *Chteniia OIDR,* July-Sept. 1872, Part II, pp. 1-60, as well as in a separate volume in Moscow in 1874.

CONCLUSION

Hugh Ragsdale

Judging by these findings, Paul is not so confusing a personality as we once thought. His guiding impulse was to snare his associates in a rigid system of high-flown principles that would make their conduct predictable and therefore manageable and harmless.

The more important human relations in his early life were anxious ones. His father ignored him and failed to name him heir. His mother initially treated him better, and she did name him heir. Subsequently, however, in Paul's imagination, she threatened him with the fate of his father and of Ivan VI. She excluded him from affairs of state. Eventually, she considered dispossessing him of the throne and probably took steps to do so.

In the meantime, Panin relentlessly drilled into him the idea that Catherine and her favorites, the persons who stood between him and his rights, were not very virtuous people. In his mind, good morals and his own well-being came to be inextricably entangled—or confused. The only environment in which Paul felt safe was one that he fantasized, a moral world.

Of course, moralizing about civic virtue was epidemic in the eighteenth century. Many of Paul's contemporaries—monarchs, ministers, and writers—were almost as concerned about proper social and political principles as he was. Even so, Paul's commitment to this style of outlook was exceptionally passionate and schematic. His thinking, prompted by Panin and catalyzed by alarm, ran a short circuit and produced almost involuntary moral sentiments rather than careful deliberations.

Paul thought, as Morane said, that he possessed a superior moral truth, and he tried to use it to achieve a measure of social and political beatitude quite beyond human reach. He took literally much of the Enlightenment morality that more sophisticated souls understood to be intended in part as a good show. He proposed to inflict a few rules on the human flux and thus to make it live happily ever after.

Most mortals of ordinary intelligence and ordinary experience would have taken the first opportunity to correct this jaded/euphoric view of the world. Paul's thought was so conspicuously simplistic as to suggest that he perhaps did not have ordinary intelligence, and both the relative seclusion in which he was brought up and the remote heights from which he ruled precluded ordinary experience.

In Kliuchevskii's opinion, Paul did not know the rules of human society, and he did not want to know them, because he did not want to be bound by them. Paul certainly did not intend to be bound by others' rules, but it seems more likely that he did know the ways of the world, even if only intuitively, and that he sensed somehow that he and they were not compatible. He must have felt that he was not of the world of the Winter Palace and probably not safe in it. He presumed to rise above it and to transform it into a world as high-minded as his image of himself. His impulse was perhaps partly escapist, but it was also an effort to impose a code of conduct that would make the world safe for eccentric autocrats.

When he came into possession of his huge power, he used it in extraordinary ways to educate and edify the people of Russia—and the people of Europe. The Bank of the Nobility was not merely a bank. It was a device for rescuing the nobility from its sloth and corruption and a means of teaching it an ethos that would better serve its own and the state's interests. Similarly, Malta was not an unlikely piece of Russian real estate: it was an ideology. Is it surprising that Paul's contemporaries were puzzled?

Paul's favorite institutional paradigm of his beloved values of order, discipline, and service was the military. His love of the *Marsovoe pole* was reflected in the militarization of the civil service and in his interest in the Maltese Knights. He would undoubtedly have endorsed the well-known confession of Nicholas:

> Here [in the army] there is order, there is a strict unconditional legality, no impertinent claims to know all the answers, no contradiction, all things flow logically one from the other, no one steps in front of anybody else without lawful reason; everything is subordinated to one definite goal, everything has its purpose. That is why I feel so well among these people, and why I shall always hold in honor the calling of a soldier. I consider the entire human life to be merely service, because everybody serves.[1]

Of course for Paul, as for Nicholas, strict unconditional legality was for others, not for himself, and it was defined by the sovereign's whim: consider the conventions and the fundamental laws of the Russian Empire that he flouted.

In summary, in spite of the oft-observed paradoxes of Paul's character, he probably was not an especially complex personality. He had surrendered his judgment to a series of schematic fantasies. But there were factors other than the purely personal in his statecraft.

Paul represents an entirely characteristic tradition of modern European monarchy, a paternalistic effort to bridle the wrong tendencies of the people and simultaneously to organize and unleash the right ones. The challenge was to apply force where it was necessary without spoiling independent initiative where that was possible, to strike a balance between coercion and good example. Catherine had favored the exemplary approach, but Paul was to prefer the coercive. While Paul needed the reassurance of the harnessing and exhorting function of monarchical power more than most monarchs, the Russian people needed it more than most peoples, as Sergeant Prishibeev and the Inspector General and their countless actual counterparts have confided to us for generations. Where Paul's policy differed radically from Catherine's, it represented different selections from the eclectic bag of tricks of the modern European model of monarchy, not a rejection of the model.

Paul evidently looked upon his economic role as that of restorer, after the fashion of Sully. He wanted to inaugurate a period of peace and prosperity after a long period of wars and heavy taxation. Peace and good order he thought sufficient for the realization of prosperity. He was more conventional, conservative, and responsible in economic and financial policy than were Sully's successors Richelieu and Mazarin, but he did not approach the energetic and systematic efforts of Colbert. In this respect, Paul was either not abreast of Catherine and contemporary ideas in the West, or, more likely, he was not comfortable with them. He probably preferred a more static society than that envisaged by Adam Smith and the physiocrats. There is no evidence of their influence in Paul's thinking—and he can hardly have been ignorant of them—but there is little evidence of his thinking about economics of any kind. He allowed non-*dvoriane* to operate factories with professional serf labor. He is credited with the improved management that saved the forests administered by the Admirality College. The new Berg-kollegiia operated the mines more advantageously in his reign than in Catherine's. In his early policy papers, there are a few brief if impassioned pleas for each class to do its economic duty for the sake of the prosperity of the nation. On the whole, however, Paul's concern with economics was slight, naive, and conservative.

His social policy was more significant. Klochkov says flatly that Paul's reign was a turning point in peasant affairs. Peter Panin and Jacob Sievers had advised Catherine to do something to improve the condition of the peasantry, but she did nothing. Bezborodko gave Paul similar advice, and he took it. Whatever the disputed truth about his famous law on three-day *barshchina* in the Ukraine, it is clear that he intended to ameliorate the situation of the serfs. At his instance the Senate undertook widespread inquiries into the size of landholdings of state peasants and attempted to establish minimal norms. Of course, to a large extent this effort was futile. Still, the peasants seem to have understood that Paul was interested in them. In spite of the suppression of peasant rebellions early in his reign, he was remembered fondly by them. In this respect, Paul's outlook was again reminiscent of Henri IV and Sully. Louis XIV, too, undertook to correct nobles' abuses of peasants in an investigation known as the Grands Jours d'Auvergne. This aspect of Paul's repudiation of Catherine's policies was based on respectable precedents, and it was well conceived to benefit Russian state and society.

More effective and more troublesome were Paul's curbs on the nobility. The seventeenth-century French experience was perhaps the classic stereotype of this kind of struggle. The Bourbon monarchy tried to curtail the inherited privileges of the nobility and to cripple its capacity to create anarchy in the state and to despoil the other classes. The Bourbons brought the nobility to court, amused it, debauched it, and kept an eye on it. They relied on the bourgeoisie for ministers of state. The nobility was subdued several times, but no one succeeded in making it useful to the French nation.

To make the nobility useful to the Russian nation was exactly what Paul aspired to do. The Russian nobility was both similar to and different from the French. The "nobles' revolt" that followed the death of Peter I, the era of cretins and freaks, was something like what recurred from time to time in seventeenth- and eighteenth-century France during royal minorities. But the privileges of the Russian nobility derived from the policies of the state itself rather than from romantic antiquity, and the state tried to impose duties to balance the privileges.

In France, the struggle of the monarchy with the nobility was aided by the cooperation of the royalist bourgeoisie. In Russia, no such social alliance was possible. Catherine had showed some awareness of this state of affairs and a disposition to develop the economic and social basis for a bourgeoisie. Paul showed none. Hence, the Russian monarchy of Paul's time had both to exhort the nobility to do its duty to the state on the one hand and to curtail its aspiration to share state power on the other. The duty demanded of it consisted, in Paul's conception, of the military service of the French and German aristocracy and the political services of the French bourgeoisie. Unlike the seventeenth-century French monarchy or Joseph II, however, Paul insisted that noble birth and cultural advantages such as a proper education were essential to prepare for the calling of the civil service. And he did not deal with his nobility in the Machiavellian fashion of Richelieu or Mazarin. It is doubtful if Paul would have countenanced the concept of raison d'état.

A related problem was the complex of issues having to do with constitutionalism and the variety of approaches to the administration of the government. Early in her reign, Catherine looked at a proposed constitution of a sort, Panin's State Council project, and rejected it. After the Legislative Assembly and the Pugachev revolt, she was persuaded of the wisdom of accepting, in the provincial reform of 1775 and the nobles' charter of 1785, a partially decentralized mode of government with carefully stipulated privileges for the nobility—in effect, a more diffusely articulated style of incipient constitution than the one that she had rejected in 1762. Catherine apparently hoped that she might thus strike a balance between coercion and inspiration that would stimulate in the nobility a cooperative spirit of political and economic enterprise and facilitate the modernization of state and economy in an orderly fashion. Paul decided upon a quite different approach. He opted for an extreme form of centralization, and he abolished most of the corporate forms that might have become the embryonic Russian counterparts of the European estates.

Constitutional ideas had been present in Russia since at least 1730. Paul and the Panin set of young journalists demanded constitutional guarantees of legality from Catherine. The conspiracy against Paul was at least partly inspired by the wish to establish in fact the legal norms of absolutism which he praised and disgraced. Alexander showed every indication of interest in a legal, or constitutional, monarchy, but in 1825, we find the Decembrists demanding it still and sometimes in phrases reminiscent of those of Paul. Russian sovereigns less forceful that Peter I could not find a means of delegating a part of their power without the risk of becoming the creature of the only class capable of entering into affairs of state. Russia did not nurture the natural checks and balances of French and English society.

Paul's views on religion were in some respects typical of those of the enlightened despots. He was committed to the standards of tolerance then thought to be so much more advanced than the religious policy of Louis XIV. Paul, however, not only willingly accepted the practice of foreign religions in his dominions, but he actually courted the Catholics and the Maltese Order in particular and distinguished them with special favors. There is some reason to think that Paul seriously contemplated the reunion of the two Churches, and it is possible that he intended to become a Catholic. This would have been only crudely analogous to the conversion of Henri IV, for Paul had no reason to be a *politique.* Religious schism did not have politically threatening proportions in Russia.

Other European monarchs and their ministers, Richelieu in particular, thought the Church an ideal institution for encouraging the virtues of obedience and conformity. Paul's interest in the Maltese Knights evidently had nothing to do with doctrinal innovations. Rather, he sought to reinforce traditional Christian moral practice. In spite of the reputation for mystical inclinations that his curious relations with Nelidova occasioned, Paul's interest in religion showed more concern with politics and practice than with the nature of belief.

Just what long-term goals were contemplated in Paul's religious policy remain somewhat mysterious, but it seems safe to say that they had few parallels in the history of Europe or Russia, and that they were perhaps unique.[2]

Finally, Paul's revolt against his mother's policies was not uniform and indiscriminate. Catherine herself began in the 1790s to repudiate her own previous work. She curtailed much of the freedom of expression that she had previously encouraged. Paul followed her lead. Similarly, Catherine had done much to encourage free trade, but when Louis XVI was beheaded, she suspended commercial as well as diplomatic relations with France. Paul continued this policy too for a time. He paid more attention to setting up and organizing the Kommerts-kollegiia than he did to the principles of trade. He followed a modestly protectionist and prohibitionist system. The most dramatic commercial development of his reign was the embargo on trade with England and the reopening of trade with France. It is obvious what a mortal blow this policy struck at the vitals of Russian commerce as a whole. Perhaps Catherine would never have broken with England, but the principle of commerce in the service of politics in peacetime she had established in 1793.

Paul's revision of Catherine's policies was part petulant but it was also a response to changing times. If the Russian monarchy had been for several hundred years virtually the sole agency of progress in Russian society, its sole model of progress for a hundred years had been Western. In the 1790s, Russians watched with some horror as the cultural standard that had previously symbolized the promise of technical sophistication, power, and social charm turned in a democratic fury against those classes and institutions that had represented to Russians the exclusive sources of respectable culture. The third estate, previously the ally of the monarchies in Europe, now asked why it should not be everything. By the time of Paul's accession, Russians recognized the threat as well as the promise of Westernization. It was an uncomfortably confusing situation. What was to be done? Paul was the first sovereign to accede to the throne in the face of this dilemma. It is in this sense, as Kliuchevskii observed, that his reign represents a program for the future.

By 1796, the new ruler of Russia clearly had to consider other policies than those in vogue in the recent past. There were a variety of alternatives available, but they were all Western. There were no contemporary Russian political programs to consider. To find a Russian program, Paul would have had to turn back to a remote and ridiculously impertinent Russian past. What he chose to do was of considerable importance for the Russian future. He chose policy options that were Western but not necessarily contemporary. More exactly, he chose an antiquated religious society, a progressive conception of a nobles' bank, and an ambitiously modern form of professionalization of the civil service. He put all of this mix of conservative and progressive devices in the service not of development but of conserving an imagined status quo from the good old days. He chose Western institutional models suitable for encouraging order at the expense of progress. He might be described facetiously as a sort of xenophile Confucian.

Much of this program for the future endured through the next two reigns. Alexander admittedly went through the motions of repudiating as much of Paul's policy as Paul had of Catherine's. At the time, it seemed the healthiest thing to do. Alexander returned to an active policy in the field of education. He "restored" the Senate and gave it the right of judicial review. More importantly, he restored almost all of the provincial administrative apparatus of 1775 and the Charter of the Nobility of 1785. Paul's assassination was apparently considered evidence enough of the wisdom of these two pieces of legislation, and the continuing liveliness of related issues was attested by the constitutional projects of the Vorontsovs, the Unofficial Committee, Speransky, and Novosil'tsev.

On the other hand, the restored Senate kept its right of judicial review just six months. Speransky found the Russian nobles no more suitable material for the administrative apparatus than Paul had, and he inaugurated civil service exams to upgrade their qualifications. Alexander increasingly looked to the West for his religious interests, which were even more eccentric than those of Paul, and the greatly expanded Russian educational establishment was eventually put in the care of the grand master of the Russian Bible Society. Speransky's constitutional aspirations "to regularize powers by laws and to assure administration by regulations and institutions"[3] were as unwelcome to the nobility that had demanded just that as Paul's similar, though unconstitutional, pretensions had been. In the interest of professionalizing the administration, most of Paul's restored colleges were retained in the form of ministries. In 1804, in furtherance of Catherine's efforts of 1796 and of Paul's subsequent ones, Alexander issued the first systematic law of preventive censorship in Russia. The legislative efforts to improve the conditions of the serfs were continued, beginning with the law on free agriculturists in 1803.

The similarity of much of Nicholas's policy to that of Paul is too obvious to belabor. It differed in that it was more nationalistic, or chauvinistic, and cheaply so. Nicholas rejected Europe, contemporary and otherwise, and he led such a frightened life that he even shied away from Paul's modern means of reinforcing old ways.

The Crimean War registered the failure of the Russian government's preference for order at the expense of development, and it posed the problem of modernization, or Westernization, in Russia in its fully mature form: that is, how to capitalize upon the promise of a Western style of technical and economic progress without succumbing to the appurtenant threat of ideas of initiative, liberalism, and perhaps democracy.

Paul's approach to foreign affairs, too, divided his and his sons' reigns from those preceding. He combated the radical principles of the French Revolution, but it must be admitted that he resorted, as he had in internal affairs, to untraditional means of doing so. Moreover, with or without the Revolution, the power vacuum on the western Russian frontier had disappeared along with Poland, and that in the northwest and the southwest was stabilized by the interests of other powers.

The foreign policy program that Paul had been taught was Panin's Northern System. Paul would have preserved Poland, and he was inclined by sentiment to favor the Prussians. Eventually, however, he grew disgusted at the cowardly inactivity of the Prussians in the face of the French threat. He took an unprecedented interest in the distinctly non-northern Italian states and Malta. In Italy he wanted to preserve a conservative balance of power and to turn the French back from the Ottoman Empire. The only thing that he wished to aggrandize at Malta was a style of conduct and service. The pious rhetoric of Miliutin's interpretation of Paul's foreign policy reflected Paul's own, and though Miliutin did not take the care, or have the information, to sustain his interpretation, he was on the right track. Both before Campoformio and before Lunéville, Paul tried to organize a league, especially with Prussia, to prevent a Franco-Austrian deal at the expense of both the German Empire in general and of the small states of Italy and Germany in particular. The League of Armed Neutrality was the product of his righteous indignation. He was angry at the abuse of the small states by the bullying English navy, but he was angrier at England's desertion of the good cause, that is, the aims of the coalition as understood by himself. Paul would willingly work with Turks, Jesuits, and usurpers to reach his goals: he was not a legitimist. He was relatively flexible about the particular territorial terms and the distribution of benefits in a European peace settlement, and he changed his terms several times. But he was not to be moved from his principles, which were stubbornly conservative. He wished to save as much stable order as possible from the chaos of revolution.

His foreign policy sometimes effectively served Russian interests, as for example in gaining a Russian establishment at Malta or in turning the French back from the eastern Mediterranean. On the other hand, it is hard to see how Russia benefited by his withdrawal from the Second Coalition or the break in trade with England. In the first instance, Paul forfeited the influence in European affairs that Russisan military victories had put within his grasp. In the second, he did grave damage to Russian trade and embroiled himself with a power whose foreign policy objectives were probably more like his own than were those of any other power in Europe.

The foreign policies of Alexander and Nicholas have not been as carefully studied as their internal policies. It would be absurd to suggest that they were patterned after Paul's, but the fascinating parallels abound. Russian foreign policy from 1801-1855, or at least from 1813-1855, was more moralistic and more conservative than it had been before 1796 or was to be after 1856.

In this sense, then, due to a certain concatenation of circumstances both inside Russia and outside it, 1796 represents, roughly, a watershed in internal affairs and a more sharply defined one in foreign affairs. In spite of a demonstrative reaction on the part of Alexander against the new direction of politics marked out by Paul, much of that direction was maintained until the ugly shock of the Crimean War. The politics of Alexander and Nicholas were variations on the themes of Paul's time, not because either of these two very different and somewhat similar people admired or even understood Paul's ideas, but because the problems of Russian politics throughout that era were posed in the 1790s. The experience of the Crimean War marks another distinct watershed both in internal and foreign affairs. Serfdom was doomed, and Panslavism was ordained. Russian foreign policy became the monster that Europe had mistakenly believed it to have been; and development became the order of the day at home, even at the price of ideological diversity and social instability.

NOTES

1 N. V. Riasanovsky, *Nicholas I and Official Nationality in Russia, 1825-1855* (Berkeley, 1961), p. 1.

2 In some instances, it is hard to find a comparison between the policies of the two sovereigns. Two good examples are education and the arts. If Paul made any mark in the arts, we do not know what it was. Of course, he built the Michael Palace. He operated Gatchina in one fashion, while Mariia Fedorovna managed Pavlovsk differently. Perhaps the reign was not long enough to accumulate a clear record in the arts. More probably, Paul was not very interested in them.

In education, after all the fanfare and flourish of Catherine's reign, Paul's efforts were miniscule. He operated peasant schools on his estates. He had that enormous faith in the value and the efficacy of education that characterized most of his contemporaries. In this sense, he was not only the first servant of the state but also the first schoolmaster. Virtually all that he did had a didactic design. But of concrete support of education, there was none.

3 Quoted in Marc Raeff, *Michael Speransky, Statesman of Imperial Russia, 1772-1839* (The Hague, 1957), p. 117.

INDEX

A

B

N

O

Q

R

S

T